PRO ENGINE
BLUEPRINTING

BEN WATSON

First published in 1997 by Motorbooks International
Publishers & Wholesalers, 729 Prospect Avenue,
PO Box 1, Osceola, WI 54020 USA

Motorbooks International books are also available at
discounts in bulk quantity for industrial or sales-promo-
tional use. For details write to Special Sales Manager at
the Publisher's address

Library of Congress Cataloging-in-Publication Data
Available

Watson, Ben.
      Pro engine blueprinting / Ben Watson.
      p. cm. -- (Motorbooks PowerTech
series)
      Includes index.
      ISBN 0-7603-0424-6 (pbk. : alk. paper)
      1. Automobiles--Motors--Maintenance and
repair. 2. Physical
measurements. I. Title. II. Series.
TL210.W354 1997
629.25'04'0288--dc21
            97-38039

On the front cover: The engine blueprinting process is
comprised of many critical steps, including measuring,
calculating, machining, and fitting. This 302 cubic-inch
Chevrolet V-8, which is at the final assembly stage, uses
a crankshaft and connecting rods from L.A. Enterprise
and JE Pistons pistons. With a standard bore, this
engine has a 12:1 compression ratio. *David Gooley*

Printed in the United States of America

CONTENTS

INTRODUCTION

What Is Blueprinting?

Blueprinting is the exact science of engine rebuilding. Whereas the art of rebuilding has been addressed as a fun pastime, blueprinting is serious business. Blueprinting is to engine rebuilding what the Culinary Institute of America is to McDonald's Hamburger University. Both manage to train people to feed the public for profit, but the CIA (that's how the Culinary Institute identifies itself) teaches the creation of masterpieces, while Hamburger U teaches the creation of quality foods for the masses.

You might be asking at this point, "Why would I want to go to the trouble and expense of blueprinting an engine . . . wouldn't a regular overhaul be good enough?" Well for normal results the answer to that is yes! Although blueprinting and the associated balancing is an act normally associated with racing engines, there are benefits to incorporating many of the procedures discussed in this book even when rebuilding the engine in the family sedan. These procedures will make the engine run smoother, and a smoother running engine inherently enjoys improved performance and fuel economy.

Perhaps the toughest part of quality blueprinting is finding an uncommonly skilled and caring machinist. Of all the automotive skills, the one that is most difficult to get good training in is machining. So how do you begin? Today, most auto mechanics never require the services of a machinist. In the 1990s, few technicians do more than tune-ups, shock and strut replacements, front end alignments, or repairs on electrical, steering, and braking systems. Most of today's engines are very dependable and generally last until the cost of an overhaul far exceeds the value of the vehicle. So the guy—or gal—that works at the local chain repair shop

Many people spend a lot of time and effort making the outside of the engine look nice. This engine was sitting in a 1930s-era Ford and looked great on the outside. But this is no indication of how it is built on the inside. Blueprinting is the precise science of getting the maximum amount of power by reducing as many of the impediments to power as possible. These include vibrations and imbalance as well as restriction to airflow.

may not be the right person to ask. Personally, I had to have more machine work done when I was working at exotic import shops than at any other time. Look around your town, are there any independent Mercedes or BMW repair shops? These mechanics would be the best ones from which to obtain a dependable referral. Although these cars are very dependable, they often hold a good resale value beyond the time that major engine work would be required. Another good place to get referrals is a truck repair shop. A $20,000 diesel truck engine is worth overhauling. Each of these sources may be inadequate in reality; however, most of the machine shops that these technicians use are skilled at performing the more common engine machining operations but may have little or no experience in performance engine work.

Okay, "Then where do I go?" you may be asking. Take a trip to the race track. Buy a pit pass and walk around the pits. Talk to the drivers and their crews. Every town that has a few Burger Kings has at least one machinist with the necessary skill.

"Can't I do it myself?" you may ask. Yes, absolutely, in fact the very purpose of this book is to help you do just that. However (you knew that there had to be a "however," didn't you?), getting set up with the equipment to do all the work necessary would be frightfully expensive.

One very important thing to keep in mind as you begin your engine building adventure is that the first 20-percent increase in power will come fairly easily and cheaply. After that, the price of each additional 1 percent will increase geometrically. That is why a good bracket engine can be put together for about $7,000 to $10,000, while a pro-stock engine will cost $40,000 and more (with the emphasis on "and more").

The lathe is a fundamental tool of engine machine work. Lathes come in all sizes; this one, at the University of Alaska-Anchorage, is large enough to handle advanced machine work for even relatively large marine engines.

CHAPTER ONE

ENGINE REBUILDING AND BLUEPRINTING TOOLS

Engine blueprinting always comes down to a matter of degrees and inches—or, more accurately, degrees and fractions of inches. It's the precise measurement and optimization of those measurements that separates a carefully blueprinted high-performance engine from a hastily bolted together production passenger car engine.

That being the case, it's easy to understand why the engine blueprinter's best friends are his tools. Blueprinters need a variety of excruciatingly accurate measuring tools to check everything from journal diameters to valve heights to port volumes.

He also needs tools to machine parts to attain specific measurements. Drills, lathes, valve grinders, hyperaccurate scales, and other equipment will all be called upon by the engine blueprinter as he attempts to maximize engine performance.

And, of course, engine builders require the generic and not-so-generic engine disassembly and assembly tools, such as piston ring pliers, ring compressors, valve spring compressors, gear pullers and installers, and possibly a variety of specialty wrenches, depending upon the particular engine being assembled.

Naturally, beyond just having the numerous tools necessary, an engine blueprinter must possess the necessary skills to utilize those tools properly. In the end, the engine blueprinter will spend countless hours scrutinizing measurements down to the thousandth of an inch in his effort to optimize every single clearance, surface, and action of the engine in hopes of gaining just a few precious horsepower.

Precision Tools

Any machine work requires precise measurements. The principle behind almost all the precision tools used in automotive machining is the screw and the gear. This is true of both the measurement tools and the

One of the more common operations of an automotive machine shop is milling, or resurfacing, the cylinder heads. This is often done because the heads have been distorted due to overheating or improper torquing. Those desiring to fine-tune compression ratios will often mill the heads to reduce the volume of the combustion chambers.

Crankshafts come from the factory as relatively precise pieces. This is particularly true of performance crankshafts. When the crankshaft becomes damaged, a machine shop can often repair it by cutting the journals undersize. When this equipment is used in blueprinting an engine, the task is a little more complex. Indexing the crankshaft ensures that each of the connecting rod journals is at the proper distance and orientation to the main journals, and that the main journals are perfectly aligned on all planes to one another.

machining tools. Imagine a shaft threaded to a pitch of 40 threads per inch. Imagine a bar, holding a cutting tool as it rides on these threads. When the shaft rotates 1/50th of a revolution, the cutting tool will be moved 1/50th of 1/40th of an inch, or 5/10,000ths of an inch. This allows for a high degree of precision.

Similarly, a gear with a diameter of 3.183 inches is meshed with a gear that has a diameter of 0.3183 inches.

The circumference of the former is 10 inches. The circumference of the latter is 1 inch. One degree of rotation on the smaller gear yields 1/10th of a degree of rotation on the larger gear. More importantly, one degree of rotation on the big gear requires a movement of about 36 degrees on the smaller gear, which would equate to an arc 0.1 inches long. If the larger gear were meshed with a geared rod, or rack, then a linear movement of 1/1000 inch would equal 0.36 degrees of movement on the larger gear or 3.6 degrees on the smaller gear. If the smaller gear were attached to a needle on a gauge, each 3.6 degrees of movement on the needle would equal 1/1000 inch of movement on the rack. These are actually simple principles that go back centuries.

Machining Tools
Lathe

The lathe is the fundamental tool for automotive machine work. The lathe takes advantage of the principle of the screw. A hardened metal bit is used to slowly scratch away metal from the component mounted in a rotating arbor. As the component rotates, the hardened metal bit is slowly moved across its surface. Gradually, metal is removed leaving behind a relatively smooth surface that will mate with another machined surface or provide a sliding surface or mounting surface for a bearing. Lathes come in a variety of sizes, some are small as though they had been designed to create jewelry (and in fact some are constructed for just that purpose), others are large enough to machine the crankshaft of an engine used to power a huge ocean going vessel. Although a lathe is a very easy piece of equipment to learn how to use, it is a very difficult piece of equipment to learn how to use effectively.

Head-Milling Machine

The head-milling machine is a special kind of lathe. Instead of rotating the component, the head is secured horizontally in a special vise with the block mating surface facing up. While the

An engine that has seen many, many miles will often have worn cylinders. These cylinders can be bored 0.010-, 0.020- or, in some cases, up to 0.050-inch oversize to repair the damaged cylinder walls. Performance engine builders will often have the engine bored to increase the swept volume or cubic inch displacement of the engine. Be careful—going oversize can kick you up one class in some types of racing.

Fly cutters are used to machine circular areas, such as the piston pin bosses, in order to lighten or balance the pistons.

head lays horizontally a set of hardened metal bits mounted on a precision rotating wheel above the head slowly moves across the surface of the head, removing metal in order to true the surface.

Crank Turning Lathe

This is a special lathe design so the component can be chucked into the arbor off-center. This allows the crankshaft center of rotation to be around one of the rod journals rather than around one of the main journals.

Fly Cutter

The fly cutter is like a miniature lathe designed to machine a surface within the end of a "cylindrical" structure. When pistons need to be lightened for balancing, one of the better places to remove metal is on the bosses where the wrist pin goes through the piston. The fly cutter can be inserted into the bottom side of the piston to make circular cuts removing metal from the bosses. Valve reliefs in pistons can also be machined with a fly cutter.

Cylinder Boring Machine

This machine resembles a large drill press. A spinning cylindrical cutting tool passes through the cylinder, machining the cylinder to a new diameter as it travels. There are two common reasons for boring an engine: to repair damage to the cylinders that resulted of wear and other forms of old age; and to increase the displacement of the engine. Some racing classes have a maximum displacement, and boring the block is a way to increase the displacement toward that maximum limit. For instance, in a class such as NASCAR Winston Cup racing where the maximum displacement is 358 cubic inches, a 350 Chevy can be over-bored 0.030 inch, increasing displacement to 355 inches. But you have to be careful, because over-boring an engine can make it too large. For example, in a class with a 305 cubic inch limit, you could not bore a 302 Ford .030 inch because its displacement would be increased to about 306 cubic inches!

Line Boring Tool

There are two primary shafts that make the engine operate: the crankshaft and the camshaft. These typically fit through the block longitudinally, with bearing supports and caps maintaining their stability. If these bearing supports and caps are not in perfect alignment, the misalignment will force the camshaft or crankshaft to flex, causing excess wear and robbing the engine of power. The line-boring tool is used to machine these bearing supports and caps into alignment.

Connecting Rod Tool

Connecting rods undergo tremendous stress in any engine, and especially in a performance engine. These stresses can cause the connecting rods to become distorted. In a true racing engine, distorted connecting rods are "soon to be replaced" connecting rods. Most machine shops have a lathe that has been specifically designed to resize both the big end and the little end of the rod and ensure that the cylinders formed by the bores of the big and little ends are in proper alignment.

Basic Measuring Tools
The Micrometer

An automobile engine is made up of dozens of closely machined parts.

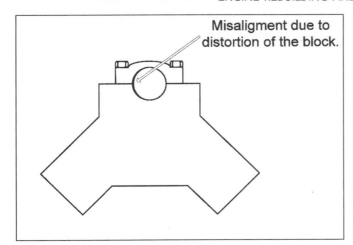

Misaligment due to distortion of the block.

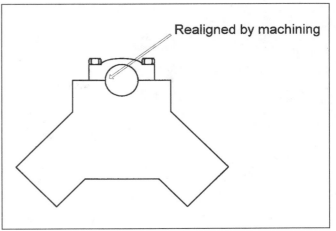

Realigned by machining

The two major shafts of the engine, the crankshaft and the camshaft, must rotate in a series of supports. If these supports are not perfectly aligned they will cause the shafts to bind as they rotate. This binding could damage the shaft or rob power. Power required to unnecessarily flex the shafts is thus not available to help turn the drive axles.

Measurements of these parts require precision to thousandths of an inch, and the micrometer provides this level of accuracy. Blueprinting an engine doesn't require measurements finer than two thousands of an inch (for instance, not as exact as to the nearest 10 thousandths of an inch), however, greater care in the accurate use of the measuring instruments is beneficial. A basic set of micrometers consists of a 0–1 inch, 1–2 inches, 3–4 inches, and 3–4 inches.

The micrometer is a very simple device, in spite of its high level of accuracy. It uses the centuries old screw-style technology discussed earlier. The basic parts of the micrometer are the spindle, the thimble, the anvil, and the barrel. The spindle is threaded to a standard of 40 threads per inch. Rotating the thimble moves the spindle 1/40th of a turn, 0.025 (twenty-five thousandths) of an inch. On the standard micrometer, there are 25 graduations around the thimble. This configuration allows an accuracy of 0.001 (one thousandth) of an inch. The barrel of the micrometer is marked off in 0.025-inch units. There is a numerical marking every four marks, indicating a movement of 0.1 (one tenth) of an inch.

How to Read a Micrometer

Using a micrometer involves placing its anvil and spindle against opposite ends of the object to be mea-

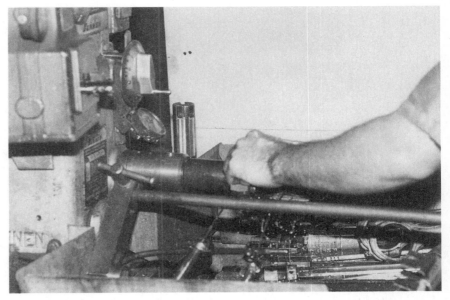

Connecting rods can also be damaged by wear. This machine repairs the rods, making the big end and the small end round again, as well as ensuring that they are on the same planes.

sured. Rotate the thimble until the spindle makes firm—but not hard—contact with the object. Over-tightening the micrometer can compress the component being measured or expand the frame of the micrometer, either of which will cause the reading to be inaccurate. Read the highest numerical marking visible on the barrel. This will indicate the nearest tenth of an inch, then count the barrel markings beyond the visible numerical mark to indicate the nearest 0.025 inch.

Finally, count the 25 marks on the thimble and how they align with the line on the barrel, thus indicating the measurement to the nearest thousandth inch.

A quality micrometer should be treated as the precision instrument it is. Over-tightening when taking measurements can stretch the frame, decreasing the accuracy of the micrometer. Often this can be remedied by adjustment using a gauge block. Dropping the micrometer can damage it beyond

Micrometers are the most basic of precision automotive measuring tools. These tools are delicate and should be treated with great care. A drop or a bump can easily affect their accuracy. Keep them well protected and in a safe place when not in use.

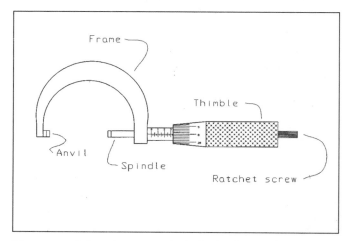

The parts of the micrometer include the frame, the stationary anvil, the moving spindle, and the rotating thimble.

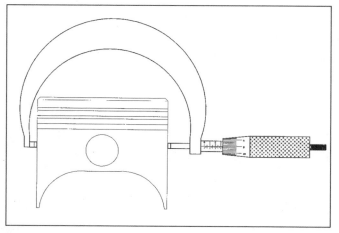

Place the anvil against the object to be measured. Rotate the thimble until the spindle comes firmly in contact with the object. Make sure the shaft of the spindle is perpendicular to the object and note the reading on the thimble.

adjustment. Top technicians may be more inclined to loan you their spouses than their micrometers.

The Inside Micrometer

The inside micrometer works just like the outside micrometer just described, however its design allows it to be used to measure the inside of a bore. These gauges are much trickier to use accurately than an outside micrometer. It is easy to put the gauge into the bore with one end lower than the other. This will cause the reading to be larger than the actual bore being measured. Also, if the inside micrometer does not bisect, or span, the widest part of the bore, in other words does not actually measure the full diameter, the reading will be inaccurate.

When the cylinder or bore is smaller than two inches, the inside micrometer cannot be used. Extremely small bores require the use of split ball gauges. Inserted into the bore of something like a valve guide, the split ball can be adjusted to the diameter of the guide. When removed from the bore, use a standard micrometer to measure the size of the split, which, of course, is the diameter of the guide.

Telescoping gauges are available in sizes up to several inches, and consist of spring loaded rods that make contact with the sides of the cylinder or bearing bore to be measured. When removed, the length of the telescoping rods can be measured with a standard micrometer to accurately determine the bore diameter.

NOTE: Using micrometers, inside micrometers, split ball and telescoping gauges requires a little skill. The measuring instrument should be extended until it makes firm but gentle contact with surfaces being measured. The measuring instrument must bisect the bore and must be perpendicular to the walls of the bore being measured. Gently move the measuring device back and forth to ensure firm contact, which will give the proper measurement.

Dial Indicator

The dial indicator consists of a precision dial gauge, usually marked in thousandths of an inch, which is moved by a plunger or rack. When clamped or mounted firmly to a block or cylinder head, dial indicators can be used to measure the amount of front-to-rear movement or end play in the camshaft or crankshaft. There are many places that a dial indicator is essential. For instance, a dial indicator may be used to measure the amount of protrusion of a piston above the deck of the block, to find the exact top dead center (TDC) positioning of a piston in its travel within the cylinder bore, relative to crankshaft rotation. Furthermore, the dial indicator can confirm that the crankshaft's connecting rod journals are indexed, or properly phased.

Additional jobs for the dial indicator include checking the flatness, parallelism, and run-out of rotating objects like the flywheel.

Dial Calipers

My fifth-grade teacher demonstrated how to measure the thickness of a human hair with a tool called a vernier caliper. This tool measures through the use of a logarithmic scale parallel to a scale based on common units of measure. The modern version of the tool uses either a dial or digital display to communicate the readings to the technician. While the modern version is no more accurate than the vernier scale-type caliper, they are easier to read and therefore there is less chance of making a mistake in the readings.

Exotic Tools
Dial Bore Gauge

The dial bore gauge combines the features of a dial indicator with those of a telescoping gauge. The

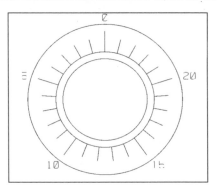

Note that the barrel is marked off in 25 increments, each of which represents 0.001 inch.

advantage of this tool is that its two guides, located on either side of the telescoping spindle, plus one above the spindle keep the gauge perpendicular to the cylinder wall and properly spanning the bore. These gauges are handy and quick to use when checking the cylinder bore for taper and out-of-round. Many of these gauges are accurate to 0.0001 (one ten-thousandth) of an inch.

Bevel Protractor

Angles are sometimes important when machining an engine. This tool can be used to measure valve angles and the machined angles after head work has been performed.

Scales

High speed engines require the reciprocating parts to be as close to the same weight as possible. A piston that is heavier than the rest will create vibration and add stress to the crankshaft. Since it takes energy to cause a vibration—energy that would otherwise be used to push the vehicle down the road—the presence of vibrations reduces the performance of the engine. In an engine with a 3-inch stroke running at 8,000 rpm, the pistons are traveling at 4,000 feet per second. One gram of weight difference at these speeds can rob the engine of over 33 potential horsepower!

Engine Disassembly and Assembly Tools
Ridge Reamer

The ridge reamer is used to remove the ridge that builds at the top of the cylinder walls. This ridge forms during thousands of miles of operation, as the rings move tiny bits of metal up the cylinder walls depositing them at the top of the cylinder, like the terminal moraine of a glacier.

Ring Compressor

Piston rings are designed to be larger than the cylinder. This helps to maintain firm contact between the

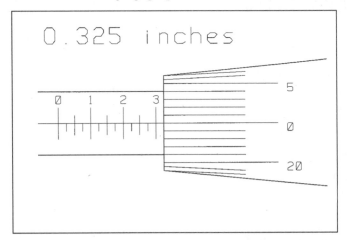

The reading here shows 0.3 inch plus 25 1-thousandths of an inch. Since the tool we used to measure the piston was a 4–5 inch mic, the diameter of the piston skirt we measured was 4 + 0.3 + 0.025, or 4.325 inches.

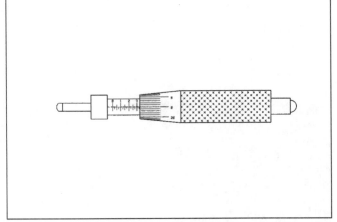

The inside micrometer works just like an outside micrometer. These are used to measure the bores of cylinders, etc. Notice the rounded ends. These are necessary to accommodate the curved inner walls of a cylinder but make the tools very difficult to become competent to use. It is often difficult to ensure that the spindle of an outside micrometer is perpendicular to the object being measured; it is much more difficult with an inside mic.

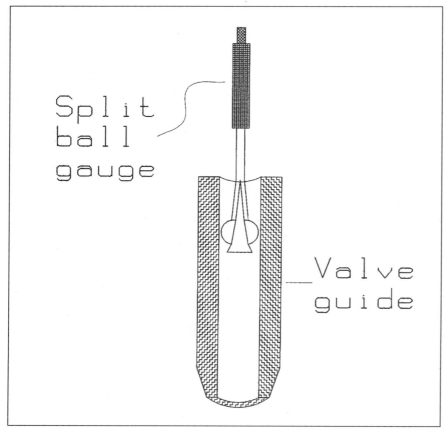

The split ball gauge is designed to measure extremely small bores, like that of a valve guide. These gauges feature a split shaft that is pressed against the bore walls as the ball is pulled up by rotating the small knob on top of the gauge. The tool is then removed from the bore and measured with a micrometer.

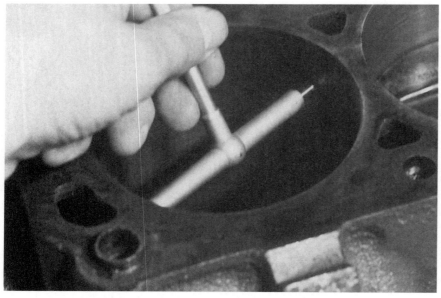

Like a split ball gauge, a telescoping gauge is fitted inside the bore then removed and measured with a standard outside micrometer.

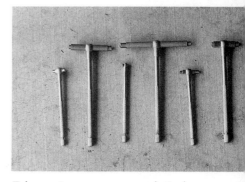

Telescoping gauges are relatively inexpensive alternatives to inside micrometers.

rings and the cylinder walls. A gap in the ring allows it to be squeezed together so it will fit in the cylinder. The open end of the rings must be squeezed together in order to get the pistons into the cylinder. This is the job of the piston ring compressor.

While any piston ring compressor will work for most engines, some engines require a special compressor. With most domestic and foreign engines, the pistons go in from the top. A few engines—like the old Volkswagen air cooled engines — require the pistons to be installed from the bottom. On these applications the connecting rod is attached to the crankshaft before it is installed into the cylinder, which would prevent a standard ring compressor from being removed once the piston is installed. Although there are ways around this problem, there is a special ring compressor available—one designed to come apart for easy removal.

Degree Wheel

The degree wheel is used to precisely measure the rotation of the crankshaft. These measurements are necessary when attempting to precisely phase the camshaft with the crankshaft. Additionally, the degree wheel can also be used to verify the proper indexing of the rod journals and the cam lobes. Verification of the proper valve timing (opening, closing, duration, overlap, separation, etc.) can also be accomplished.

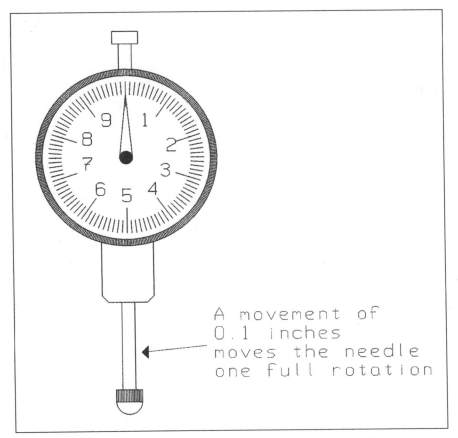

A movement of
0.1 inches
moves the needle
one full rotation

Dial indictors are used to measure depth and surface variations. On this dial indicator, a movement of 0.1 inch will cause the needle on the gauge to rotate one full revolution. Therefore the movement of one hash mark is equal to a movement of 0.001 inch.

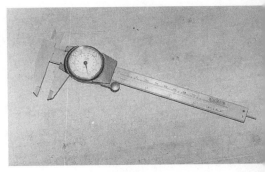

I was introduced to the vernier caliper at the tender age of 10. At the age of 14, my ninth-grade science teacher was having us calculate the circumference of a needle using this tool. Thank goodness a dial has replaced that vernier scale, which was very difficult to use. These tools are handy for quick measurements, where limited precision is required.

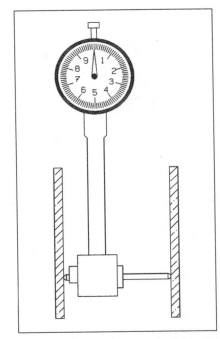

The bore gauge is used to measure the diameter and trueness of the cylinder bore.

Valve Spring Compressor

This tool looks like a large C-clamp with a set of hooks on one end to cradle the valve spring. When tightened, the valve spring is compressed, allowing the valve keepers to be removed. Although not absolutely necessary during the disassembly process, the valve spring compressor is indispensable during the reassembly process.

Some overhead cam engines have the valves recessed in the head. These engines require special valve spring compressors.

Burette

A burette is a glass tube marked in milliliters. At the bottom of the tube there is a petcock. When the burette is filled with mineral oil and slowly drained through the petcock into the combustion chambers of the cylinder head, it is possible to measure the volume of the combustion chambers. When blueprinting an engine, the equality of combustion chamber volume is critical to achieving equal power from each of the cylinders.

Electric Drill

A powerful electric drill is one of the most universal tools that any handyman or technician can possess. Cleaning, buffing, grinding and enlarging are all tasks that can be performed by this simple and common tool.

High Speed Grinder

Like drill motors, these tools come in a wide range of sizes. Small, low horsepower grinders are great for the detail work of deburring and removal of "flash" (excess metal) from a casting. Anyone who has built a model car or model airplane is familiar with the flash that results from seep-age of the plastic into the joints between the sections of the mold. When building a plastic model, this flash must be removed to make the final product look neat.

Similarly, many engine parts have flash at the junction between the pieces of the mold. Removing this flash is important for more than just

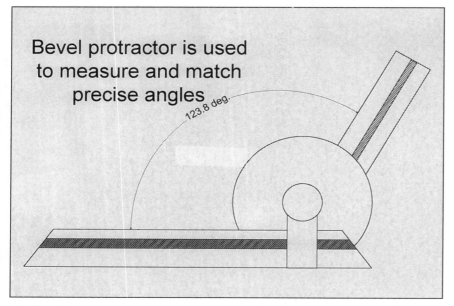

Bevel protractor is used
to measure and match
precise angles

123.8 deg.

The bevel protractor is used to measure valve angles and the machined angles after head work has been done.

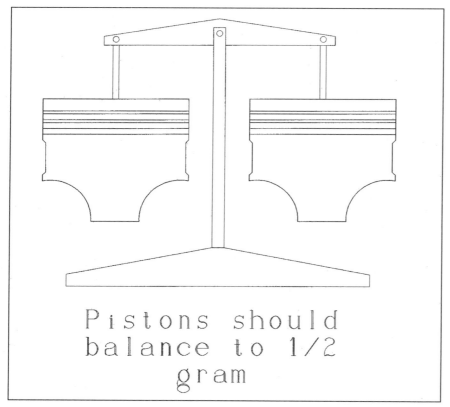

Pistons should
balance to 1/2
gram

Balancing is the second part of the common expression "blueprinted and balanced." All of the reciprocating components should be within one-quarter to one-half gram of one another.

cosmetic purposes: The ridges formed by the flash provide a starting point—known as a stress riser—for cracks and stress fractures.

A rotary file in an electric drill motor is the perfect tool for grinding off flash. Air drills are acceptable if the motor has a variable speed, but most single-speed air drills spin so fast that the unwary hand could accidentally grind away the block and leave the flash behind. Remove any flash evident on the interior of the crankcase or the intake valley. Other places to look for flash include the lifter valley drain holes to the crankcase. Don't get carried away with "deburring" a component, however, because the idea is to remove the flash, not polish the inside of the block. While a polished block may seem like a nice idea, in reality the removal of all the little dimples reduces the surface area of the block and reduces heat transfer from the oil to the block.

There are places in the block where a rotary file will not fit. In those areas, a flat-tipped punch will usually work well. A file should be used to debur the edges of the main bearing caps. Deburring the lifter holes can be done with a wheel cylinder abrasive ball hone. It is not advisable to use a flat stone wheel cylinder hone for this purpose.

Piston Ring File

Many high-performance piston rings are built with a negative gap. This allows the engine builder to choose and create the ring gap that best suits the application. Below is a chart of typical gaps for specific engine uses.

Piston Ring Expander/Installer

Two of the trickiest operations of rebuilding an engine are removing and installing the brittle piston rings without breaking them. While the rings can easily be spread far enough to go over the piston head and slip them into the ring grooves of the pistons, they can also be easily spread far enough to break them. While the piston ring pliers

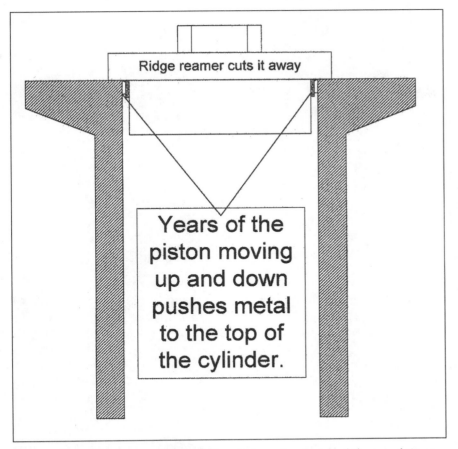

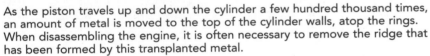

As the piston travels up and down the cylinder a few hundred thousand times, an amount of metal is moved to the top of the cylinder walls, atop the rings. When disassembling the engine, it is often necessary to remove the ridge that has been formed by this transplanted metal.

The ring compressor is a necessary tool for reassembly. The piston rings must be held within the perimeter of the ring grooves so that the piston can be installed in the cylinder.

do not eliminate the possibility of breaking the piston rings, they do decrease that risk significantly.

Pullers

Pullers are one of those things in life that no matter how many you have, you never have the one you need. Several categories of pullers are needed to complete an engine disassembly: slotted bolt pullers, claw pullers, and slide hammers will all be needed.

Ductile iron top rings	Readings below in inches	Plain iron second rings	Readings below in inches
Supercharged/ injected nitro engine	0.022–0.024	Supercharged/ injected nitro engine	0.014–0.016
Supercharged/ injected alcohol engine	0.018–0.020	Supercharged/ injected alcohol engine	0.012–0.014
Supercharged/ injected gasoline engine	0.022–0.024	Supercharged/ injected gasoline engine	0.012–0.014
Oval track (rectangular ring) carbureted engine	0.018–0.020	Oval track carbureted engine	0.012–0.014
Oval track (head land rings) carbureted engine	0.024–0.026	Modified drag racing carbureted engine	0.012–0.014
Oval track (pressure back rings) carbureted engine	0.020–0.022	Stock, Super Stock drag racing carbureted engine	0.010–0.012
Modified drag racing carbureted engine	0.018–0.020	Street carbureted engine	0.010–0.012
Stock drag racing carbureted engine	0.016–0.018		
Street carbureted engine	0.016–0.018		

The degree wheel is used to accurately phase the crankshaft with the camshaft. Synchronizing the camshaft with the crankshaft, and therefore with the pistons, is one of the most important ways of improving or maximizing performance.

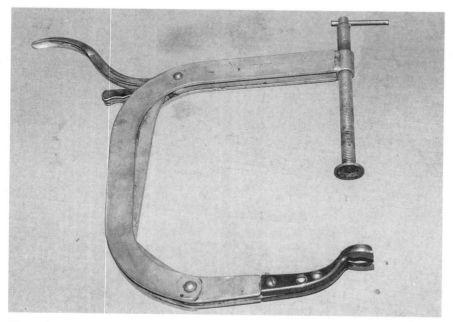

The valve spring compressor is needed to both remove and install the valves in the cylinder head. The most common design looks like a large C-clamp; some are air operated.

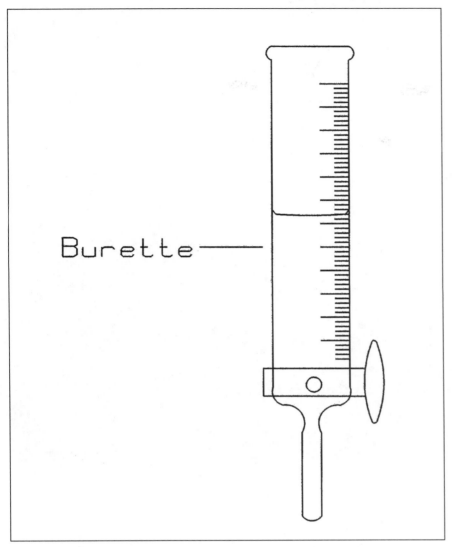

Burette

In 265 BC, Archimedes discovered that if you fill a bathtub too full and then get in it, it will overflow. According to legend, he cried "Eureka!" when he discovered this. Although the physicists and engineers are mostly concerned about why things float, with regards to this discovery, it also proves that a liquid conforms to the shape of the vessel it is in and also to items placed in it. Carefully measuring the amount of liquid that can be poured into the combustion chamber of a cylinder head, for instance, will tell the engine builder the exact volume of that combustion chamber. A burette is used to measure how much fluid is poured into the port or chamber.

Most electric drills are designed, as the name implies, to utilize another discovery of Archimedes. The screw is the basic principle of the drill. Drilling holes is an operation that needs to be conducted at relatively low speeds. When grinding, higher speeds are required. A high-speed grinder is essential for removing metal for balancing weights and volumes in an engine.

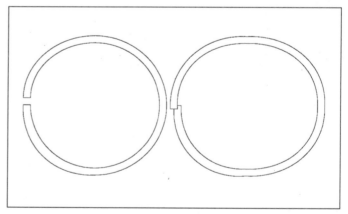

Most performance rings are manufactured either with no ring end gap or even with an overlapping gap. A ring file is used by the engine builder to provide the desired gap.

Piston ring expanders, or pliers, are used to install piston rings on the pistons. Rings are very brittle and can easily be broken when spread apart for installation; these pliers reduce that risk.

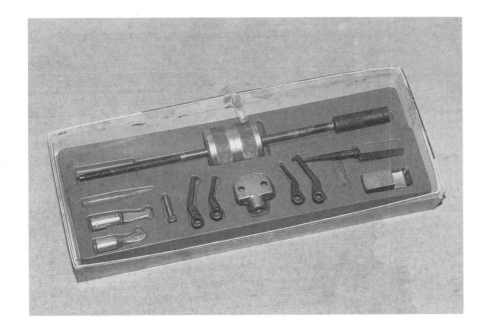

A selection of slide hammers and pullers makes the process of disassembly much easier. An interesting rule of the industry is "no matter how many pullers you have, you will never have the one you need."

CHAPTER TWO

CYLINDER BLOCKS

As the very foundation of your engine, it could easily be argued that the cylinder block is the single most important part. After all, without the block, you don't have much of an engine—just a pile of parts laying in a big puddle of oil and coolant.

The block for your new engine must be carefully chosen and painstakingly prepared if you expect it—and thus your engine—to last a good, long while. With that in mind, you will have to weigh the advantages of going with a new block against those of using a seasoned, used block. You'll also want to consider the block material, as well as the presence or lack of specific machining or features, such as four-bolt main bearing caps.

And once you know what you want, you've got to find a suitable example of it that you can then prepare exactly as needed to suit your requirements, whatever those may be.

There's a lot to think about when you're thinking about cylinder blocks.

The following information should help steer you in the right direction by giving you a few pointers.

Selecting a Block

Engine blocks are not created equal, and they certainly are not equal after they have traveled down the road a few thousand miles. Some blocks are treated with kindness and care. Other blocks are treated very poorly, indeed. In my own history there was an episode where I was traveling from Yakima, Washington, to Twin Falls, Idaho. I had a full day to make the 479-mile journey, plenty of time. About 80 miles out of Yakima, the upper radiator hose blew. Because of the traffic and lack of a safe place to stop, the engine got extremely overheated. After shortening the hose and borrowing an inadequate amount of water from a passing state trooper I made it into the next town. The engine was

There is some debate over whether you should begin building your performance engine with a new block or with an old block. New blocks can be somewhat depended upon to be free of defects. Used, or "seasoned" engine blocks are typically free of stress areas that promote cracks and defects. Sometimes a real gem can be found. This old Mustang engine sat on a friend's garage floor for nearly 20 years before being reborn.

Cleaning is one of those tasks that can be very time consuming. I usually just send the block, heads, and miscellaneous components to a machine shop equipped with good cleaning equipment and devote my mental processes to loftier targets—cam lift, duration, cc measurements of combustion chambers, to name a few.

The engine block is usually the largest and heaviest component in the engine. Yet, as heavy as it is, it is still prone to distortions and damage due to heat and wear. Inspect the block for cracks and evidence of poor maintenance and overheating. The two white lines highlight cracks in the cylinder wall of this block.

extremely hot. After letting it cool down for about an hour, I replaced the offending hose and the thermostat. Leaving town, I felt confident that I would be able to make it to Twin Falls. But the route I was traveling required driving across the corner of Oregon, and about 70 or 80 miles into Oregon I came to a place known by the locals as Cabbage Hill. For about 20 miles, Interstate 84 travels up a six percent or steeper grade. About half way up the grade, the engine overheated again. This time, by the time I got to a place where I could shut the engine off, the block and cylinder head were so hot that the engine was behaving more like a diesel engine than a gas one. This event repeated itself twice more that day. I finally ended up trailering the car another 1,800 miles home. The point of all this is that even an engine owned by a conscientious individual might have been subjected to severe trauma during its life. Even though this was not a performance application, the reuse of this engine block was out of the question.

Begin your search by looking for a well-maintained late-model vehicle featuring the engine block you need. If your search leads you to the wrecking yard (a.k.a.: the automotive parts recycler), look for a car that is residing in that yard as a result of being rear-ended. The hot blocks—the small-block Chevrolets, Fords, and Chryslers—are getting ever harder to find. Technology has progressed at a very rapid pace over the past ten years. Some of these technological changes have been a real benefit to the automotive enthusiast. Electronic fuel injection, electronic timing control, and other high-tech systems have resolved many of the operational compromises that have plagued engine designers and builders since the dawn of history. But along with these changes have come changes in the basic design of the engine. In fact, these blocks are slowly being phased out in new cars. Many of the newer engine blocks have very limited potential for performance modification.

New Versus "Experienced" Block

Based on what you just read, you might assume that a new engine block would be the best way to begin. But there are considerable advantages to using an "experienced" or "seasoned" engine block. Casting something like an engine block leaves it with many unseen stress points and lines. As an engine is run, heat and the repeated stroking of the cylinders with the pistons tend to relieve these stresses. Therefore engines tend to get stronger as they age.

Older castings, however, may have been made at a time when automakers were trying to reduce both costs and weight. Some blocks made during the 1970s were made with thin cylinder walls and crankcases. Eventually, the automakers realized that this was bad business and have increased the weights and thicknesses. What little increase there is in weight is more than offset by greater strength and better heat dissipation.

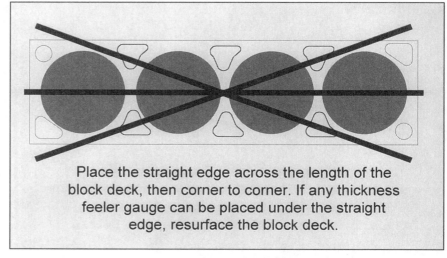

Place the straight edge across the length of the block deck, then corner to corner. If any thickness feeler gauge can be placed under the straight edge, resurface the block deck.

A machinist's straight edge is used to check the flatness of surfaces like the cylinder head and block deck.

Perhaps the ideal situation is to find a used—but not abused—heavy-duty engine. Some of these so-called heavy-duty engines are quite famous. "Four-bolt main" 302's and 351's are among these. Other heavy-duty engines are less well known. Most truck engines from the 1960's and 1970's were built with much heavier castings than their automobile counterparts.

Preliminary Inspection and Disassembly Cleaning

Cleaning is one of the least glamorous operations, but it is one of the most necessary in quality engine building. There are a number of effective ways to clean engine parts: The good old hot tank acid bath is a very effective method, because the parts are left as oil-free, bare metal. Unfortunately, this method produces an environmentally toxic waste product.

There are several practical approaches that can be taken with cleaning. Perhaps the easiest and most practical is to let someone else do it, if they can do it better than you. Solvents and cleaners can have a tremendous environmental impact—even the ones available to the typical consumer may have special disposal instructions that range from being a hassle, to being exorbitantly expensive to dispose of. Most machine shops provide a for-fee service that will clean the parts far better than you or I could ever dream of doing.

There are several cleaning systems available that do an excellent job. These include chemical acid-based, chemical caustic-based, citrus-based, enzyme-based, high-pressure water,

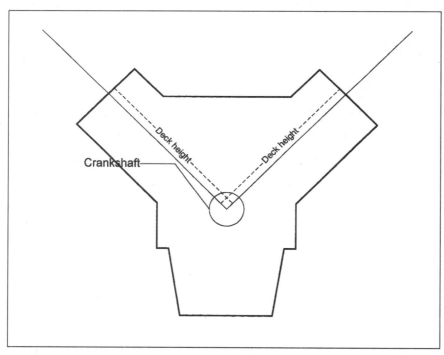

The deck height is the distance from the rotating center of the crankshaft main journals to the top of the cylinder head mating surface of the block. In most cases this should be exactly, or almost exactly, the same distance as from the center of the connecting rod big end to the top of the piston head (not dome). If the engine block you are contemplating using has ever had machine work such as deck resurfacing or line boring done, these operations may limit your flexibility for new machine work.

Cracks many times will leave telltale signs. Although pressure testing should be done, this only ensures the integrity of the water jacket. Cracks that may cause breaking of the block outside of the water jacket area must be found with the eyes.

and high-pressure steam. In most cases, the equipment your machine shop uses will be adequate. If it weren't adequate, they probably would have purchased something else, because chances are good that the machinist is just as finicky—if not more so—than you are.

A few final words of advice: There's a right cleaning tool for every cleaning job. Keep this in mind the next time you think of using the dishwasher to clean parts. After all, you wouldn't use your electric drill as a hammer, would you?

Preliminary Inspection

You are probably not blueprinting your engine because of a deep-seated desire to spend more money than you really need to during your overhaul. The engine is almost doubtlessly destined for some sort of high-performance application. "High performance" can be

defined in several different ways. Most people think of fire-breathing track rockets, but high performance can also mean good fuel economy or smooth operation during long duration cruise conditions. In any event, only parts close to the nominal spec on their tolerance should be used. These parts should be free of cracks and other damage, of course. Additionally, wherever there are multiple units of a component type, such as pistons and connecting rods, it is always best to start with as nearly balanced a set as possible. Many machine shops will have literally drums full of good used connecting rods and pistons for common engines. Bring a set of one-gram accurate scales and a six pack of the machine shop manager's favorite beverage and spend an afternoon weighing out a set of parts.

It just doesn't make sense to use certain seasoned parts, however.

Camshafts, lifters, piston rings, and main rod and cam bearings should always be replaced during any overhaul; therefore close inspection of these components is not necessary. Crankshafts, pistons, the block, connecting rods, heads and most other engine parts should receive close inspection before being reused. Over the next few pages visual and preliminary inspection of the primary non-replacement engine components will be discussed.

Engine Block Inspection
Deck Height

The engine block is, of course, one of the primary components of the engine. It is usually the most expensive component, unless you are opting for a forged crank. Purchasing a new block may considerably reduce the risk of putting a lot of time, effort, and money into what might ultimately prove to be a defective chunk of iron. As already discussed, however, there are benefits to using a previously "seasoned" block.

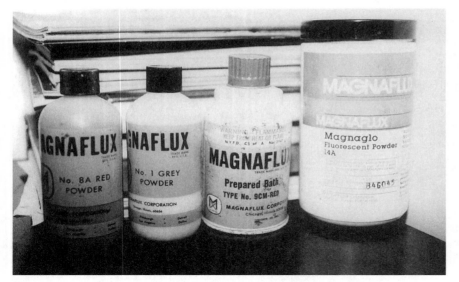

There are many chemicals and devices designed to help the builder find evidence of cracks in metal components. Some that use magnetic fields are only effective on iron components. Others, like these dyes, can be used on cast iron, steel, aluminum, and alloys. A residual stain remains in the crack after application of the dye and the solvent, which make the crack easy to see.

Look at the block closely for evidence of work that may have been done to the deck, or head-mating surface. Inspect the main bearing saddles and caps, looking particularly for evidence that the block may have been align bored. While shaving the block's "deck" surface (the block-to-head mating surface) increases the likelihood that the piston-to-deck clearance at top dead center (TDC) will be incorrect, align boring can also affect this "deck height" because it actually raises the crank centerline closer to the deck surfaces. Of course, it is possible that the machining that was previously done on the block, with regard to these to parameters, is exactly what you want done, which would then save you some money. But it's not very likely.

And keep in mind that any previous machine work will limit the machining you can have performed during your rebuild. It is always best to start with a "virgin" part—something as close as possible to the way it was cast. This gives you the most flexibility and option of changing your mind, reconfiguring, and experimenting.

True Surfaces

There are many important surfaces on an engine block, but two of the surfaces are critical: The block's deck surface—where the head mates with it—must be parallel in all planes to a centerline drawn through the main journal cradles; and the head's deck surface—where it mates to the block—must be smooth, flat, and even. If you lay a machinist's straight edge on the top of the block deck, bisecting each of the cylinders, you should not be able to slide a feeler gauge—even the thinnest gauge you have—between the straight edge and the deck surface. If a gauge fits, the block deck should be machined. This zero-tolerance policy for this specification might seem somewhat severe to some people, but a blueprinted engine is usually asked to endure great pressures and forces, and settling for anything less than perfect is settling for something less than dependable. If a 10-thousandths feeler gauge (or larger) fits under the straight edge, consider another block.

Repeat the test with the straight edge turned from one corner to the other (e.g., upper-left to lower-right) then between the opposite corners. Again, the feeler gauge should not fit.

The crankshaft journal alignment is also critical. Lay the straight edge in the trough of the main bearing webs. You should not be able to insert a feeler gauge between the straight edge and the bearing saddle.

If a feeler gauge does fit, it could indicate that the engine block is distorted, and that could indicate that the engine was severely overheated in the past. It might be advisable to find a different engine block. Severe overheating can cause changes in the metallurgy that will either strengthen or weaken the block. These effects are unpredictable, aren't easily measured, and are definitely uneven. At the very least, the quality and strength of the engine block will be uneven. At the very worst, it will be very weak.

Cracks and Integrity

This is a job for the keen of eye, the determined of will and the long of patience. Cracks have a way of being elusive to the untrained eye. One of my favorite machinists, a fellow I used to use all the time in the Seattle area, had an uncanny eye for finding even the smallest crack or non-conformity. As good as your eye may be for finding these problems, your eye will never beat that of a trained professional, or, if you are a trained professional, the eye of another trained professional.

There are also many methods of checking for cracks and other damage that are a little more scientific in nature. One of the best methods is called magnafluxing. The component being tested is placed on or against a large electro-magnet. The electro-magnet is then switched on. If the component being tested has a relatively uniform structure, the magnetic lines of flux from the electro-magnet will be disbursed evenly throughout the component. Iron filings are then sprinkled on the component. The iron filings will distribute in a pattern following the magnetic lines of flux. If there are no cracks or anomalies, the pattern of the iron filings will be fairly uniform. If there is a crack, the iron filings will line up in a pattern that outlines the crack.

Magnafluxing does not work very well on aluminum, though. For non-ferrous materials, a dye method is used, which involves spraying a colorful dye on the component being tested, and the dye is allowed to soak in for a few minutes. A solvent is then used to remove the dye from the surface of the component. If there are any cranks, the stain will have seeped into them and a jagged line of the dyes color will be easily visible.

Sonic Testing

Sonic testing is one of the newest and, naturally, one of the most high-tech ways of testing the block. Where this technology shines is in its ability to confirm the thickness of the block, which is important because castings are not always exactly the same thickness. Some castings may be thinner in critical stress areas than others, and sonic testing can detect these anomalies and head off a potential disaster.

CONTENTS

CHAPTER THREE

CRANKSHAFTS

If the cylinder block is your engine's foundation, then the crankshaft would have to be the equivalent of a house's floors. Build your house with weak, poorly constructed floors, and they'll creak and groan and bounce until one day—*CRACK!!*—they break apart beneath you, scattering debris everywhere.

Ironically, good crankshafts, like good floors, aren't hard to come by, they just cost a little more. But isn't this an area that's well worth an added expense? After all, the crankshaft is the very thing that keeps those connecting rods and pistons moving, and sends the power rearward to help you keep moving ahead, ever faster.

As an engine blueprinter, you'll face certain challenges with the crankshaft—reducing weight, reducing friction, improving lubrication, increasing strength, increasing durability, just to name a few. And there are right ways and wrong ways to achieve any of these goals. The information you'll find on the following pages should make your decisions a bit easier and make your engine that much better.

Types
Cast

There are several quality ranges of crankshafts available. The lowest range is the simple cast crankshaft. These are by far the most common and least expensive of the available crankshafts. The cast iron crank has been the mainstay of the automotive engine industry for decades. The main shortcoming of the cast iron crank is its strength. If you were to break a cast iron crankshaft in half you would see a rather non-homogeneous pattern to the metal, and this random non-homogeneity weakens the structure of the crankshaft. Some castings are worse than others, but without special X-ray equipment, it's impossible to tell these worse cranks from the better ones.

The cast iron crankshaft has been the mainstay of the automotive industry for decades. It remains a cheap and relatively strong choice. In fact, a stock, cast iron crankshaft is quite adequate for most street performance and bracket racing applications.

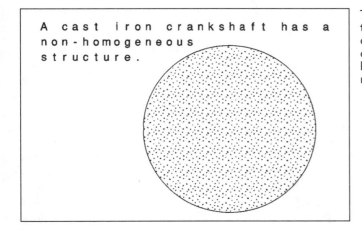

A cast iron crankshaft has a non-homogeneous structure.

The structure of the cast iron crankshaft is low-density and non-homogeneous in nature.

Forged

Forged crankshafts feature a much more homogeneous structure. This homogeneity adds to the strength of the crankshaft. Forging aligns the structure of the metal. The principle is the same as the strength gained when bricks in a wall are properly aligned versus being aligned in a haphazard fashion. Forged crankshafts can be very expensive, but they should be strongly considered when a high-power, high-performance engine is being built.

Billet

Billet crankshafts are machined from a solid and uniform block of steel, and thus they make the ultimate crankshaft. The solid billet steel provides maximum strength. When installed with custom connecting rods—rods that have been designed specifically for use with that crankshaft design—the rod journals can be made with a smaller diameter. Smaller journal diameters, plus lighter rods and pistons can mean smaller crankshaft counterweights. Smaller crankshaft counterweights can mean less rotating mass in the engine, and that can mean more power from the engine.

As you might imagine, billet and forged cranks can be very expensive and are not available for every application. A standard cast iron crank has done a superb and lasting job for street performance engines for decades. In fact, the strengthening processes available for cast iron crankshafts can improve the strength of the cast iron crank so much that your street performance dollar will always be better spent on heads, pistons, rods, and balancing.

Problems and Fixes
Out-of-Round Journals

Crankshaft journals have to be round. To check whether yours are truly and uniformly round, you need to measure each journal in several places to get an accurate picture of the journal's shape. Start by measuring one end of a journal with a micrometer (your "A" measurement), then rotate the micrometer 90 degrees and check it again (the "B" measurement). Take these measurements again at the other end of the journal ("C" and "D" measurements). The difference between the "A" and "B" measurements or the "C" and "D" measurements is the out-of-round of the journal. Repeat the procedure for each rod and main journal. Out-of-round wear should be less than 0.0005 inch. If any of the journals shows greater wear, the crankshaft will have to be machined. If only the main bearing journals exhibit excessive wear, only the main journals will need to be machined. And if only the rod bearing journals exhibit excessive wear, only the rod journals will need to be machined. In fact, after showing the measurements to your machinist, he may even advise you to machine the specific rod and main journals to different undersizes to correct the problem.

This is a forged crank from a small high-performance four-cylinder engine. Forged crankshafts offer superior strength and durability, if you can afford the higher price tag.

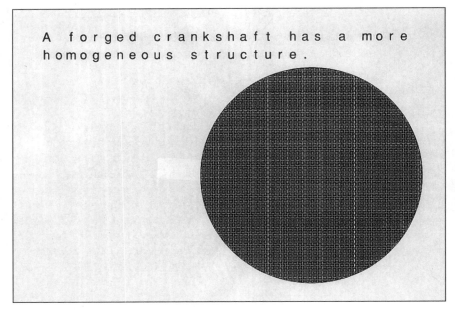

A forged crankshaft has a more homogeneous structure.

Forged crankshafts have a much denser and homogeneous structure.

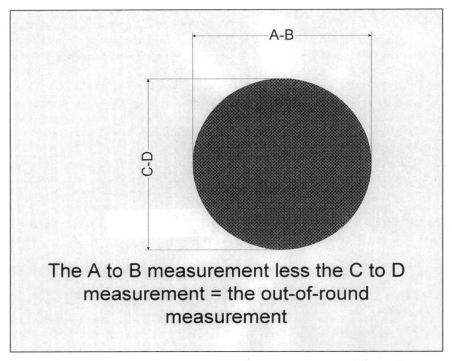

A-B

C-D

The A to B measurement less the C to D measurement = the out-of-round measurement

Many crankshafts will not wear evenly. Before installing a used crankshaft, there are several measurements that should be made. With a micrometer, take a measurement from A to B, and then again from C to D. Subtract the larger measurement from the smaller. If the difference is greater than 0.0005 inch, have the crankshaft machined.

Journal Taper

The taper on each journal is the difference between measurements "A" and "C" and from "B" to "D." Maximum allowable tolerance for taper is also 0.0005 inch.

Regrinding the Crank

When the machine shop grinds the crank to 0.010 undersize, it means that 0.005 inches of metal has been removed from around the journal. Because the metal has been removed from the radius of the journal (from its center to its outside edge), the diameter of the journal (from outside edge to outside edge) has been reduced by 0.010 inches.

Most machine shops do not have crank grinding capability. If you confirm that your crank will need to be ground and the machinist you have chosen to use does not have this capability, he will need to send it to another machine shop. This is a common practice and should not deter you from using your chosen machinist. Crank grinding equipment is very expensive and difficult for a small machine shop to realize a return on. However, you may want to take the crank to your machinist a few days before the rest of the components you will be taking to him, which should allow you to pick up all your machined parts at the same time.

Casting Flash

Anyone who has built a model car or model airplane is familiar with the seepage of the plastic between the sections of the mold. The sharp edged residue of this is called flash. When building a plastic model this flash must be removed to make the final product look neat. In engine components, the flash also marks the junction between

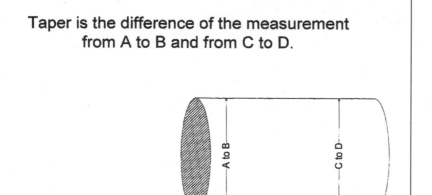

Taper is the difference of the measurement from A to B and from C to D.

Taper is the difference between a measurement from A to B, above, and from C to D. The maximum amount of allowable taper is also 0.0005 inch.

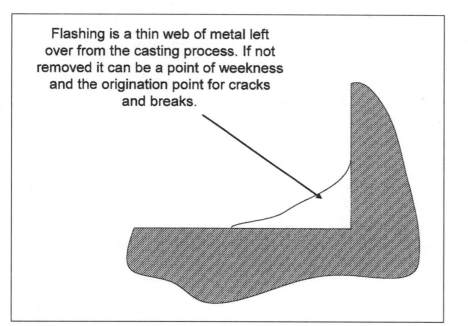

Flashing is a thin web of metal left over from the casting process. If not removed it can be a point of weekness and the origination point for cracks and breaks.

Anyone who has ever built a plastic model car is familiar with casting flash—the thin web of metal (or plastic, on the models) left over from the casting process. Use a high-speed grinder to remove this point of weakness. If not removed, flash can be a source of weakness and an origination point for stress cracks and fractures.

the pieces of the mold. However, in a cast iron or aluminum engine component, you remove this flash for more than just cosmetic reasons—removing casting flash makes engine components stronger, because as you grind away flash you're actually removing stress risers, which are starting points for cracks and stress fractures.

Cracks and Integrity

Crankshafts must withstand tremendous forces, and because of this, damage to a crankshaft is usually quite obvious. However, magnafluxing and dye testing are still good ideas. Obviously, any crankshaft that is cracked or otherwise compromised should be discarded.

A great deal of money can be spent on connecting rods. Some forged aluminum rods can cost thousands of dollars. Unless your goal is to squeeze every last microwatt of horsepower out of the engine you are building, then a well-balanced set of steel rods will be quite adequate. While forged aluminum rods sound cool and exotic, they are not as durable as steel and, thus, require periodic inspection.

CHAPTER FOUR

CONNECTING RODS AND PISTONS

Connecting rods are subjected to some of the greatest forces in the engine and, not surprisingly, when they break they tend to do the greatest amount of damage. A broken and loose connecting rod flying around inside the crankcase at 5,000+ rpm can do a lot of damage *real fast!* Connecting rods have to be carefully chosen and meticulously prepared for a blueprinted, high-performance engine. For a standard engine overhaul, used or rebuilt connecting rods are quite acceptable. For performance engines, at least during the original build, only new connecting rods should be used. Regardless of the age of your rods, it's your sworn duty as an engine blueprinter to ensure that they are inspected for signs of twisting, warping, and cracks. But the work doesn't end there, and this chapter is all about explaining just what goes into blueprinting your connecting rods to improve power, performance, and durability.

Connecting Rod Basics

Each connecting rod has a big end and a small end. The small end fits into the piston where the power is transferred from the piston to the connecting rod by means of a wrist pin. The wrist pin can be installed in one of three methods: It can be pressed into the piston and left "floating" in the rod; it may be pressed into the rod but left floating in the piston; or it may be "full floating" in both the piston and the connecting rod.

The big end of the connecting rod connects to the crankshaft. Around the inside of the big end is a replaceable bearing shell. Due to the enormous stress exerted on these bearing shells, they are among the engine components most prone to failure.

Types of Connecting Rods
Cast

Cast iron connecting rods are similar to Zoot Suits, they were quite

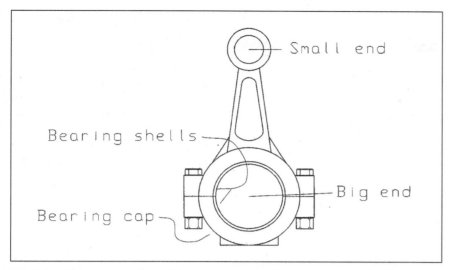

The job of the connecting rod is to connect the forces generated by the rapidly expanding gases of combustion to the crankshaft. These forces can be extreme. This illustration shows the main parts of a connecting rod.

the item in their day, but now they are severely outmoded. Cast iron connecting rods were great in the days of low-horsepower, low-rpm engines, but they are totally unsuitable for today's stock engines, much less high-performance or racing engines.

Steel

Steel connecting rods are the standard of the industry today. They provide high durability, low wear, and high resistance to deterioration and distortion from heat. Although steel connecting rods are far superior to cast ones, they still have a non-homogeneous nature to their structure. Again, this non-homogeneous structure limits their strength.

Forged

Like forged crankshafts, forged connecting rods offer great strength without a large increase in weight. There are two primary metals that are used in the construction of forged connecting rods: steel and aluminum.

Billet

Billet connecting rods, like billet crankshafts, offer great strength because they are machined from a solid and uniform piece of metal. If you are strictly interested in high-performance and racing use, then there is

no other logical choice than to spend the money for billet connecting rods.

Problems and Fixes
Distortion

There may be several contributing factors to connecting rod distortion. Catastrophic engine failure is the most dramatic cause, but in most cases even a slight twist in the rod can weaken its structural integrity. Minor distortion in connecting rods can usually be corrected, but this amounts to simple straightening and does nothing to restore the strength of the rod. In performance engines, twisted connecting rods should never be re-used, they should be replaced.

The job of a connecting rod is to connect the power generated by the explosion of the air and fuel in the combustion chamber, above the piston, to the crankshaft. Like the pistons, the connecting rods can either be cast or forged. Forged pistons are stronger, and more precisely manufactured; therefore, they are normally reserved for performance engines. Connecting rods for less-ambitious passenger cars are made of cast iron. Cast iron connecting rods represent an enormous reciprocating mass, robbing the engine of precious power and rpm. Racing engines and other high-performance engines often use aluminum

connecting rods. The 1950s and 1960s saw the introduction of aluminum connecting rods on performance engines, allowing higher maximum rpm and reducing parasitic loss of power to the reciprocating movement of the connecting rod mass.

Materials

There are two basic materials that have been used in modern connecting rods, steel and aluminum. Steel connecting rods are still the industry standard for factory OEM (Original Equipment Manufacturers) engines. These engines are designed to take mom and pop to the bingo parlor or to provide the illusion of speed/performance while making sure that even with the roughest abuse the engine will at least outlast the 50,000 to 70,000 warranty. Connecting rods connect the power of the controlled explosion on top of the piston in the combustion chamber to the ground. Since each of the cylinders fires consecutively, each of the connecting rods is individually responsible for moving several tons of iron, steel, aluminum, glass, and plastic down the road. A typical steel connecting rod features an "I-Beam" construction. This maximizes the strength of the rod while minimizing the weight. These steel connecting rods offer extreme durability in the roughest and most long-term service.

Performance connecting rods (remember that "performance" is a term that can mean either speed or economy) are generally made of aluminum alloy. My first experience with aluminum connecting rods was very positive. While in trade school, we were required to overhaul the engine from a "real customer's" car—an early 1960s Plymouth Valiant. The engine made no noise beyond the normal engine running noise during our initial inspection. Upon tearing the engine down, we found that all of the bearings in the big ends of the connecting rods had spun. In spite of this, the car's owner had elected to have the engine overhauled only because the school would do it inexpensively and she wanted to keep the car—not

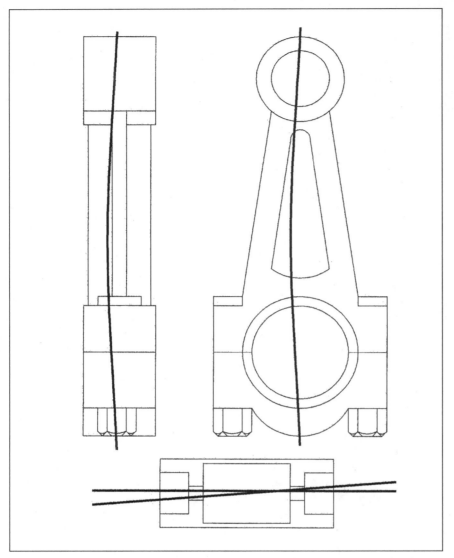

Used connecting rods usually give excellent service, but during a rebuild they should be inspected for cracks, casting flash, and distortion. Check for distortion along the front axis and side axis and twisting along the centerlines of the small and big ends. Any well-equipped machine shop will have equipment to repair connecting rods. These machines not only see to it that the rods are not bent but also that the holes of the big end and the small end are in proper alignment.

Casting Versus Forging

The automotive world is filled with confusing terminology. Take the following sentence: "Yeah, I rebuilt my engine, put in a 3/4 cam, forged pistons, and forged rods." That sounds great, but what's a 3/4 cam? Is it a V-8 camshaft with four lobes rounded off? Actually, it's a slang term for a mild-grind performance camshaft. The term "forged," however, has a much more specific meaning, but is no less misunderstood.

To understand "forging," you really have to start with understanding the basics of iron casting—pouring molten iron into a mold to form a specific item—which dates back as much as 6,500 years ago to the Bronze Age, and the methods of which have changed little since.

Steel, on the other hand, is a relatively new development. Basically steel is an alloy, or blend, of iron and carbon. It's production dates from only the fourteenth century, while casting steel dates from only the 1800s.

Casting bronze, iron, steel, or any other metal requires a mold into which the molten metal can be poured and allowed to cool. Casting creates a fairly strong—although often poorly structured—metal. Think about the structure of sandstone. There are great mountains of sandstone around the world; they hold up relatively well against erosion and the other forces of nature. Sandstone is brittle and breaks easily, however, when subjected to lateral, shearing forces.

Forging, on the other hand, hammers and forces the metal into a uniform, well-structured material. This is similar to the process that transforms sandstone into quartzite. Quartzite is a much more homogeneous stone, almost like a gem. It is far more resistant to weathering and the stresses of nature and has a much greater shear strength. Forged is to cast as quartzite is to sandstone. Forged connecting rods will therefore have a much higher tensile strength, or resistance to stretching, and a much greater lateral, or shear strength. Aircraft connecting rods are almost always forged.

because she had symptoms that would warrant an overhaul. Although most of the engine, including the cylinder head, had to be replaced, only two connecting rods required replacement. This clearly illustrates the durability of aluminum connecting rods.

The primary advantage of aluminum connecting rods is their minimal inertial mass. Since they're lighter than steel, aluminum rods can significantly improve acceleration, because a lighter component offers less resistance to acceleration than does a heavy one. Lighter connecting rods also allow crankshaft counterweights to be lighter, which reduces the rotating mass.

Despite their many advantages, aluminum connecting rods should really only be considered for engines that are destined for frequent overhaul maintenance. The typical bracket racer may find that the need for routine tear-down and inspection will offset the additional speed potential gained with these rods.

Checking Connecting Rods

If you plan on re-using a set of connecting rods, especially if the rod has been in a racing engine or an engine that has suffered a catastrophic failure, there are several things each rod must be tested for, including

- Cracks
- Bends
- Heat Damage
- Nicks and Burrs
- Residual Magnetism
- Alignment

Cracks

It should be obvious by now that installing a connecting rod that is cracked will doom an engine to early and perhaps catastrophic failure. The question is: How do you ensure that the rods being installed do not have a hidden or microscopic crack? The problem is that you can't. Even a new connecting rod could have an undetectable manufacturing flaw that could cause the engine to disassemble itself in a matter of milliseconds. The best we can do is reduce this likelihood through careful inspection.

Visual

This is where the *Star Trek: The Next Generation* character Data or maybe the Six Million Dollar Man would come in handy. Cracks that may do damage to the connecting rod and therefore the engine can start life extremely small. A good visual inspection requires a well-lit work area, a good magnifying glass, and a lot of patience. Not to mention a good eye or two. In every shop and every family there is a person who can find things no one else can find, a person who can see things no one else can see—this is the person who should do the inspection!

Magnafluxing

Even the most discerning individual can miss cracks that give themselves away only as the slightest discoloration. More scientific methods are available, methods that can even detect cracks hidden below the surface. This technique is called "magnafluxing." The connecting rod is placed on a powerful electromagnet. Fine iron powder is

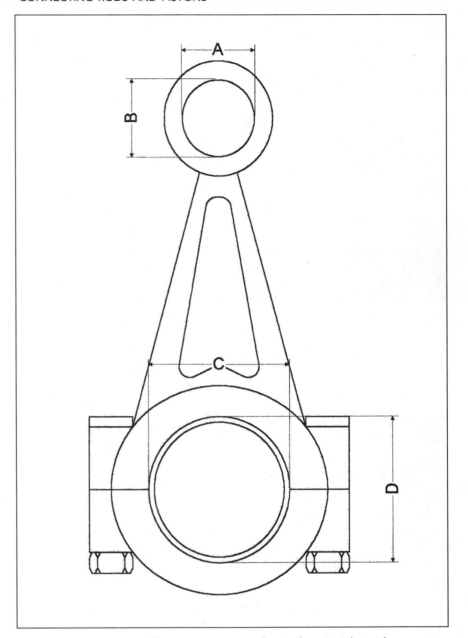

The stresses experienced by a connecting rod as it does its job tend to elongate the big end and small end bores. Should the small end become elongated, it will be necessary to enlarge, then sleeve, the bore. If the big end becomes egg-shaped the machinist will file the ends of the rod bearing cap until the hole is slightly smaller than factory-standard in the D dimension then machine a new, round hole.

sprinkled on the connecting rod. The magnetic field will align the iron powder in a very distinctive pattern, but a crack will interrupt this pattern. When the technician sees this interruption in the even distribution of the powder, he knows that a crack is present. The powder will actually highlight the crack, itself.

Because magnafluxing depends upon magnetism, you can't magnaflux aluminum components, since aluminum isn't affected by magnetism. There are ways of checking aluminum components for cracks, although these methods cannot locate cracks hidden below the surface, as magnafluxing can.

Pistons are an expensive commodity; however, they are a commodity that should not be scrimped on. On the first build of your blueprinting project, new pistons should be purchased. If you must use "veteran" pistons, make sure that they are of proper dimensions and free of cracks and damage.

Dye Penetrant

How many times has this happened to you? You're drinking a cup of coffee from a porcelain mug, and as you get close to the bottom of the cup you see a narrow but long crack in the porcelain. This crack is brown. Your coffee, in fact the coffee from the last several hundred cups, has stained the ceramic material exposed by the crack. This is exactly how dye penetrant works. The crack exposes the relatively coarse and porous inside of the connecting rod to the dye. The dye soaks into the porous material, but is easily cleaned off of the relatively non-porous outside, just like the coffee cup washes cleanly, except for where the crack is.

The procedure for using dye penetrant to inspect for cracks involves coating the surface of the connecting rod with a colored dye. After allowing the dye to dry, as per instructions on the can, the dye is cleaned off of the rod, usually with some sort of solvent. The dye on the outer surface of the rod will clean off easily, but any dye that found its way into a crack will remain, making the crack visible. But again, this only points out surface cracks. It does nothing to point out imperfections beneath the surface of the metal.

So What If It Is Cracked?

If you have a cracked connecting rod, or any other engine component, you really have only two choices of what to do with that component. The first choice—and usually your best one—is to replace the part, and use the old one as a paperweight. In most cases, it's easier and less expensive to get a replacement part than it is to subject yourself to the expense and trouble of trying to repair the cracked item. In the end, the repaired item will rarely be as reliable as a new, uncracked replacement (don't just assume a new part will be crack-free—it may not be!).

Of course, replacement parts are only a viable solution if replacement parts are available. If you're building up an engine from a 1948 Studebaker, you may be unable to find anyone with a good connecting rod for the engine. Then your only choice is to repair the damaged rod, which can be done by a master machinist or welder, but these folks are extremely rare so be careful—not everyone with a pair of goggles and a bottle of acetylene is a master. Ask several of the local racers and aircraft mechanics in your area for recommendations and go with the most recommended person.

Bends

Connecting rods are subjected to a number of extreme forces that act in several different directions. As a result, connecting rods need to be checked for bends on all three axes, because the forces can cause the rod to become
- Twisted
- Flexed
- Stretched

Twisted Connecting Rods

A twisted connecting rod is one where the small end and the big end of the rod are skewed with respect to one another, in a manner similar to how you might wring out a wet towel. Obviously, the big end of the rod, which is connected to the crankshaft, will remain on the proper plane, but the small end is connected only to the piston. When the piston is pushed up the cylinder on the compression stroke, it will be pushed up with the force off center and angular, causing uneven wear. When the piston is forced down by the combustion gases, the force on the thrust side of the piston will also be angular and off center, possibly causing the piston to rotate slightly. The piston is designed to receive forces in a very specific way. When forces are received angular and off center, it will cause stresses in and on the piston that can cause poor wear patterns and may crack or damage the piston.

Flexed Connecting Rods

Imagine that you have borrowed your brother's umbrella and have taken it to the race track. Due to a lack of grandstand seating you find that you will have to stand for the duration of the race. Sitting is the grass is out of the question, since the ground is muddy. Remembering the umbrella you borrowed, you stick the point in the ground and sit on the handle. All goes well until you shift your weight slightly. Suddenly, the middle of the shaft of the umbrella shifts to the right, while the point in the ground and the handle, firmly planted against your behind, remain in their original relative positions. The umbrella is bent. This can happen to a connecting rod for many reasons, including: high combustion pressures, or more

This veteran performance piston carries an "030" mark, which indicates that the piston is a 30-thousandths oversize, or larger, in diameter than a stock piston.

likely, coolant in the combustion chamber during the compression stroke.

Stretched Connecting Rods

A stretched connecting rod is an unlikely event in the typical family sedan, but at high rpm in a performance or racing engine, the mass of the piston, rings, wrist pin, and the rod itself attempt to keep the rod moving upward as it nears top dead center of the bore. But then the crankshaft swings downward, tugging the rod back down with it. Somewhere between the wrist pin and the big end of the rod, the rod experiences tremendous stretching forces, just like a rubber band being pulled from both ends stretches in the middle. These forces, at high speed and high temperatures, or with help from even a minor defect in the rod, can actually stretch the connecting rod. The amount of lengthening that occurs is quite small, but may result in an unbalanced compression ratio. More importantly, though, stretching weakens the rod in the area where the stretching occurred, making it more likely to twist, flex, or simply snap the next time it is subjected to extreme forces.

And What If a Rod Is Bent?

As with so many other things, the answer to this question depends on the destined use of the engine. Connecting rods can be straightened. For most engines, such as those bound for use in a family sedan, where rpm will be kept low and loads will be minimal, a straightened rod will generally work just fine.

A connecting rod that has been bent has had the integrity of its structure disturbed. Therefore the rod is weakened. When the rod is bent back, its structural integrity is disturbed again, again weakening it. Without a doubt the better policy is to replace bent connecting rods. This will be discussed further later.

Heat Damage

Remember in the old Western movies when the protagonist would ride up to the local blacksmith shop and the smithy was always pounding a horseshoe on an anvil with a hammer, then he plunged the red-hot shoe into cold water, then heated it up again. If you ever wondered what he was doing, you are about to find out. The smithy was forging the shoe by beating with a hammer, and then he heat treated it with the forge and the cold water. Heat, properly applied, strengthens the metal. Heat, improperly applied, can weaken the metal.

In many cases, a heat damaged component can be identified by a bluish shading on the surface of the affected metal. The presence of a blue shading confirms the probability of heat damage, however the lack of the blue shading does not necessarily confirm a lack of heat damage. The best defense against a catastrophic failure is to replace any components that have possibly been subjected to extremely high temperatures. This is especially true for pistons, which receive the brunt of the combustion chamber temperatures.

Nicks and Burrs

Nicks and burrs are flaws on a component that provide a starting point for cracks and breaks. Torsional and tensile loads that are normally spread out over a large area tend to become concentrated at the flaw, which serves as a stress riser.

Inspecting connecting rods for nicks and burrs is a job best suited for the anal retentive. Gauge your personality type. I tend to be more oriented toward getting the engine assembled and getting the vehicle on the road. Realizing that this is a weakness, there are two things I do to compensate: First, I force myself to inspect every component, square centimeter by square centimeter. Second, I find an individual, perhaps not even an expert, who is very detail oriented. This type of person sees the universe as the sum of its parts, they see the trees, not the forest. This is exactly what the ideal inspector needs to be. The ideal inspector, however, may spend so much time on the minute details of the job that the engine will never get completed. On the other hand, someone with a personality type like mine, who puts an emphasis on completing a job, has to be deliberate about inspection of the parts.

While inspecting for nicks and burrs, look closely at the casting seams of the component. Residual flash can concentrate stresses the same as other minor defects. When these flaws are found, they should be filed smooth. Obviously, you should use your judgment to determine whether removing the defect will weaken the component more than the burr, flashing or nick. If so, then the part should simply be replaced.

Residual Magnetism

Residual magnetism is a problem that is often not considered, even by the most experienced of engine builders. Iron and steel components can become magnetized as a result of the hammering caused by excessive clearances before the engine was disassembled, or as a result of machine work. Magnetic inspections, magnafluxing, and the like can also magnetize components. When a component is magnetized, it attracts all the little bits and flakes of metal that result from normal engine wear. These bits and flakes of metal belong in the bottom of the oil pan, attached to a magnetic oil pan drain plug, not attached to expensive engine parts.

A magnetized part can be identified by laying a thin sheet of paper over the part and sprinkling iron filings or dust on the sheet of paper. If the iron filings arrange themselves in distinct patterns, the part is magnetized. To demagnetize a component, borrow a trick from the television repairman: Use a tool called a degausser, which creates a powerful magnetic field designed to scramble the magnetic fields of other objects. A similar, but less powerful device used to erase audio and video tapes can be purchased from stores like Radio Shack. Some electronics technicians were taught to use a powerful soldering gun to degauss picture tubes and other components, and that process can work on magnetized engine parts, as well.

Whichever tool you have access to or choose to use, the technique is the same: Energize the degaussing device away from the component to be demagnetized, then pass the degausser back and forth across the components in random patterns, making sure each pass stops well beyond the component. After degaussing the part, check it for magnetism again by using the iron filing technique described earlier.

NOTE: Be careful not to allow any iron filings to get on the component. If they do, make sure that they are thoroughly cleaned off before installing the component.

Big End and Small End Alignment

A twisted connecting rod can occur as a result of a wide range of events, including: detonation; blown head gaskets that allow water or coolant to enter the cylinder, causing "hydro-lock"; foreign objects in the cylinder, such as broken valves; broken timing chains or belts and overrevving.

A precision gauge is required to test for a twisted connecting rod. These gauges can cost several hundred dollars, and it is unlikely that you will want to purchase one if you only need it for just one engine. On the other hand, if you are going to be rebuilding engines frequently, or will rebuild this engine often, then it may be worth the investment.

Many technicians have a strong desire to perform expensive inspection procedures in inexpensive manners, and thus they—or you—may be tempted to employ several "tricks" they may have learned over the years to check the alignment of connecting rods. Unfortunately, none of these tricks is very effective. The bottom line is that, especially in the case of connecting rods, the right tool is the only tool. If you suspect that the connecting rods are bent or twisted, take them to a machine shop that is prepared to straighten them, or replace them.

Big End and Small End Eccentricity

You have already read about the effects of inertia on the piston and connecting rod assembly several times in this book. Those inertial forces can cause either end of the connecting rod to become egg-shaped. A good example of how this happens is illustrated by a common dog toy, which is a lot like a rubber connecting rod with a shaft in the middle and loops on each end. When a dog bites one loop in his teeth and you hold the other loop, and you each pull, the loops elongate. This is exactly what can happen to connecting rods after years of use—or just seconds of abuse.

Since the end connected to the crankshaft is larger, there is more of a tendency for it, the "big end," to elongate. Use an inside micrometer or telescoping gauge to determine if either end of the connecting rod is out of round by measuring the bore of the big end at two points that are 90 degrees apart from each other. The measurements should be within 0.001 inch of each other.

Repairing (Rebuilding) a Connecting Rod

If the big end of the connecting rod does not meet the specs for eccentricity, or if the connecting rod is bent, they can sometimes be repaired. When considering the repair of a connecting rod, also consider how the engine for which the connecting rod is destined will be used. Performance engines and engines used in wilderness areas should have new connecting rods to replace those that are damaged. Your life is worth more than the few hundred dollars you'll save by not replacing questionable connecting rods.

However, for mundane uses, such as in a low-powered commuter car, connecting rods that have a minor bend or twist in them can be corrected by simply reversing the bending process. To do so, pad the jaws of a vise with soft wood and clamp the rod in the vise. The wood will protect the rod from the teeth of the vise. With the piston mounted on the connecting rod, slide a long, thin pry bar into the wrist pin. Gently apply pressure to the connecting rod in the direction in which you wish it to straighten it. Gradually increase the pressure. You may feel the rod bend or you may not. Try to bend the rod only a little at a time. Just like the time-honored tradition of bending beer or soda can pull-tabs, each time you bend the rod it

weakens, so you do not want to over-bend the rod beyond being straight, then have to again bend it back. And heed this warning: Do not attempt to straighten the connecting without the piston and wrist pin installed, or you risk severely damaging the connecting rod.

Connecting rod ends with eccentric big or small ends can be repaired by most machine shops. The procedure begins by machining the mating surfaces of the connecting rod cap and the connecting rod. That reduces the average diameter of the big end, but will not necessarily remove the eccentricity. The big end bore is then machined back to the original, truly round diameter. Small-end repairs involve enlarging the bore then sleeving it to achieve the original, necessary diameter.

All this talk about rebuilding connecting rods belies the fact that if an engine is being built for performance or durability new rods should be used. This is especially true if there is any question about the structural integrity of the old rods.

Pistons
Selection and Inspection

In most cases, if you are blueprinting an engine it means that you are going through a great deal of trouble to make the engine as perfect as possible. So, it really makes little or no sense to spend a great

deal of time or effort sorting through used pistons to find a set that meets your needs.

The exception, of course, would be if you were going to blueprint a rare engine, like that from an old MGA or some experimental engine for which there probably aren't boxes of pistons lying around to sort through, anyway. In those sort of cases, if the pistons you have are unusable or you simply desire to change the shape of the piston dome, then you may be forced to bite the bullet and have a set custom made by a company such as JE, Wiseco, or Arias.

Beginning with a set of new pistons will always put you a step ahead in the blueprinting process. With new pistons, you can be relatively sure they will be defect free (however, don't just assume they are—test them!) and that they aren't abnormally worn. You'll also find that modern, new pistons will be more closely matched in terms of weight, and, thanks to advances in piston machining that are largely attributable to the use of Computer Numerically Controlled (CNC) tools, the pistons will be identical in terms of shape, which contributes to balanced power production from cylinder to cylinder. Still, you may find it beneficial to have a couple of sets of pistons to pick through, in order to more exactly meet your goals for balance.

CHAPTER FIVE

CYLINDER HEADS

Just like us, your engine breathes air. And the more power you want your engine to make, the more air it will require. Of course, it's no secret that most production cylinder heads pose a significant restriction to airflow at high rpm, so your task as an engine blueprinter is to improve the airflow through your cylinder heads without compromising any aspect of performance any more than necessary.

Beyond how much air a given cylinder head will allow to enter your engine, cylinder head design dictates how that air enters—whether it moves quickly and efficiently, or whether it moves large volumes slowly and turbulently. A good cylinder head will help maximize an engine's efficiency by speeding the air/fuel charge into the cylinder during the intake stroke, and will pose little restriction to exhaust

gases as they are ushered out of the cylinder on the exhaust stroke. The better your heads are at achieving these two goals, the more power your engine will be capable of making.

Besides air flow, you'll need to think about valve sizes, valve angles, additional machining necessary to "rebuild" the head, as well as machine work that can be performed to improve a cylinder head. For many engines, there are numerous cylinder head designs available, too, which complicate the head selection process by confronting you with a sometimes mind-boggling array of heads from which to choose.

Attempting to select, rebuild, and modify cylinder heads without some understanding of just what makes a cylinder head work well for a particular engine is likely to result in disappointing

Cylinder heads are among the most critical parts of a performance engine. The head on the right is a stock head from an elderly Ford 289, while the one on the left is a custom-built head for a NASCAR Winston Cup engine. The ability of the cylinder head to permit air and exhaust gases to flow freely is perhaps the most critical part of making sure that the engine can reach its power potential.

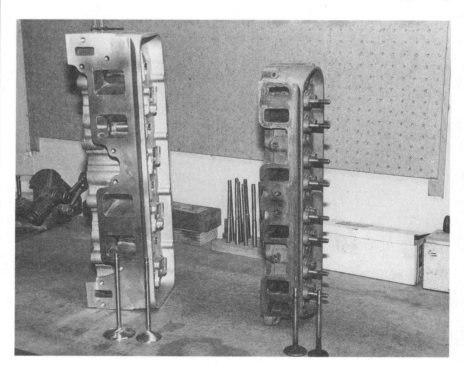

Since the cylinder head is, like the block, a major and expensive item, you will often find yourself using a "seasoned" head, which makes careful inspection essential. This head has been cut in half to show the location of a crack in an angular area of the head's top surface. The chalked area shows how the crack runs from the top of the head to the water jacket.

Over the years, cylinder heads have featured a wide variety of combustion chamber designs in an effort to make the flow of air and exhaust gases more efficient. In the late 1950s, the hemispherical combustion chamber was an answer to that challenge. Hemi-heads continue to be seen in many smaller engines today.

performance. So read the following information carefully and keep it in mind as you shop for cylinder heads and prepare them for installation. A little effort now will be well worth it, in the long run.

Selection and Inspection

Some of the more popular domestic engines have had a variety of cylinder head configurations. For these engines, there were changes in the cylinder heads to meet various requirements of use. There were high-performance heads for Camaros, Mustangs, Corvettes, and the like. There were special heads designed for more torque or smoother or faster acceleration. Begin your cylinder head selection process with a good review of the literature available on performance modifications for the engine in question. Don't forget that the literature reviewed should include people who have modified the same type of engine in the past. Other engines had only a single cylinder head design, which limits your possibilities.

Once the type of head design is selected, you will find yourself on the hunt for a suitable example (or two) of that head.

Pressure Testing

Perhaps the most important operations that can be done by the machine shop is testing the integrity of the water jacket in the block and head. Most machine shops are equipped to do pressure testing.

To begin the pressure test, all of the water ports in the head or block are plugged. Air or water is forced into the cylinder head or block. If air is being used, soapy water is sprayed on the surfaces in question. If there is a leak, air bubbles will be seen.

Aluminum heads sometimes become porous. When this occurs coolant will literally seep through the metal when pressurized. Should your machinist find this situation, he can sometimes seal it with a resin. Like so many other things in rebuilding an engine, because of the amount of work required to repair mistakes or bad judgment, a porous head should just be replaced.

Magnetic Crack Inspection

This technique only works on ferrous metals because it depends on the dispersion of the magnetic field through the metal. The principle is similar to the famous high school physics experiment that illustrates magnetic flux fields: A magnet is placed under a sheet of paper and iron filings are sprinkled over it; as the iron filings fall, they line up along the magnetic fields of flux. The same basic technique is used in magnetic crack inspection: Iron filings are sprinkled on the head, then a large electro-magnet is held a fixed distance above the head. Cracks in the cylinder head create distortions in the magnetic field and thus affect the alignment of the iron filings.

Dye Crack Testing

In dye crack testing, a penetrating dye is sprayed on the surface of the item to be tested. After being allowed to soak in and dry, a cleaner is used to remove dye from the surface. Like the coffee stains in the crack of the cup, the dye will remain in the cracks of the component being tested. The dye method is especially effective on non-ferrous metals, such as aluminum and magnesium.

While overhead cam engines have been rather rare in domestic applications until recently, they have been popular in import applications for more than two decades. Their primary advantages are a simpler valvetrain composed of parts that tend to flex less, plus increased flexibility for the engine designer in positioning the intake and exhaust valves.

This is actually a very sophisticated cylinder head design from a rather inexpensive Japanese car. A single overhead cam operates the exhaust valve and a pair of intake valves in a hemispherical combustion chamber. Considering the size of the engine, performance was rather amazing. Today's designs squeeze far more horsepower out of fewer cubic inches than was ever really dreamed of for street cars in the 1960s.

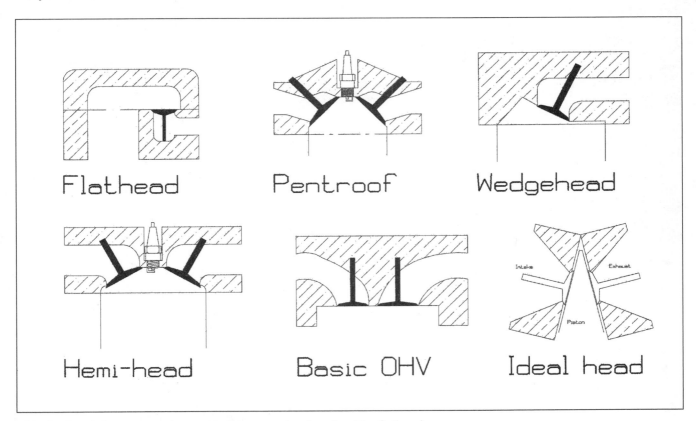

Cylinder heads have sported many designs over the decades. The flathead was the most popular design for much of the first half of the century. The most common design through the 1950s and 1960s was the wedge head. Today, cross-flow pentroof and hemi designs seem to be dominant.

Carefully remove the burrs and casting flash from the block. These form weak points where cracks can begin.

CHAPTER SIX

PREPARING CYLINDER BLOCKS

Whether you're rebuilding the engine for your 13-year-old winter beater pickup truck or assembling a fresh engine to make blistering assaults on a quarter-mile dragstrip somewhere, you'll need to make sure that the engine's cylinder block is properly set up for the job.

Naturally, the amount of effort and preparation required for a relatively modest engine, such as one for a daily-driven beater, should be less involved than for a race engine from which you need to extract every last horsepower. But the processes that you perform for each must, nevertheless, be carefully and accurately carried out, or you will run the risk of causing rapid wear, reduced durability, or even complete and catastrophic failure of the engine.

Fortunately, a good deal of cylinder block preparation will be performed by machine shop technicians, out of necessity—they have the needed equipment and skills, and you

do not. But don't let a little hands-off time lull you into thinking you don't have any part in block preparation. On the contrary, depending on your knowledge and comfort level, you can specify the measurements you want the machinist to work within, and what procedures to perform. And when you get the block back from the machine shop, you'll need to verify that all the work was done properly and to your satisfaction.

Like nearly every other aspect of engine blueprinting, the time and effort you put into the project now—in this case, preparing the engine block—will yield worthwhile rewards later, in the form of increased power, reliability and performance.

Deburring

Deburring a block is the process of removing sharp edges, such as casting flash, from a block or other part, in hopes of eliminating areas where

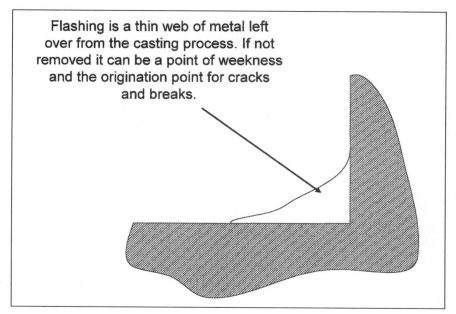
Flashing is a thin web of metal left over from the casting process. If not removed it can be a point of weekness and the origination point for cracks and breaks.

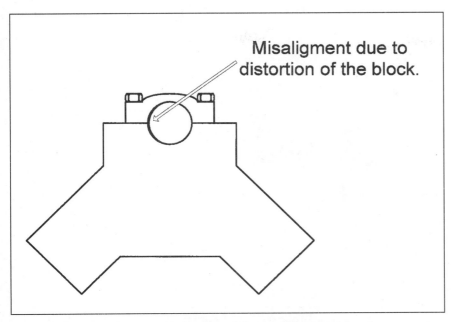

Misaligment due to distortion of the block.

Engine blocks can become damaged and distorted for a variety of reasons, the most common of which is heat. The distortion can cause the bore of the main journal saddles to become misaligned. If there is enough distortion, the crankshaft will not turn when torqued into the block. Lesser degrees of distortion can cause power that was intended to be transferred to the ground to be consumed by flexing the crankshaft as it rotates.

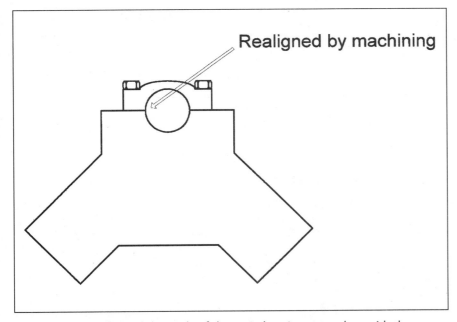

Realigned by machining

The machinist will grind the ends of the main bearing caps, then with the machined caps bolted and torqued in place, he can machine the bore to a precise, imaginary cylinder.

cracks will be likely to form. Like on a plastic model, casting flash on engine parts occurs where mold halves meet and excess material (metal for an engine, or plastic for the model) seeped in to any gaps between those mold halves. Almost anyone can debur a block by simply grinding away this flash with an electric drill and various sanding cones. (Air drills are acceptable if the motor has a variable speed, however, most single-speed air drills spin so fast that the unwary hand could accidentally grind away too much material, ruining the block!)

With a rotary file mounted in an electric drill, remove any flash evident on the interior of the crankcase or the intake valley. Other places to look for flash include the lifter valley drain holes to the crankcase. But don't get carried away with this procedure—the idea is to remove the flash, not polish the inside of the block. While a polished block may seem like a nice idea, in reality the removal of all the little dimples reduces the surface area of the block and reduces its ability to transfer heat to the oil.

There are places in the block where the rotary file will not fit. In such cases, a flat-tipped punch will usually work well. A file should be used to debur the edges of the main bearing caps, while the lifter bores can be deburred with a wheel cylinder abrasive ball hone. It is not advisable to use flat stone wheel cylinder hone for this purpose.

Continue the deburring process until all the flashing is removed.

Align Honing and Boring

This operation corrects for misalignment of the crankshaft journals in the block. Extreme heating and cooling of the engine block can cause warping. Even a slight misalignment of 0.0015 inch (less than 1/640th of an inch) can cause a power loss and premature failure of the main bearings and can ultimately break the crankshaft. A block should be line bored any time the engine is being rebuilt as a result of a broken crankshaft.

Line boring equipment is very large and very expensive. Many machine shops will opt to sublet this operation to a larger machine shop. The block is placed in a boring machine and small amounts of metal are removed. As the metal is removed the main journals are aligned. If too much metal is removed during the boring process, the crankshaft is moved too far up in the block, which alters the compression ratio and slackens the timing chain. If the engine has

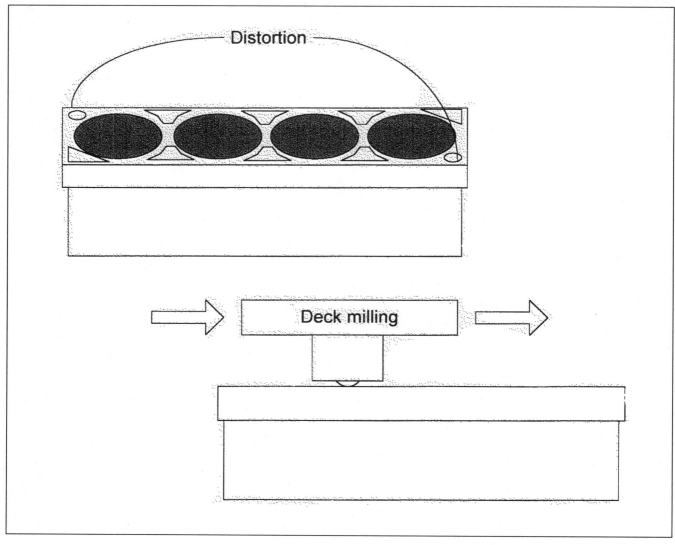

Distortion of the deck of the block is not nearly as common as distortion of its equivalent surface on the cylinder head. However, it sometimes does occur. A machine shop can resurface the block's deck, which will make the block's mating surface with the cylinder head true again. Keep in mind however, that removing metal from the block's deck will change the deck height of the block. Decking the block should be done in conjunction with line boring the main journals, incorrect deck height can be corrected through this procedure.

a timing chain tensioner to compensate for the slack chain, cam timing will still be retarded. If the cam timing is controlled through meshing gears, special gears will have to be purchased, as the tooth penetration of stock gear will be too deep, which would cause premature wear. Seek the advice of your machinist on whether or not to replace the block, instead.

Decking

Decking the block makes sure that the surface on which the cylinder head mates is flat and even. It's really senseless—especially in a performance engine—to pay money to have the cylinder heads machined flat and then install them on a distorted cylinder block surface. This process, when done properly, also ensures the angles of the head mating surfaces are correct. For most "V" engines this angle is either 60 or 90 degrees. The accuracy of this angle is important to allow proper fit of the intake manifold to the cylinder head. Speaking of which, intake manifolds often must be milled slightly when cylinder heads or cylinder blocks are decked, to restore proper port alignment.

For most performance minded individuals, the purpose of decking the block is to provide the proper clearance between the piston at the top of the stroke and the bottom of the cylinder head. Without giving it a great deal of thought one might feel that the piston should be flush with the top of the block when it is at the top of its stroke (top dead center). This would be true if the metal of the connecting rods were not slightly elastic, but as we've discussed previously, the piston is an inertial mass moving at approximately 2,000 feet per minute (nearly 23 miles per hour) as it travels up and down the cylinder at only 2,000 rpm. As the piston reaches the top of its travel, it must stop and reverse

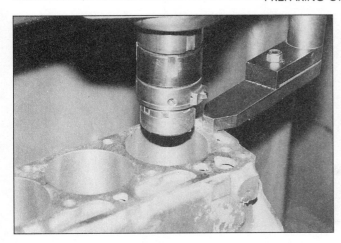

Boring the cylinders is done for two primary reasons. First, enlarging the cylinder bores alters the cubic inch displacement of the engine. Second, boring cylinders allows a machinist to correct for any distortion of the cylinders that may have occurred, often as a result of wear, but possibly from excessive heat.

Honing the cylinders is an operation that should be performed after the cylinders are bored, to ensure exact sizing of the cylinder diameter. Most machine shops will use a machine, such as this one, to perform this task and ensure accuracy.

direction in as little as 3 milliseconds. During that time, there are tremendous forces working on the connecting rod, causing it to stretch. When building an engine for street use, the static clearance between the top of the piston and the deck should be 0.035 of an inch. Due to potentially much higher engine speeds, this clearance should be 0.045 inch on racing engines. If the engine is being reassembled with aluminum connecting rods, which stretch even more, the clearance should be 0.060 inch to prevent catastrophic damage.

When deck-to-piston top clearance is being checked, you should consider the thickness of the head gas-ket, too. If you were building a stock street engine using a head gasket with a compressed thickness of 0.035 inch, a piston-to-deck clearance of zero would be about right (0.005 inch more would be better). Keep in mind that a compression ratio loss will not occur at higher engine speeds, because of the stretch in the connecting rods.

Boring

Damaged cylinders must be repaired before the block can be reused. If the problem is excessive taper or out-of-round, the cylinders can be repaired by re-boring them. Since the procedure alters the diame-ter of the cylinder, and since changing the diameter affects the combustion chamber volume, the re-bored diame-ter of the cylinders must all be equal. Often cylinders are re-bored to increase performance. This increases engine displacement. A classic Ford 302 "punched out" 0.030-inch over (stock) will then displace 306 cubic inches. At the same time, the com-pression ratio rises slightly because the volume of the cylinder rises. Boring the cylinders also removes from the cylinder walls metal that is an essential part in the removal of heat. Engines with cylinder walls that are too thin can run hot—too hot.

Before discussing with your machinist how much you are going to have the cylinders bored, check the sizes of replacement pistons that are available. Typical replacement sizes are 0.020-, 0.030-, 0.040- and sometimes 0.060-inch oversize. The most com-mon re-bore is a 0.030-inch oversize.

Honing

When blueprinting an engine, honing serves two purposes. First, as in a standard overhaul, honing is done to remove the glaze from the cylinder walls. As the engine is run over the years the old piston rings polish the walls of the cylinders. Honing breaks up this glaze and provides the rings with an abrasive surface to help seat them. When blueprinting an engine, honing also serves to ensure that the cylinder walls are as round and straight as possible. The berry ball hone dis-cussed earlier is only used to break the glaze on the cylinder walls and cannot be used for truing the cylinder walls.

Correct honing technique will produce a crosshatch pattern on the cylinder walls. Only a flat stone hone can be used to true the cylinder walls. Although a flat stone hone mounted in a drill motor will do a reasonable good job for a stock engine, maximum pre-cision for performance engines can only be achieved with your machinist's honing machine.

There is a "home" version of a precision honing machine that does an excellent job. If you have a lot of time

Since the installation of the cylinder head will often cause minor distortions in the engine block, accurate honing of the cylinders requires the use of torque plates. These are bolted to the deck of the block to simulate the presence of the cylinder heads. Then, since the distortion that would be caused by the cylinder head is simulated by the torque plates, the machinist can perform an accurate honing job.

Hand honing should be reserved only for the task of creating a cross-hatch pattern on the walls of the cylinders. This cross-hatch is necessary to help the rings seat properly. Although it is possible to size the cylinders by hand honing, it would be a slow and tedious process. Also note that if you did choose to hand hone for sizing, you must use a stone type hone. The berry-ball hone cannot ensure proper linearity of the cylinder walls.

and a lot of money, or if you are going to be building a lot of engines, then investing in a "home" honing machine might be worthwhile. Proper performance honing requires that the block be submerged in oil during the process, to both cool the part and the hone, as well as clean the honing stones. Along with the honing machine buy an old bathtub and several gallons of honing oil. Also, since there is likely to be 0.004 to 0.006 inch of metal to remove from each cylinder, verify that there is nothing you want to see on television for the next week.

If you are having the block bored, it's standard procedure for the machinist to then hone the cylinders. The boring machine will bore the cylinders 0.004 to 0.006 inch undersize. A hone will then be used to remove the remaining metal for proper bore size. While it is usually standard procedure for a bore job to include honing, it wouldn't hurt to confirm that honing would be part of the procedure when you drop the block off with the machinist.

Honing with Torque Plates

When the cylinder heads are bolted into place, the block will distort ever so slightly. This distortion is not a concern in a regular overhaul or rebuild. In a performance engine, minor distortions may have minimal detrimental effects on performance. But don't forget that minor negative effects on performance are exactly what we are trying to eliminate by blueprinting the engine.

Torque plates are machined flat steel plates that are bolted and torqued onto the block in place of the cylinder heads. Unlike the cylinder heads, torque plates have holes in them to allow a hone to access to the cylinders. When bolted in place, the torque plates distort the block in the same manner that properly installed and torqued heads will distort the block. When the cylinders are subsequently honed, they will result in cylinders that are true to the crank and cylinder head *as assembled*, even though the bores may be out-of-round when the bare block is measured just prior to the buildup.

Hand Honing

Hand honing the cylinders is an operation that can be done by anyone. An engine cylinder hone can be purchased for as little as $20 and can be used effectively to remove the normal glaze that occurs on cylinder walls from years of piston rings polishing them. Hand-honing simply breaks up this glaze and provides the rings with an abrasive surface to help seat them.

Correct honing technique will produce a crosshatch pattern on the cylinder walls. Place the hone in a low-speed electric or air-powered drill. It should be noted that in order to produce a 45-degree crosshatch pattern with an air powered drill motor rotating at 20,000 rpm, your arm must be capable of reciprocating about 330 times per second. So, unless you're the Bionic Man, make sure you use a slow drill speed, then simply hold the drill and hone vertically and move it in and out in slow even movements. Continue the process until there are conspicuous 45-degree crosshatch marks in each of the cylinders.

Because it is somewhat of a less-than-totally-accurate procedure, hand honing is not part of the engine blueprinting procedure except, perhaps, as part of a post-blueprinting inspection or repair. Machine honing is part of the engine blueprinting procedure, because the machine can be set to achieve a specific, accurate size.

Automatic Honing

Automatic, or machine, honing is used to precisely size the cylinders for

Most busy machine shops will have a cylinder honing machine that is capable of being set for a precise diameter that relates to the specific diameter of the piston. Once set, the machine will automatically hone the cylinder to the proper and exact diameter. This particular honing machine is the Sunnen CK-10, one of the most common and trusted hones in use.

the pistons to be used. Typically, the cylinders are bored to a diameter a few thousandths of an inch below the desired final measurement. A honing machine is then used to do three things: precisely size the desired diameter; smooth the roughness left from the boring process; and establish the crosshatch necessary to allow the rings to wear in properly.

Nominal sizing is a matter of several variables. To measure piston clearance, subtract the maximum piston diameter from the diameter of the cylinder. The difference between these measurements is the piston clearance. The clearance for pistons to be reused should always be less than 0.0035 inch. If the clearance is excessive, consult with your machinist about the advisability of having the pistons knurled, which raises the metal on the skirt of the piston to reduce the piston to cylinder wall clearance.

To find the piston taper, measure the diameter of the piston just below the oil ring and again at the bottom of the skirt. The difference between these measurements is the taper. Taper should not exceed 0.010 inch, otherwise the piston will be able to rock excessively in the bore, possibly dam-

aging the bore or the piston or both.

If the piston clearance is insufficient, the piston can literally seize in the bore. Keep in mind that the piston is cam ground, or oval shaped. As most substances will, the piston will expand when heated. Since the structure of the piston is not concentric, the amount of expansion will be different on the wrist pin axis and 90 degrees from the wrist pin axis. The oval shape when cold will allow the piston to be round when the engine is warmed up. The difference, when cold, between these two axes is only about 0.020 to 0.040 inch.

Most pistons are also tapered 0.005 to 0.010 inch. The bottom of the piston skirt has less metal to expand than does the area closest to the head. For that reason the top of most piston skirts is smaller than the bottom of the piston skirt. There are also pistons that have a barrel grind, meaning that their skirts are narrow on the top and bottom, and wide in the middle.

Another factor is the material the piston is made of. If money is not a problem you might invest in ceramic pistons. These may not expand at all, the far more common aluminum pis-

tons will have expansion rates that will vary depending on the alloy's blend of silicon, magnesium, manganese, nickel, copper, and other elements.

The last three paragraphs lead to this simple fact: To ensure proper piston-to-cylinder wall clearance, the diameter of the piston must be measured at the point recommended by the manufacturer of the piston. Furthermore, the clearance should be that specified by the piston manufacturer, not by the factory service manual.

Begin the process of checking piston to cylinder wall clearance by reviewing the measurement recommendations supplied by the piston manufacturer. This recommended measurement will often be taken 90 degrees from the wrist pin at the top of the skirt, though some piston manufacturers dictate measurements from other areas. Measure this diameter carefully with a micrometer. Then, with an inside micrometer, measure the diameter of the cylinder at several places along the length of the cylinder. The places checked should be on the same axis as the piston manufacturer recommended for checking piston diameter. Of course, the places checked should be located within the area of travel of the measured point on the piston.

A simpler, though often just as effective, method to measure piston-to-cylinder wall clearance is with a feeler gauge. The best way to use the feeler gauge for this method is the go-no-go method. Read the piston manufacturer's recommendations for clearance. Select a feeler gauge that is equal to the minimum recommendation and a feeler gauge just larger than the maximum recommendation. The thinner feeler gauge should slide easily between the cylinder wall and the piston, while the thicker gauge should not fit at all.

Whatever the method you use, be sure to make these measurements exact. Remember that failure to follow the piston manufacturer's recommendations exactly can cause piston slap or seizing of the piston.

An engine that is destined for the world of muffler-less open headers on the drag strip has different requirements

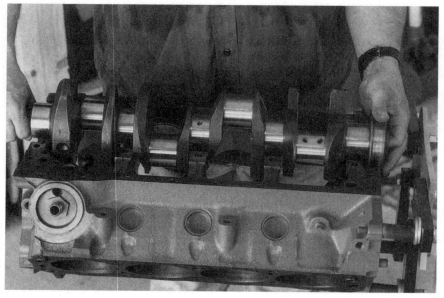

Painting the engine, and in particular the block, is more then just a matter of aesthetics. The paint reduces the possibility of corrosion. Painting the inside of the block also smoothes the rough and irregular surfaces of the block's insides, which permits the oil to drain back into the oil pan faster. The faster the oil returns to the pan, the more oil is available to lubricate and protect the engine.

from a typical commuter car. On these performance engines, the sound of the exhaust will muffle any piston slap that might occur. For these engines it is recommended that the piston-to-cylinder wall clearance be exactly at the maximum limit. The larger clearance will prevent piston scuffing as a result of high heat and pressures at high rpm, during competition.

Block Painting

Painting the block has no proven effect either in a positive manner, or in a negative one, on the performance of the engine. Personally I like to paint the block both inside and out. Paint on the outside of the block has mostly aesthetic purpose. Although it does reduce rust on the block, in all but the most severe climates and situations, the rust that forms on the outside of the block is little more than a light surface coat.

Painting the inside of the block, on the other hand, actually has a more practical value: A couple of coats of paint will seal the pours that might otherwise trap small particulates that may ultimately end up forming dam-

aging sediments. Additionally, the paint provides a slicker surface than the bare metal. Some people feel that this allows for easier return of the oil to the pan, and therefore the pump, and may allow for better lubrication. There are special paints designed exclusively for painting engine parts. Check with your engine machinist for their recommendation.

Restricting Oil Passages

The very though of restricting oil passages may sound a bit odd. After all, why in the world would you deliberately restrict oil passages in the engine block? The answer, of course, is that normally you wouldn't. But racing engines have different needs and are faced with different demands than stock engines. And sometimes fulfilling those needs and demands calls for unorthodox thinking.

Before you go tinkering with your engine's oiling system, you need to have an accurate grasp on just how the oiling system operates, starting with the commonly misunderstood concept that oil pumps—even so-called "high-pressure" oil pumps—don't really create any oil pressure. All oil

pumps do is move a volume of oil. Restrictions to that oil flow are what creates the pressure in the engine. These restrictions are located at many points throughout the engine. When the oil is forced between the main bearing and the crankshaft journal, there is a restriction, so pressure builds up. When the oil is forced between the rod bearing and the crankshaft journal, there's another restriction. If the oil clearance gets too large or if oil pump volume is insufficient to make up for any loss that occurs because of the excessive oil clearance, oil pressure will drop. Anywhere oil flow is not completely blocked is a point where oil pressure loss will occur. And, like electricity, oil will always flow along the path of least resistance. If you open up a pathway, the oil will flow through that path rather than to components that need lubrication. Restrict a pathway and the oil flow to other components will tend to increase.

When engineers design a stock engine, they must calculate the oil pump flow rate and determine the oil paths and how much of an effect each has on oil flow. If they misjudge, then some of the lubricated components will be starved for oil. One of the points classically starved for oil in an engine is the upper end of the valvetrain, including the rocker arms. If—and only if—solid or roller lifters are to be used in the blueprinted engine, then some of the oil destined for the rockers can be redirected to the crankshaft bearings. One of the advantages of roller rockers is their reduced need for lubrication. Oil destined for the rockers in the stock engine can therefore be redirected to other places in the engine where it will do more good. If hydraulic lifters are used in the engine then restricting oil flow to them could result in the lifters collapsing, causing serious valvetrain damage.

Study the oil flow paths to and from the upper part of the valvetrain. Limit the flow of the oil to the rockers and force the oil to return to the pan via a path that bypasses the camshaft. In some engines, installing a restricting plug in the supply passage can do this.

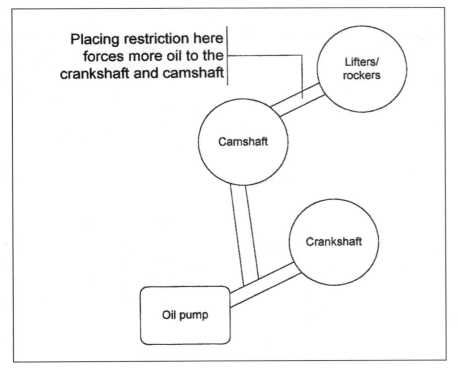

Placing restriction here forces more oil to the crankshaft and camshaft

Lifters/rockers

Camshaft

Crankshaft

Oil pump

In a performance or racing engine, it is sometimes desirable to force oil to the components that require the most lubrication. Study the oil delivery paths and determine if the rocker arms are receiving more oil than they require. Reducing—by means of a restriction—the amount of oil destined for the rocker arms may reroute additional oil to the rod journals and main journals.

Epoxy screen over oil return holes to prevent debris from returning to the pan in the event of engine failure.

I am sure you are not building this engine in hopes that it will fail; however, there is always a possibility that some component might fail. If the failure occurs in the top end of the engine, pieces may find their way back through the oil return ports of the block and do additional damage to the bottom end. A little epoxy an some fine screen (down South we call this chicken wire) can prevent this potential problem.

Moroso, for example, sells a plug set that reduces the normally 0.250-inch passage to 0.060. This forces more of the oil to the crank bearings and reduces the amount of oil that has to find its way around the crankshaft, back to the pan.

Oil that is pumped to the rocker arms has to return to the oil pan, too. On many engines the path is along the rocker arms to the lifter valley where the oil drips through holes on top of the camshaft. The spinning camshaft then flings oil into the crankcase as a mist. This oil mist is more difficult for the crankshaft and its counterweights to swing through than air. This added resistance to rotation is technically called "windage" loss, but whatever you call it, it's a loss in horsepower.

Always keep in mind that as you restrict oil flow, you are decreasing the lubrication to vital engine components, too, so only make these oil routing modifications if horsepower is more important than durability.

Debris Screens

Some engine blocks have a large opening over the camshaft. It is often impractical to seal this opening to reduce windage problems, yet there is a more serious issue than windage to consider. This large opening provides a path for large metal chunks to find their way to the camshaft, crankshaft, and other important engine components. Installing a debris screen prevents hard metal pieces from failed components in the top end of the engine from damaging components in its bottom end.

A common way to install this screen is to simply epoxy it in place. The materials necessary to perform this task are available commercially or can be assembled from products readily available from a hardware store. Some fine, heavy-duty wire screen and epoxy are all that are required.

Rod and Crank Clearance

A popular modification during a performance overhaul is the installation of a stroker crank. Anytime a

49

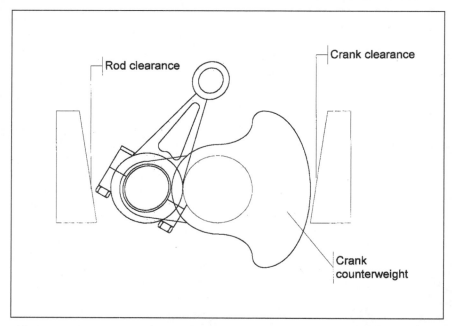

Rod clearance

Crank clearance

Crank counterweight

When a stroker crankshaft is used it changes the relative clearances between the crankshaft, the connecting rods and the engine block. Carefully measure these clearances when using a crankshaft for connecting rods that are not of factory dimensions. Remember that even a crankshaft that has stock journal and stroke dimensions may have counterweights that are larger (or smaller), which would result in reduced clearances between the counterweights and the engine block.

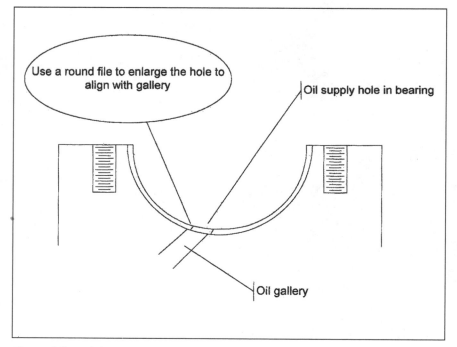

Use a round file to enlarge the hole to align with gallery

Oil supply hole in bearing

Oil gallery

The saddles of the main journals have holes drilled to supply oil through holes in the main bearings to the crankshaft main journals. Often these holes do not align properly with the holes in the bearings. Use a round file to enlarge the holes in the bearings for proper alignment.

crankshaft other than the original factory unit is installed the clearance between the new crankshaft, the installed connecting rods, and the block should be checked. Aluminum connecting rods are much bulkier than stock connecting rods and therefore may reduce clearance to the block. There should be about 0.050-inch (one-twentieth of an inch) clearance between the rotating and reciprocating components and the block.

If there is insufficient clearance, use a high-speed grinder to remove the necessary metal. Anytime you start grinding on the block you need to remember that there is a short distance between the area where you are grinding and the water jacket. As a precaution, the block should be sonic tested again after the clearance grinding is completed to ensure acceptable wall thickness.

Oil Hole Alignment

It would seem that the engine block manufacturers and the manufacturers of engine bearings would get together on the location of the oil supply holes. To a large extent they have, but the situation is far from perfect. Set the bearing you are going to use in position in the block, then use a sharp rat-tail file to enlarge the hole in the bearing so that there is no interference with oil flow from the supply hole in the block to the crankshaft journal.

Final Cleanup

After all the machine work is complete, the block must be thoroughly cleaned and free from all metal particles and residues. In a professional environment, there are high-pressure steam cleaners that scour the tiniest pores in the metal. I find that thorough washing with something as unsophisticated as soap and water applied liberally with a stiff brush does a really nice job. Blasting with compressed air or exposure to sunshine will also do a very nice job of drying the components after they are clean. Thorough drying is very important because of the possibility of corrosion.

After all of the block blueprinting tasks are completed, and prior to painting the block, it should be cleaned thoroughly with hot soapy water. All grime, metal shavings and dirt should be removed, then the block should be painted, inside and out (don't paint any machined surfaces, however, such as cylinders, lifter bores, and main bearing saddles.

Deburring is a task performed to remove the casting flash and thin casting ridges left behind by the casting process. This is done for more than just aesthetic purposes. These areas provide a starting point for stress cracks and breaks.

CHAPTER SEVEN

PREPARING CRANKSHAFTS

Blueprinting and preparing a crankshaft for use in an engine—any engine—involves a great deal more than just turning the crank's rod and main journals. The crankshaft must be checked for straightness and trued if necessary. It needs to be checked for twist, and corrected as needed. Counterweights must be attended to with both essential and optional procedures, and oil passages can benefit from a number of subtle, easy modifications.

On top of all that, there are all sorts of clearances to check: Rod bearing oil clearance, main bearing oil clearance, end play, counterweight-to-piston skirt clearances, counterweight-to-block skirt clearances, and more.

These factors, alone, make crank preparation a time-consuming process. But a crankshaft isn't a component to cut corners with—the very survival of your engine is at stake with every single degree of rotation. And you don't necessarily need to spend a fortune to prepare a nearly bullet-proof crank.

You just need to know what you're doing, and what needs to be done. And that's what this chapter is all about.

Deburring

As with the block, burrs and flash on cast crankshafts become the focal points for weakness and cracks to begin. These leftovers from the casting process should be removed using a sharp grinding bit and a high speed electric or air-operated drill.

Anyone who has built a model car or model airplane is familiar with the seepage of excess plastic between the sections of the mold. The sharp edged residue is called "casting flash." When building a plastic model, this flash is typically removed to make the final product look neat. In engine components, the flash also marks the junction between the pieces of the mold. However, in a cast iron or aluminum engine component, removal of flash is done for more than just cosmetic purposes—it's done to make the engine

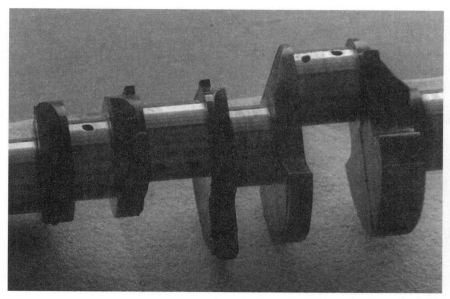

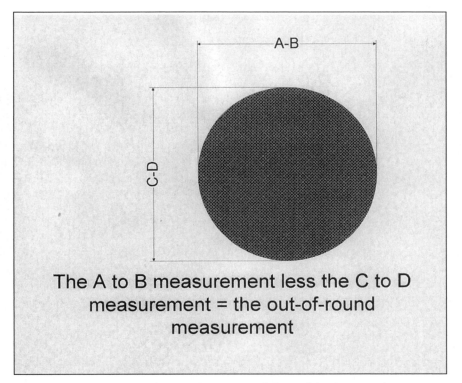

The A to B measurement less the C to D measurement = the out-of-round measurement

An out-of-round crankshaft journal can cause failure of the bearing that mates with that journal. Even a relatively minor discrepancy can result in a power loss. Crankshafts can be machined to make the journals perfectly round again.

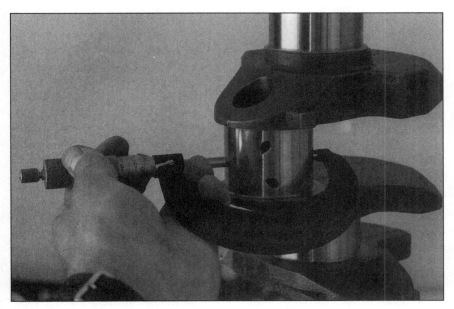

components strong, since the ridges formed by the flash provide a starting point for cracks and stress fractures.

Shot Peening and Stress Relieving

The most common method of strengthening the crankshaft is through shot peening. After masking the journals to protect them, high velocity shot is targeted at the other areas of the crank. Particular attention is paid to the fillet or radius areas of the main journals. The impact of the shot relieves stress in the metal that could cause microscopic cracks that could later become a broken crankshaft.

After polishing, the connecting rods can be further strengthened through shot peening. After masking the bearing mating surfaces to protect them, high velocity shot is targeted at the other areas of the connecting rods. Particular attention is paid to the fillet or radius near the rod bolts. Again, the impact of the shot relieves stress in the metal. The principle is not unlike stopping at the massage booth at the Seattle airport to have your back pounded on to relieve stress. Additionally, shot peening compacts the surface of the rod, providing a homogeneous surface that doesn't allow potential cracks any place to begin.

Crankshaft Grinding
Out-of-Round Journals

Use a micrometer to check the diameter of a rod or main journal at one end of the journal (this will be your "A" measurement). After checking the first diameter, rotate the micrometer 90 degrees and check it again (your "B" measurement). Then take similar measurements at the other end of the journal (your "C" and "D" measurements, respectively). The difference between the "A" and "B" measurements, or the "C" and "D" measurements, is the out-of-round of the journal. Out-of round wear should be less than 0.0005 inch. Repeat the measurement process for each rod and main journal.

If any of the journals is worn greater than 0.0005 inch, the crankshaft will have to be machined. If only the main bearing journals exhibit excessive wear, only the main journals will need to be machined. Likewise, if only the rod bearing journals exhibit excessive wear, only the rod journals will need to be machined. In fact, after showing the measurements to your machinist, he may advise you to machine the rod and main journals to different undersizes.

Tapered Journals

The taper of a journal is the difference between measurements "A" and "C," or from "B" to "D." Maximum allowable tolerance for taper is also 0.0005 inch.

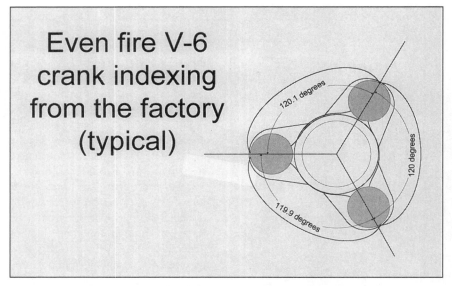

Even fire V-6 crank indexing from the factory (typical)

120.1 degrees

120 degrees

119.9 degrees

Each crankshaft rod journal should be arranged a specific number of degrees apart from the other journals, when viewed from either end of the crankshaft. In most cases, the number of degrees between each of the rod journals will be equal. Indexing the crankshaft ensures that the number of degrees between rod journals is exactly what was designed for the engine. Additionally, it ensures that the center of each of the rod journals is equidistant from the center of the main journals.

Regrinding the Crank

When the machine shop grinds the crank to 0.010 undersize it means that 0.005 inch of metal has been remove from around the journal. The 0.005 inch reduction in the journal's radius yields a 0.010-inch reduction in the journal's diameter, when measured with a micrometer.

Most machine shops do not have crank grinding capability. If you confirm that your crank will need to be ground and the machinist you have chosen to use does not have this capability, he will need to send it to another machine shop. This is common practice and should not deter you from using your chosen machinist. Crank grinding equipment is very expensive and difficult for a small machine shop to realize a return on. However, you may want to take the crank to your machinist a few days before the rest of the components you will be taking to him, which will allow for the crank to be machined and returned to the shop in time for you to pick up all your machined parts at the same time.

Indexing

Crankshaft indexing is a difficult concept to understand, and even more difficult to explain. Each of the main journals of the crankshaft has an exact rotational center. When these centers lie on a single geometric line they are perfectly indexed. That's the easy part to explain. What is really difficult is the indexing of the connecting rod journals. If a line is drawn between the center point of each rod journal and the rotational center of the main journals the point of intersection (the rotational center of the main journals) should form a precise engineered angle. On a typical V-8 engine this angle should be 90 degrees. On a typical inline or flat four-cylinder engine this angle should be 180 degrees. Also, the centerline of each of the rod journals should be exactly the same distance from the centerline of the main journals. Although the intent during the manufacturing process is to make these angles and distances as precise as possible, it does not always happen.

Straightness

This term describes the loss of precise indexing due to post-manufacturing deterioration of the crankshaft. Many things can alter the straightness of the crankshaft, but the primary offender is heat, this is especially true when the crankshaft has the characteristic incongruities of cast iron. This non-homogeneous metal will have areas that vary from one another in thermal expansion rates. These variations in expansion rate will cause distortion to occur during heating and cooling.

Cross-Drilling

In the typical crankshaft, each rod journal has only one hole to supply oil to the bearing. This means that oil is only delivered to one of the bearing shells at a time, therefore, each bearing shell will receive oil only once per crankshaft revolution. Improved lubrication, and therefore extended bearing life, results from cross-drilling the rod journals. In this procedure, each rod journal oil supply hole is drilled straight through the journal to the other side.

Chamfering Oil Holes

Use a small, medium-grit grinding stone mounted in a drill to chamfer the opening of the crankshaft oil holes. Chamfering permits smoother flow of oil to the journal. The oil does not have to turn a sharp 90-degree corner and the chamfer provides a reservoir. The result is better lubrication to the rod and main journals.

As a bonus, chamfering oil holes removes sharp edges that may act as stress risers, and a likely spot for a crack to form.

Counterweight Modifications

An engine's crankcase is a pretty hostile environment in which to spin a crankshaft. A mist of fine particles of oil impedes the movement of the crankshaft as the oil droplets contact the crankshaft. Fortunately, there are several steps you can take to minimize any losses.

The simplest step, though only a first one, is to install a windage tray

The crankshaft is subjected to extreme forces and changes in temperature. This can cause distortion, especially in cast iron crankshafts. The most accurate way to straighten a distorted crankshaft is to machine it on a lathe.

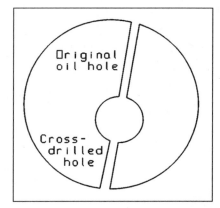

Lubricating oil is only supplied through most crankshafts through a single oil port on each journal, which means that each point on the bearing surface is only lubricated once per crankshaft revolution. By cross-drilling the journals—drilling the oil supply hole completely through the journal—each point on the bearing surface is lubricated twice per revolution.

above the oil level in the oil pan to both catch and hold onto oil draining back to the oil pan, as well as to prevent oil in the pan from sloshing up on the crankshaft. Windage trays are available commercially from a number of manufacturers of oil system components.

A second step is to polish the rough as-cast counterweight surfaces of the crankshaft, which simply enhances the crank's ability to shed itself of any oil that it encounters, either as a mist or from sloshing. Without a porous surface to cling to, the oil will quickly flow off the rapidly spinning crankshaft, and be caught and trapped by a windage tray.

If the goal is a fire-breathing, quarter-mile-gobbling, racing engine, there are three additional procedures that may be advisable. A popular procedure for such engines is to knife-edge the counterweights, which involves removing metal to form a 45-degree leading edge to the counterweight. In much the same way the sloped nose of a Chevy Lumina APV has better aerodynamics than a 1962 VW microbus, a knife-edged counterweight slips through the air and oil mist of the crankcase much easier. Knife-edging, however, removes material (i.e., weight) from the counterweights and should only be done if the crank, rod and piston assemblies are to be balanced, as well.

Counterweight Radius

One of the most effective operations that can be performed on the counterweights to improve performance, is to reduce their radius. Removing the metal to reduce the radius lightens the crank, making the engine more responsive to speed change requests from the driver and reduces the wind resistance that results from the counterweight swinging the air and oil mist in the block. The ideal crankshaft would feature counterweights near the centerline of the crankshaft. The further the weight is from the centerline, the greater the amount of energy required to change the speed of the engine. Reducing the radius not only decreases the mass, but it also moves the center of gravity for the mass closer to the centerline of the crankshaft.

Counterweight Windage

Anybody who remembers soft drinks in bottles has probably blown across the mouth of such a bottle. The sound that is created is evidence of wind resistance. When the factory and your machinist balanced the crankshaft they did so by drilling holes in the counterweights. These holes increase the wind resistance of the counterweight. During the final stages of preparation, the crank, rod, and piston assembly is balanced, and the counterweight holes should be closed by welding special freeze plugs over them. After these plugs are welded in place, they should be machined smooth, under a process called "smooth balancing."

All of the counterweight modifications you want to make should be made at the same time, as modifying the crank later will affect other machine work. So, sit down with your machinist, calculate how much each procedure will cost, then figure out how many meals your spouse and children will have do without before contracting what will be done.

Gas Nitriding, Hard Chroming, and Tuftriding

Gas nitriding is a process that can improve the hardness of a soft crankshaft. This process increases the nitrogen content of the surface layer of the crankshaft. Generally, this process can only be performed on components that have been previously hardened. Nitriding a component that has not been previously hardened can result in warpage. When the metal is heated to between 500 and 580 degrees Celsius (932 to 1076 degrees Fahrenheit) nitrogen comes to the surface layer, which can produce a layer several millimeters thick that will have a Vickers rating of 700 to over 1200 HV.

Hard chroming addresses the journals of the crankshaft. After all the machine work on the crank is completed the journals are masked and the entire crankshaft is submerged in wax.

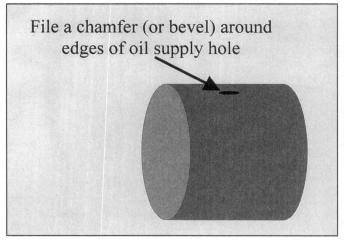

File a chamfer (or bevel) around edges of oil supply hole

When you come to a corner when driving your car, you don't actually change direction with an abrupt 90-degree turn. Instead, you make a gradual turn. This is because early in your driving experience, you probably learned that it's easier to make a smooth, rounded turn that an abrupt, sharp turn. The same is true for the lubricating oil trying to pass from the oil galleries of the crankshaft to the bearing surfaces. By chamfering (beveling) the oil supply holes, the oil can more easily spread to the bearing.

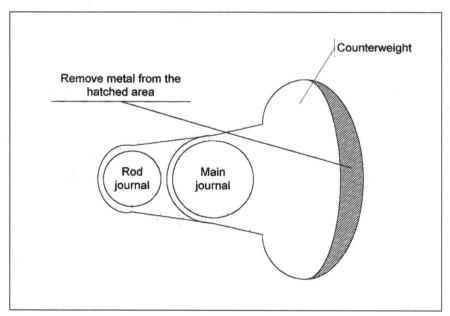

Remove metal from the hatched area

Counterweight

Rod journal

Main journal

Power is consumed through the act of rotating the crankshaft. The greater the inertial mass of the crankshaft, the greater the amount of wasted power. Removing metal to decrease the radius of the counterweights reduces the rotating mass. Keep in mind, however, that the benefits of doing this can quickly be lost if the balance of the crankshaft is affected, so lightening the counterweights should be done prior to balancing, and only by someone knowledgeable enough not to destroy the crank.

This coats the entire crankshaft, except for the journals, to prevent them from being electroplated along with the journals. After all these surfaces are suitably waxed, the masking is removed, excess wax that may have seeped into the journal areas is removed, and the crank is them submerged into an electro-plating bath. A word of caution: If the process is not done properly, the chrome plating may peel off or the crankshaft may become brittle, either of which could have devastating consequences.

Tuftriding is a hardening process that involves submerging the crankshaft in a molten cyanide salt bath. The entire crankshaft, not just the journals, is thereby heat treated and hardened. This is a very effective process, so effective, in fact, that a hardening depth of as little as 0.0001 inch is all that is required to significantly increase surface hardness. A tuftrided crank can be recognized by a gray color that pervades over the entire crankshaft. To verify that the crank has been tuftrided, use a file on a non-bearing surface. If the file easily cuts through the gray surface, then the crank is gray for a reason other than having been hardened through tuftriding.

Pilot Bearings

The pilot bearing is basically unimportant when the clutch pedal is released. However, the pilot bearing should be inspected while the crankshaft is being serviced. It is strongly recommended that the bearing be replaced even if no defect is found. The main reason for replacing the pilot bearing has more to do with the transmission than the engine. When the vehicle is stopped and the clutch pedal is depressed, the input shaft of the transmission should not be spinning. If it is, then the transmission will tend to load the engine and will be difficult to get in and out of first gear. Additionally, the input shaft may continue to spin even after the clutch is depressed during a shift, which will, at very least, cause wear on the transmission and may cause difficulty in gear changes that may cost a race if the vehicle is destined for that use.

While the crankshaft is being machined, it might be advisable to ask your machinist to fit a roller bearing in place of the bronze bearing that probably came standard from the factory. Some applications feature a roller bearing from the factory and this may be a simple drop in replacement.

Stroke Changes

There are many reasons that you may choose to change the stroke of the crankshaft. You may have decided to use the car in competition, in which case class rules may limit the cubic inch displacement, causing you to switch to a

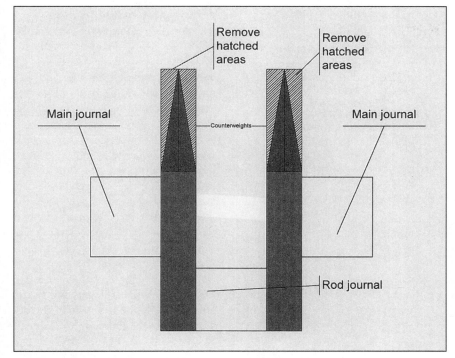

Which cuts through wood quicker: a hammer or an ax? A hammer has a large, blunt face that's great for smashing things and pounding them, but it's pretty tough to cut through wood in a hurry with one. An ax, on the other hand, has a wedge shape that splits the wood and spreads it apart, letting the ax quickly cut through the wood. Stock crankshaft counterweights act a lot like hammers as they smash into oil in the crankcase. By machining a knife-like edge on the leading side of the rotating crankshaft, air and oil will be spread apart, reducing power-robbing friction. Keep in mind though, that knife-edging a crank is one of those expensive and/or time-consuming operations that will have a small, but sometimes important, effect on your elapsed time.

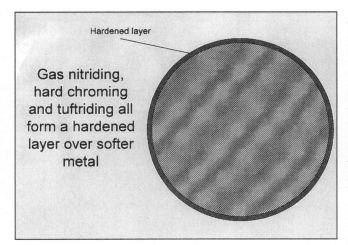

Gas nitriding, hard chroming and tuftriding all form a hardened layer over softer metal

Although most crankshafts are hardened already, high rpm or extended rough use may defeat this hardening. Talk to your machinist about alternative hardening processes. Though these processes are often expensive, they are considerably cheaper than the typical forged or billet crankshaft.

shorter stroke. Or the use of a turbocharger or supercharger may cause you to alter the compression ratio through a stroke reduction to avoid detonation.

A simple means to this end is called "offset grinding," which is a procedure that involves regrinding the rod journals to relocate the center of their radius. On some crankshafts this offset can be as much as 0.010 (ten thousandths) of an inch, which means that a 302 Ford engine, for example, could be changed to either a 311 or a 292 cubic inch engine, depending on your requirements.

Regrinding the crankshaft to a new stroke measurement is not an operation to be indulged in lightly, though. Many machinists will probably have experience in changing the stroke of a small-block Chevrolet crankshaft, but they may not have experience with—nor know the limitations of—more unusual crankshafts. Also keep in mind that changes in the block deck and perhaps even the cylinder head may be necessary to adjust for the new crankshaft dimensions.

If more exotic or drastic changes in the stroke are required, or desired, it will be necessary to purchase a "stroker kit" or have a new crankshaft designed and cast. While the former can often be little more than the price of a high-quality replacement crank, the latter may be necessary for less common engines. If you are considering stroking your 1953 Studebaker engine, you will probably need to be prepared for the mid- to high-four-digit price range, if not more.

Micropolishing

Micropolishing reduces the microscopic imperfections on the bearing surfaces of the crankshaft. The crankshaft is mounted in a grinding machine, instead of using a cutting bit the machinist will use a high-speed motor-driven abrasive belt. This technique will leave behind shiny and pretty bearing surfaces, but more importantly it will remove the tiny imperfections that remain as a result of the machine work that was done on the crankshaft.

For minor polishing chores, a homemade version of a crankshaft polishing tool can be created from a piece of 600 grit wet-dry emery paper and a leather thong. Simply wrap the emery paper around the journal, then wrap the thong around the emery paper one complete loop. Pull back and forth on opposite ends of the thong to rotate the emery paper, thus polishing the journal.

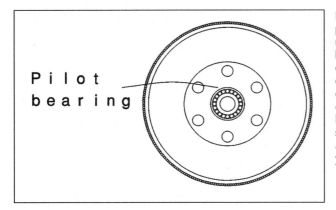

Pilot bearing

It is standard procedure to replace the pilot bearing when the clutch is replaced or during an engine overhaul. A defective pilot bearing can cause shifting problems and greatly affect your elapsed time.

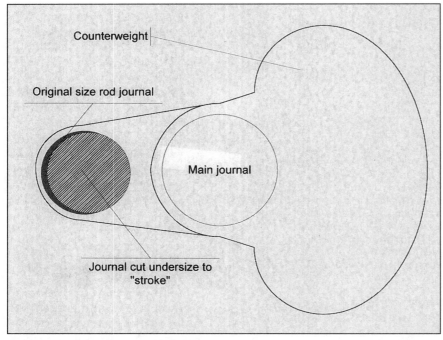

Counterweight

Original size rod journal

Main journal

Journal cut undersize to "stroke"

Minor changes in the stroke of the engine can be accomplished by grinding the rod journals off-center. Since the depth of the hardening on the journals is only a few thousandths of an inch thick, the amount of stroke alteration that can be accomplished with this method is extremely limited, unless the journals are re-hardened.

Journal surface before micropolishing

Journal surface after micropolishing

Micro-polishing smoothes out the tiny imperfections in the surface of the crankshaft journals. A smoother journal surface means less rotating resistance, therefore less heat buildup and a little more power to the ground.

Crankshaft Straightening

In most cases, when the crankshaft becomes distorted, bent or warped, it would be necessary to have the anomaly machined out. Installing the crankshaft in its normal position in the block and firmly tapping the end of the crankshaft with the hammer can sometimes eliminate relatively minor distortions. This realigns the structure of the crankshaft and will often remove the distortion as it does so. Since it is the metallurgical structure of the crankshaft that will allow the precise realignment to occur, this technique will work far better on forged crankshafts than on cast. When the main bearings are properly torqued the crankshaft should turn freely by hand. If the crankshaft is difficult to turn or locks up when the caps are torqued the crank is warped.

Stroke Checking

If you have more than moderate resources, a special dial indicator fixture can be purchased to measure the stroke of your crankshaft. This fixture saddles the main journals on either side of the rod journal being measured. The dial indicator must have a travel greater than the stroke of the crankshaft. With the saddle fixture in place, rotate the crankshaft and observe the movement of the dial indicator. The movement will be a measurement of the stroke. Repeating this procedure for each of the rod journals will confirm the stroke of the engine and also prove whether the crankshaft is or is not properly indexed.

If you are not a professional engine builder, you may find a better use for your money than purchasing a special saddle for checking stroke. Also since you are not a professional engine builder, it is probably not essential that your engine building process be completed in a hurry. Therefore you can take the time to install the crankshaft and pistons in the engine and measure the difference in the position of the piston with respect to the block when the piston is

Sometimes a crankshaft with a minor warp, or distortion, can be straightened by installing and torquing the crankshaft in its normal position in the block then smacking the end of the crank with a hammer, causing the crank's structure to realign and straighten itself.

at top dead center, as opposed to bottom dead center. The difference in deck height between top dead center and bottom dead center is also the stroke. This procedure can only be at its most accurate when the pistons and bearings that are to be used in the final build are used when the measurements are made.

Bearing Clearances

In a regular engine overhaul, precise bearing measurements and matching of clearances and thicknesses is not significantly important. But when blueprinting, it is desirable to make sure that all of the journals are lubricated equally. There are two valid ways of measuring the oil clearance of the crankshaft bearings. The method most familiar to the amateur or general line technician is to use a product called Plastigage, which is a soft waxy thread that is laid on the crankshaft journal before the bearing cap is torqued in place. As the cap is torqued, the strip of Plastigage is crushed between the upper bearing surface and the journal. As it is crushed, it spreads out. The width of the thread when the bearing cap is removed indicates the oil clearance.

A more sophisticated, yet more difficult method involves precisely measuring the diameter of the crankshaft journal, plus the inside diameter of the assembled and torqued bearing cap and saddle. Additionally, the thicknesses of the bearing shells must the measured. This method prevents inaccuracy as a result of any slight warpage that there might be in the crankshaft. Of course, at this point, there really shouldn't be any distortion in the crankshaft to make a difference in a Plastigage measurement.

Install the bearing caps on the saddles of the block and on the connecting rods. Measure the diameter of the hole through which the crankshaft will be mounted with an inside micrometer. Now measure the diameter of the corresponding crankshaft journal. The difference between the journal diameter and the saddle / cap diameter will give you the information you need to select bearings with the proper thickness to achieve your desired oil clearance. The difference in the two diameter measurements (bore size minus journal size) divided by two, minus the desired oil clearance, will equal the desired thickness for the bearings.

High-performance engines usually have an oil clearance that is greater than those designed for pushing the family sedan to the grocery store. A non-performance engine will typically have an oil clearance between 0.001 and 0.003 inch. Performance engines usually have clearances between 0.0025 and 0.0035. This is to the upper end and just beyond those of the non-performance engine. The larger clearance allows for freer rotation than is typical on non-performance engines.

If the clearances are not equal, you can take advantage of the fact that no two engine bearings are exactly identical to one another. Measure the thicknesses of the various bearing halves that you purchased. If the clearance is greater than desired, it may be possible to purchase bearings that are 0.001 or 0.002 inch thinner and therefore will give you the desired additional clearance. Another alternative is to try a different brand of bearings. Although different brands are supposed to be made according to common specs, the reality is that there are often measurable differences between brands. Another method that is sometimes used involves using one bearing half of one size and the other bearing half of another size. Find the combination of bearing shells that will give you the desired clearance. This process is sometimes referred to as "half-shelling."

Thrust Clearances

The thrust clearance is the measurement of front rear movement of the crankshaft. In most engines, one of the main bearings features tabs that hang down each side of that main bearing's saddle. These surfaces limit the crankshaft's linear movement. For most engines, an acceptable clearance is 0.005 inch to about 0.010 inch. To check the thrust clearance, install all of the main bearings in their saddles. Lay the crankshaft in its proper position. Install the bearings in the bearing caps and torque them in place. Set up a dial indicator on the oil pan mating surface of the block. Rotate the dial indicator

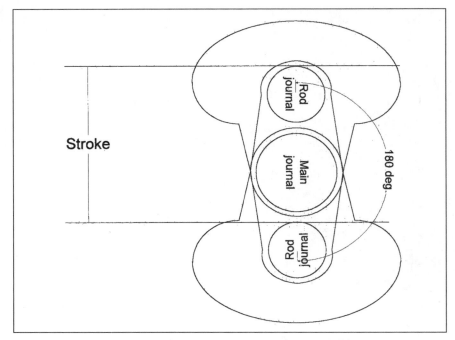

Install the crankshaft and pistons in the engine. Measure the difference in the position of the piston with respect to the deck of the block when the piston is at top dead center, and again when the piston is at bottom dead center. The difference in deck height between TDC and BDC is the crankshaft's stroke.

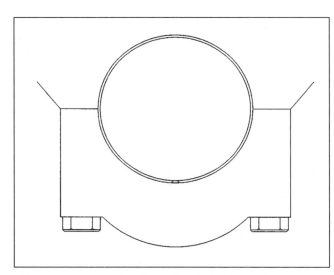

A non-performance engine will typically have an oil clearance between 0.001 and 0.003 inch. Performance engines usually have clearances between 0.0025 and 0.0035 inch—figures that are usually at the upper end of the specified range for non-performance engine clearances. The larger clearance reduces friction, allowing the crank to rotate more freely than can a typical non-performance engine's crank.

so that the measurement probe rests against one of the counterweights of the crankshaft. Using a screwdriver or small pry bar, gently force the crankshaft to its rear most position and set the dial indicator to zero. At this point a light tap with a medium-size, soft-faced hammer will ensure that the crankshaft is fully to the rear. Next, pry the crankshaft toward its forward-most position. Again, tap the crankshaft with the soft hammer to seat it in the forward position. Observe the change in the dial indicator reading. The amount of movement shown on the dial indicator is the thrust clearance.

In some engines, the thrust surface is separate from the main bearings. They are actually more like thrust washers than they are bearings. The measurement procedure is identical, but extreme care should be taken to ensure that the washers are in their proper position when the measurements are taken.

Many engine builders use a feeler gauge to make these measurements. This is not a bad practice, but it is not quite as accurate. With the crankshaft pried in either the forward-most or rear-most position, try to insert feeler gauges between the thrust surface of the bearing and the thrust surface of the crankshaft. The clearance will be the measurement between the largest feeler gauge that will fit and the smallest feeler gauge that will not fit.

If the thrust clearance is too great, a machine shop can weld additional metal on the crankshaft's thrust surface, then re-machine a new, thicker thrust surface. If the thrust clearance is too tight, then a machine shop can simply machine a satisfactory clearance on the crankshaft thrust surface. However, if the clearance is close but just slightly too small, you may be able to simply machine the thrust bearing surface by placing a piece of 600 grit wet-dry sand paper on a flat, thick glass surface and carefully rubbing each side of the thrust bearing against it. Make sure that the sandpaper has been well lubricated with solvent or light oil.

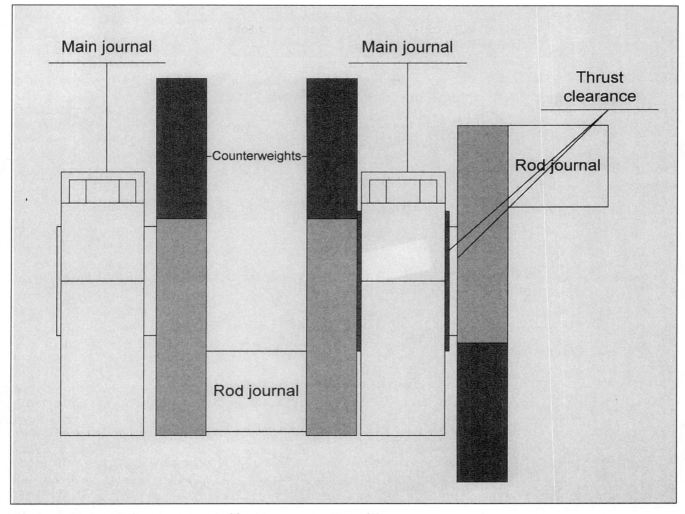

The thrust clearance is the measurement of front-to-rear movement of the crankshaft. For most engines, an acceptable clearance is 0.005 to about 0.010 inch.

In my career, I have had two extreme experiences with thrust surfaces. The first time was on a Datsun 310's A-14 engine. During a routine overhaul we replaced not only the major engine components but also the clutch assembly. Over the next few weeks, we overhauled the engine two additional times. Each time, the thrust surface had been severely worn in the direction that the clutch applies pressure. During the second re-overhaul, we discovered that the replacement pressure plate applied way too much spring force against the crankshaft when the clutch was depressed. After replacing the pressure plate, the engine had no further problems. When an engine is being built for performance use and you are planning on using a manual transmission with a high spring tension clutch assembly, the thrust surface clearance measurements are critically important.

In another incident, a 318 Dodge engine was rebuilt for a van. This was a "performance" build focused on improving fuel economy. The van was equipped with an automatic transmission, but the torque converter was defective. During normal operation of the transmission, the torque converter ballooned and applied pressure against the rear thrust surface of the crankshaft. Careful measurement of the thrust clearance is essential on both performance and standard engine overhauls.

Oil Hole Alignment

Oil hole alignment is one of those things that is just assumed to be correct in a standard overhaul. But when blueprinting an engine, you need to make sure that there is as little restriction to oil flow as possible. Begin by installing the main bearings in their saddles in the block, then note the alignment of the oil passages from the interior of the block to the bearing surfaces. If these holes are not aligned properly then use a small rat-tail file to enlarge and reshape the bearing's hole for proper alignment.

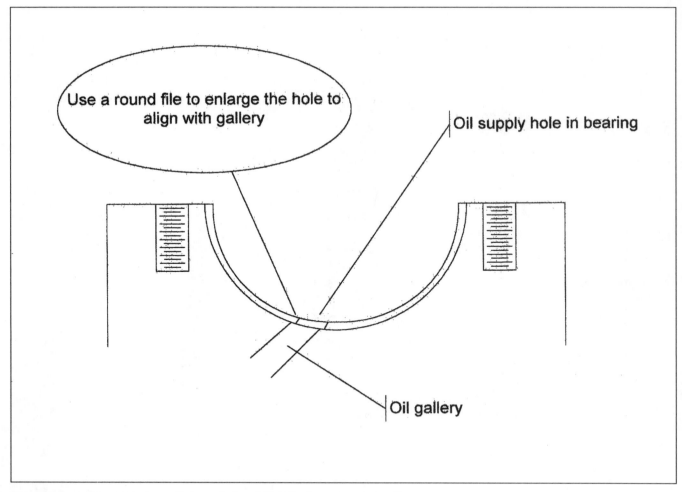

The saddles of the main journals have holes drilled in them to supply oil through holes in the main bearings to the crankshaft main journals. Often these holes do not align properly with the holes in the bearings. Use a round file to enlarge the holes in the bearings for proper alignment.

Balancing the connecting rods is an effort to equalize the reciprocating mass of each throw of the crankshaft. This reduces both load factors on the crank and vibrations of the crank. A reduction in either of these areas means less power loss.

CHAPTER EIGHT

PREPARING CONNECTING RODS

The forces at work inside your engine all conspire, perhaps unintentionally, to destroy your connecting rods. The rods are accelerated upward toward the top of the cylinder, straining to compress gases as they go, then suddenly, those gases explode creating intense pressure forcing those pistons back down the cylinder. As the pistons reach the bottom of the cylinder they almost instantaneously have to reverse direction and start back upward, which causes the rod to compress, and when it reaches the top of the cylinder again, the opposite happens—they want to keep going up, but the crankshaft yanks them down, causing the rod to stretch. Millions and millions of cycles of compressing and stretching fatigue the rods, weakening them.

It's your job to prepare your rods to withstand these pressures and forces for however long you need your engine to stay together. By carefully examining the rods, performing the necessary massaging and machining, then using good quality parts and procedures to hang them on the pistons and install them in the engine, you swing the odds in your favor that a rod failure won't bring your fun, or work, to an abrupt end.

Balancing

Frankly, the best way, and often the cheapest way, for the individual interested in street performance to balance connecting rods is to buy them that way. However, if the challenge is more important than common sense, and for a true motorhead that is the way it should be, or if this

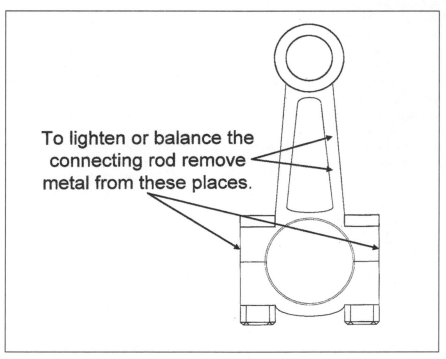

To lighten or balance the connecting rod remove metal from these places.

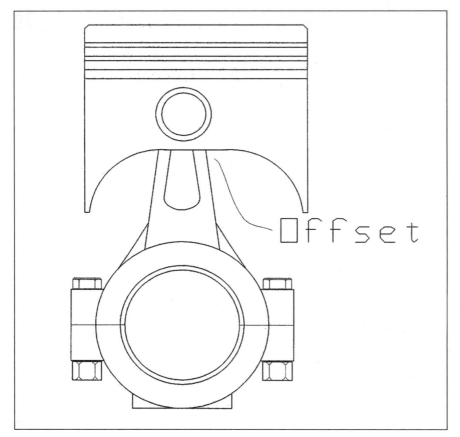

Many, perhaps most, connecting rods are not perfectly symmetrical in design. If the connecting rod is installed on the piston backward, it may touch the side of the block or the skirt of the piston when the engine runs.

engine is truly destined for the race track, then balancing skills are required. The key to balancing an engine is to ensure, as much as possible, that each set of reciprocating masses is equal.

The first and most essential piece of equipment for balancing connecting rods is a good set of scales. These scales should be accurate to about one-half of a gram—that's about half the weight of a dollar bill. It may seem obvious to some, but you begin by weighing all the connecting rods to find the lightest one, which should be used as your "standard"—the weight to which you'll reduce the heavier rods. At each end of the connecting rod is a flat area. You may have thought that the purpose of this flat area was to allow you to stand the connecting rod on end, but actually they are called balancing pads, because to

balance the connecting rods you grind or file small amounts of metal from these pads. Keep in mind that the heat generated while grinding the balance pads can change the nature of the metal, usually weakening it. Filing, although much slower, generates far less heat and therefore is far less likely to do damage to the connecting rod. If you choose to grind, as I confess I often do, limit the time the connecting rod is on the grinding wheel. Limiting the time will limit the risk of damaging the rod with excessive heat.

When all the connecting rods weigh the same to within half a gram, you are ready to install the pistons.

Earlier, we discussed the balancing of the pistons. Logically, if the balanced pistons are installed on balanced connecting rods, the reciprocating masses will be balanced, right?

Weigh the parts for each reciprocating assembly, including bearings, prior to final assembly, in order to confirm balance. If you find that the assemblies are not balanced, fine tune the balance before assembly.

Connecting Rod Offset and Installation

Several years ago I was teaching a class about automotive electronics in Canada. When I teach, I often use examples of professional mistakes I have made. After several weeks of these stories, one of the students commented: "You must be a terrible mechanic." Perhaps at one point I was, but I've learned a great deal from those mistakes. For instance, after rebuilding the engine of a Volvo 265 that had been submerged in water, the engine exhibited a rapping noise that seemed to be coming from the mid-portion of the block, near cylinder number one. Henry, a rather round and highly experienced mechanic whose basic philosophy of life was that work interfered with fishing, said: "Sounds like a piece of carbon in the number one cylinder." When I reminded him that I had just rebuilt the engine, he said, "Well, I guess you should have cleaned the heads and intake better." He recommended that I just drive the car, and that the carbon would soon pass like a kidney stone. I decided to tear the engine apart again.

After careful inspection, I determined that I had somehow installed the connecting rod on the number one piston backward. When the engine was not running, there was plenty of clearance between the moving parts. However, when the engine *was* running, combustion forces on the top of the piston shortened the connecting rod just enough to cause the skirt of the piston to tap lightly on the head of the rod bolt. The rods in this engine had enough offset that the skirt would tap when the rod was installed backward.

Most connecting rods have a mark on them to identify the proper direction of installation. These marks

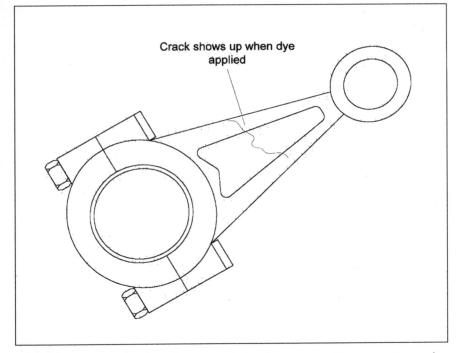

Crack shows up when dye applied

Magnafluxing is a procedure that uses a large electromagnet to magnetize each connecting rod. A special magnetic fluid is then saturated into the rod. When examined under a black light, surface cracks will be revealed. These surface cracks can be the starting point of much more serious cracks and breaks.

are sometimes in the form of a delta or an arrow. Care should be taken during disassembly to identify each of the connecting rods and note the direction of installation. Newly purchased connecting rods often come with installation instructions.

Buying Performance Connecting Rods

Speaking of newly purchased connecting rods, the best way to reduce reciprocating mass, lower energy loss and increase power is by purchasing high-performance aluminum connecting rods. This is especially important when you have purchased new pistons.

At this point, it would be easy for this book to turn into a catalog of the connecting rods available. Rather than provide free advertising for countless companies across the country, let's take a look at the decision-making process.

Essentially, there are six applications for an engine:
1. Taking mom and pop to the grocery store
2. Street performance
3. Circle-track short track racing
4. Circle-track duration racing
5. Competition drag racing
6. Maximum power drag racing

Common connecting rod options include cast iron, forged steel and cast aluminum, each of which has its advantages and disadvantages.

Cast Iron

The beauties of cast iron connecting rods are that they are both inexpensive and durable. These connecting rods are the ones normally found in stock engines. With a little work, cast iron rods can perform very effectively in a street performance application or even a bracket racer.

Forged Premium Steel

Forged steel connecting rods were the mainstay of the performance engine industry for many years. They have the combined advantage of strength, lightness, and durability, making them generally one of the best rods available for use in street performance machines.

Cast Aluminum

Aluminum connecting rods are light and very strong. Their weakness, though, is their low fatigue strength, which means poor durability. Frequent replacement of aluminum connecting rods is necessary. Aluminum connecting rods should not be used in engines where durability is of the essence, so they're not appropriate for endurance racers, aircraft, or even family cruisers.

Performance Preparation of a Stock Connecting Rod
Magnaflux Inspection

Magnafluxing is a procedure that uses a large electromagnet to magnetize each connecting rod. A special magnetic fluid is then saturated into the rod. When examined under a black light, surface cracks will be revealed. These surface cracks can be the starting point of much more serious cracks and breaks.

NOTE: After performing a magnafluxing procedure, be sure to demagnetize the rod using the procedure addressed earlier in this book. Leaving it magnetized will allow it to attract steel and iron particles after the engine is started, accelerating wear.

X-ray Inspection

If you are blessed to be one of those rare individuals who has more money than their wife and kids expend, then X-raying the connecting rods will reveal not only surface cracks, but cracks below the surface, as well. But X-raying is an expensive procedure that isn't even available in many towns. Still, it is well worth the expense for the peace of mind it affords. On the other hand, if you are really in doubt about the connecting rod, in doubt enough to consider the expense of having the connecting rods X-rayed, save the money on the X-ray and replace the rods instead.

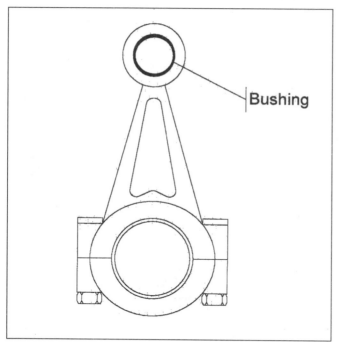

Bushing

When the connecting rod small end is damaged, the only practical repair is to enlarge the bore and install a bushing, or sleeve. This returns the bore of the small end to its nominal size without significantly affecting strength or durability.

Polishing

Polishing is done to strengthen the connecting rod, not to make it look nice. Some rules in stock racing classes do not permit polishing. If the engine you are building is not bound by any rules, or if the rules it is bound by do not prohibit polishing, polishing them is time well spent. Polishing is also cheaper than spending $1,000 on a set of performance connecting rods.

Use a high-speed die grinder and a carbide cutter to remove the casting flash or forging marks from the sides of the connecting rods. This operation is often referred to as deburring. Then, with a stationary belt sander, grind the casting pits and marks off of the connecting rods. By smoothing the rod beams, you remove the small pits and crevices that provide a starting point for cracks, so the rods are instantly stronger.

Shot Peening

After polishing, connecting rods can be further strengthened through shot peening. After masking the bearing mating surfaces to protect them, high velocity shot is targeted at the other areas of the connecting rods, particularly the fillet or radius near the rod bolts. The impact of the shot relieves stress in the metal that could cause microscopic cracks and could later become a broken rod. The principle is not unlike stopping at a massage parlor to have your back pounded on to relieve stress. An additional benefit is that shot peening compacts the surface of the rod, providing a more homogeneous surface that further denies cracks a place to begin.

Bushing

A lot of attention has been paid thus far to the big end of the connecting rod. The small end can also be subjected to damage and require repair. Since the small end of the rod cannot be separated like the big end, repairing the small end is not as easy as repairing the big end. The small end must first be machined round. Then a bushing can be driven in place and flushed off with the side of the rod, completing the repair.

New Bolts

Installing new connecting rods or rebuilt connecting rods without using new rod bolts is like splicing an anchor chain with a piece of twine.

Although it will initially serve the function, it may prove to doom the life of the work that has been done by providing a weak point for failure.

Rod-to-Cam Clearance

When a crankshaft is rotating at its maximum speed, there is a great deal of flexing and stretching occurring. On an overhead valve engine with the cam in the block, the sides of the connecting rods get very close to the camshaft. This is especially true of performance aluminum connecting rods that are typically much larger than iron or steel rods. The broader big end of an aluminum rod may swing dangerously near or even touch the camshaft, especially with some high-lift performance camshafts.

To check the connecting rod-to-cam clearance, install and torque the crankshaft in the block. Install the pistons on the connecting rods and install them properly in the engine. Torque all bearing caps. Place a thin layer of modeling clay on the sides of the connecting rod where the narrow portion expands to the big end. Now adjust the cam timing. This is an essential step to ensure that the phasing of the connecting rod with the camshaft will be as it is destined to be after the final build. Finally, rotate the crankshaft at least four or five times, then carefully remove the connecting rods and pistons, making sure that the clay is not rubbed against the block or cylinders during their removal. By carefully cutting a cross-section in the thinnest area of the clay, you can measure its thickness, which is the clearance between the rod and the cam.

If there is at least 0.050 inch of clearance, then this will be sufficient to keep the connecting rod from colliding with the camshaft when the engine is operating at maximum speed.

If, however, the clearance is not sufficient, then there are two viable alternatives. The first choice is to replace the camshaft with one that has a smaller base circle, but this may

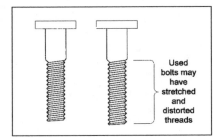

Used bolts may have stretched and distorted threads

Something that is almost never done during a standard overhaul is replacing the connecting rod bolts and nuts. The fasteners have been subjected to extreme and long-term stresses and should be replaced in a performance engine with every tear down. Why risk dozens of hours of work and thousands of dollars for the sake of a few dollars worth of nuts and bolts?

not be desirable because you have probably already spent a great deal of time selecting exactly the camshaft that will maximize the type of performance that you desire from this engine. Nonetheless, a small base-circle will ensure that the strength of the connecting rods is not compromised. The second option is to use a grinder to remove metal from the connecting rod bolts and shank, but this may be a bit disconcerting when you consider that the money spent on these new performance connecting rods could have paid a lot of green fees or could have bought a lot of fishing bait. There is no doubt that grinding away metal from the bolts and shank does weaken the rod.

Piston-to-Rod Clearance

Where non-stock pistons or a stroked crankshaft are used, there is an increased possibility of a lack of clearance between the counterweights of the crankshaft and the skirt of the piston. Stroker crankshafts also increase the angle between the vertical line of the piston and the connecting rod; in other words, when the throw of the crankshaft is 90 degrees from the vertical line described by piston movement, there is a possibility of the connecting rod hitting the skirt of the piston.

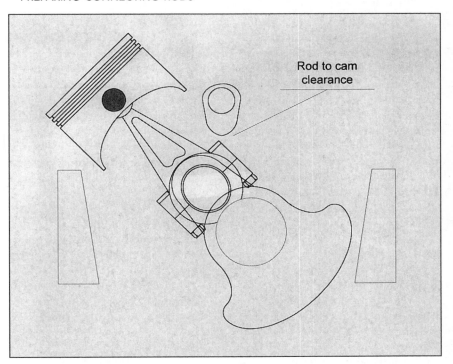

On an overhead-valve engine, the side of the connecting rod gets very close to the camshaft. This is especially true of performance aluminum connecting rods. These rods are designed to have improved strength by making the normally narrow part of the rod as it nears the big end broader. The broader big end may swing dangerously near or even touch the camshaft—especially high-lift performance camshafts.

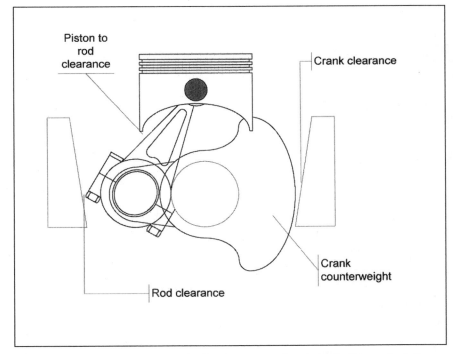

With performance connecting rods, the narrow area between the big and small ends is usually wider than on a stock rod. This compensates for the inherent weakness of some exotic, light-weight alloys when compared to steel. This additional width can cause the rod to touch the skirt of the piston when that journal reaches 90 degrees and 270 degrees during its rotation. Check for adequate clearance and modify (grind) the connecting rod as required for proper clearance.

Again, the modeling clay trick comes to the rescue. Press modeling clay along the sides of the upper part of the connecting rod (the beam). Install the crankshaft, rods and pistons; torque everything to their proper specifications, then rotate the crankshaft at least two full rotations. After cutting a cross-section into the clay at its thinnest point, measure the thickness to determine the clearance. The thickness should indicate a clearance of at least 0.050 inch to avoid trouble.

Rod Bearing Clearance

As with the main bearings, it's necessary to provide enough room between the surface of the crankshaft's connecting rod journal and the connecting rod bearing to allow for a thin film of oil. The term "bearing" is interpreted by most people to mean a surface that has a low coefficient of friction when placed against another surface. In reality, the bearing and crankshaft should never make direct contact when the engine is running—the two surfaces should always be kept apart by a film of oil exactly as thick as the clearance between the two surfaces. There is a common misconception that the oil clearance between two parts must always be minimal to prevent a loss of oil pressure. In reality, the clearance can be relatively large providing the oil pump has sufficient volumetric capacity to overcome the oil loss from the large oil clearance built into your engine.

Bearing clearances are a trade-off between free rotation, maintenance of alignment, and maintenance of adequate lubrication.

Rod Side Clearance

Whether dealing with an inline engine or a "V" engine, connecting rods require a certain amount of clearance to allow them to spin freely on their respective rod journal without binding either on the crankshaft itself, or, in the case of "V" engines, on the adjacent connecting rod.

To check the connecting rod side clearances, hold the connecting rod as far to one side as possible, then measure the clearance on the opposite side using a feeler gauge (for "V" engine, measure the clearance between rod pairs, while spreading the rods apart). Verify the acceptable range of clearances with the specifications listed in a shop manual. Typical side clearances are 0.010 to 0.020 inch. If the side clearance is outside the specified range for your application, replace the connecting rod or both rods, if replacement of one is not sufficient. If the side clearance is still incorrect, there is a problem with the crankshaft.

Piston-to-cylinder wall
clearance is critical to the
proper operation of any
engine. Too much clearance
and the piston will tend to
rock excessively as it
reciprocates. Too little
clearance and the normal
thermal expansion that occurs
as the engine runs may cause
the piston to seize. Different
alloys will have different
thermal expansion properties,
therefore the only real expert
on what the proper clearance
for a given piston choice is the
manufacturer of that piston.

CHAPTER NINE

PREPARING PISTONS

There's an old saying: If you can't take the heat, get out of the kitchen. Well, your pistons don't have that option: they *must* take the heat. Unfortunately, if they can't, they make a far less graceful exit than just casually exiting. Holes burned through their tops, broken ring lands and even pistons that seize themselves against the cylinder walls are all very real possibilities if you slip up while preparing your pistons for the rigors of service in your new or rebuilt engine.

Still, piston preparation is far from being a mysterious form of black magic. The steps you need to take have been taken before by countless engine builders, and the kinks have pretty much been worked out, so if you work carefully, you can rest assured your pistons *will* take the heat of every combustion cycle they see.

Of course, pistons that survive do little good if their supporting components don't do so, too. So while you strive for piston perfection, you'll need to devote attention to piston ring and even cylinder preparation, too. A well thought-out combination of parts, coupled with sound preparation techniques can make all the difference in the world for your new engine, not too mention your reputation as a Hot Rod Hero . . . or a Hot Rod Zero.

Piston-to-Wall Clearance

Excessive piston-to-cylinder wall clearance will allow the piston to rock excessively in the cylinder bore. If the clearance is insufficient, the piston can literally seize in the bore as the two expand in reaction to being heated. Keep in mind that the piston is cam ground, or oval shaped. Again, as most substances do, pistons expand when heated. Since the structure of the piston is not concentric, the amount of expansion will be different on the wrist pin axis than it will 90 degrees from the wrist pin axis. The oval shape when cold will allow the piston to be round when the engine is warmed up.

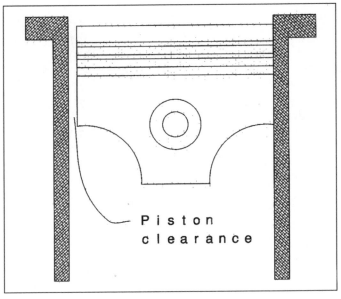

Piston
clearance

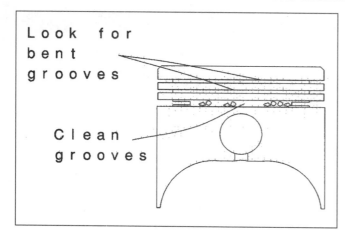

Use an old ring and a feeler gauge to measure the width of the ring groove. Damaged ring grooves can prevent desired flexing of the rings during engine operation and result in oil consumption or compression loss. If re-using old pistons, you also need to ensure that the grooves are completely free of any carbon build-up or other debris.

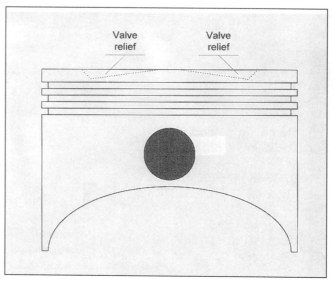

In a low-compression engine, there is usually plenty of clearance between the factory valve reliefs in the top of the piston and the bottom of the intake valve, when it is open. In a high-compression engine, however, it may be necessary to machine or modify the factory valve reliefs to provide a space in the top of the piston for the valves to occupy when the piston is near top dead center.

The difference, when cold, between these two axes should only be about 0.020 to 0.040 inch.

Most pistons are also tapered from 0.005 to 0.010 inch. The bottom of the piston skirt has less metal to expand than does the area closest to the head. For that reason, the top of most piston skirts is smaller than the bottom of the piston skirt. There are also pistons that have a barrel grind, which means that their piston skirts are narrow on the top and bottom but wide in the middle.

Another factor you need to consider is the piston material. If you can afford to invest in ceramic pistons you will find that they may not expand at all as the engine warms. The far more common aluminum pistons will have expansion rates that will vary depending on the alloy's blend of silicon, magnesium, manganese, nickel, copper, and other elements.

To ensure proper piston to cylinder wall clearance the diameter of the piston must be measured at the point recommended by the manufacturer of the piston. Furthermore, you should use the clearance specified by the pis-

ton manufacturer and *not* the factory service manual spec.

Begin the process of checking piston-to-cylinder wall clearance by reviewing the measurement recommendations supplied by the piston manufacturer. This recommended measurement will often need to be taken 90 degrees from the wrist pin at the top of the skirt (but some manufacturers have different recommendations, so don't take this for granted). Measure the piston diameter carefully with a micrometer, then, with an inside micrometer, measure the diameter of the cylinder at several places along the length of the cylinder. The places checked should be on the same axis as the piston manufacturer's recommendation for checking piston diameter. Naturally, the places measured should be in an area through which the measured point of the piston can travel.

A simpler, though often just as effective, method of measuring piston-to-cylinder wall clearance is with a feeler gauge. The best way to use the feeler gauge for this is the go-no-go method. Read the piston manufac-

A good way to check for adequate piston-to head-clearance is to place a lump of modeling clay on the top of the piston, install the head gasket and head, then rotate the crankshaft 720 degrees. A cross-section of this clay will reveal the piston-to-head clearance.

turer's recommendations for clearance. Select a feeler gauge that is equal to the minimum recommendation and a feeler gauge just larger than the maximum recommendation. The thinner feeler gauge should slide easily between the cylinder wall and the piston, while the thicker gauge should not fit at all.

Whichever method you use, be sure to make these measurements exact. Remember that failure to follow the piston manufacturer's recommendations exactly can cause piston slap or seizing of the piston.

Racing Piston Preparations

An engine that is destined for the world of muffler-less open headers on the drag strip or circle track has different requirements from one that is designed to haul mom and the kids to the local store. On these performance engines, the sound of the exhaust will muffle any piston slap that might occur, so it is recommended that the piston to cylinder wall clearance be exactly at the maximum limit to minimize friction. The larger clearance will also prevent piston scuffing as a result of high heat and pressures experienced at high rpm.

Honing for Exact Cylinder Diameter

Proper honing of the cylinders can ensure that the cylinder bore is exactly the correct diameter for each piston. Correct honing technique will produce a cross-hatch pattern on the cylinder walls. Only a flat stone hone can be used to true the cylinder walls. Although a flat stone hone mounted in a drill will do a reasonable job for a stock engine, maximum precision for performance applications can only be achieved with your machinist's honing machine.

There is a "home" version of a precision honing machine that does an excellent job. If you have a lot of time and a lot of money, or if you are going to be building a lot of engines, then investing in a "home" honing machine might be worthwhile. Since proper performance honing requires that the block be submerged or constantly bathed in oil during the honing process, you may want to consider buying an old bathtub and several gallons of honing oil along with the honing machine. Because each cylinder should have a determined ideal bore, each cylinder should be honed for a minute or so then measured. This may need to be repeated dozens of times,

but you don't want to proceed too quickly, which may result in accidentally exceeding your target diameter. Also, since there is likely to be 0.001 to 0.006 inch of metal to remove from each cylinder, be sure to verify that there is nothing you want to see on television for the next week or so.

If you are having the block bored, it is standard procedure for the machinist to then hone the cylinders following the boring process. The boring machine will bore the cylinders 0.004 to 0.006 inch undersize, then a hone will be used to remove the remaining metal to achieve the designated bore size. While honing is generally included in the cost of boring a cylinder, it wouldn't hurt to confirm that honing will be part of the procedure when you drop the block off with the machinist.

Ring Grooves

Of all the areas of a piston, the ones that probably require the most accuracy and precision are the ring grooves. The metal area between two grooves is known as a ring land. The head of the piston and the lands are several thousandths of an inch smaller in diameter than the rest of the piston. The bottom and top surfaces of the lands must be as smooth and parallel as possible. Any roughness or uneven surface on the lands can cause compression leaks and decrease power. The piston ring lands should be protected like negotiable stock certificates. A small ding or warpage of a land can literally render that piston—or possibly even a full set of pistons—useless. If the ring grooves of the pistons in a street engine are coated with carbon, you scrape the carbon using a special tool or with an old, broken ring. Performance pistons with carbon-coated grooves should just be replaced. Of course, if the engine is being used on the track, it probably will not get enough mileage on it to have carbon build-up. Until the pistons are ready to be installed in the engine, keep the lands and grooves protected with gaffers tape or something similar. Do not use duct tape as it leaves behind a sticky damaging residue. This is crucial

on pistons destined for use in competition engines. Building a performance engine is definitely a job for the detail-oriented individual.

Valve Pockets

The piston needs to be at the top of its stroke when the intake valve is open or opening to ensure that when the piston begins its downward journey, the fresh air/fuel charge can fill the cylinder. The problem is that the intake valve must be at least partially open when the piston arrives at top dead center in order to ensure that the cylinder can fill properly with air. Because a cylinder tends to be most efficient at drawing in air while the piston is accelerating down the first half of the stroke, many performance engines will have the intake valve open quite a bit before the piston reaches top dead center on the exhaust stroke. The valve must be fully open well before the piston reaches its point of maximum velocity at the halfway point of the stroke. In a low compression engine, there is usually plenty of clearance between the factory valve reliefs in the top of the piston and the bottom of the intake valve, but in a high compression engine it may be necessary to machine or modify the factory valve reliefs to provide additional clearance required by high-lift cams, oversize valves, or just high rpm.

Piston-to-Head Clearance

Measuring piston-to-head clearance is another of those times when modeling clay comes in handy. Lightly coat the surface of the piston and combustion chamber with a light oil. Place a small ball of modeling clay in the center of the piston and make sure that the ball is large enough that it will be compressed between the top of the piston and the bottom of the head. You also need to make sure that the ball is not so large that the piston cannot go over top dead center—there's no sense in damaging connecting rods before you even fire-up the engine. Install the cylinder head with the type of gasket that you will ulti-

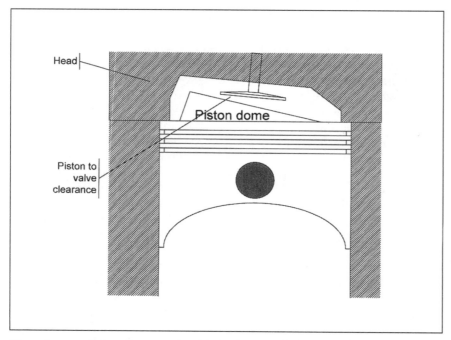

The valve-to-piston clearance should also be noted when checking the piston-to-head clearance. A minimum specification should be at least 0.080 inch clearance for the intake valves and at least 0.100 inch for the exhaust valves.

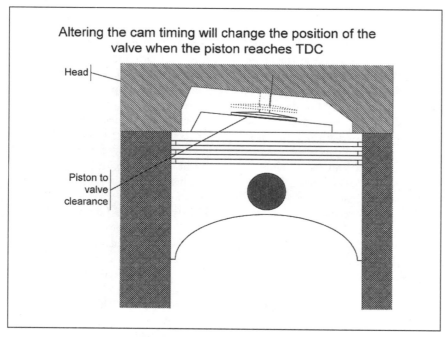

If there is insufficient piston-to-valve clearance, you can try advancing or retarding the cam phasing. This may sacrifice some performance, however (though not as much as if you don't provide the proper clearance and the valves hit the pistons). The valve seats can be reground, but this, too, will affect airflow and therefore power. The best solution is to deepen the valve reliefs in the piston head and dome.

mately use during final assembly, torque the cylinder head, then rotate the crankshaft through 360 degrees of rotation. The minimum thickness of the modeling clay will be your minimum piston-to-head clearance.

Piston-to-Valve Clearance

Oddly enough, piston-to-valve clearance is less critical on a racing engine than it is on a street performance engine, because racing engines feature valvetrains that are very positive in action. In racing engines, the valve springs are extremely stiff to prevent valve float at high engine speeds. But don't think that you can improve your street performance engine with these extremely stiff valve springs, however, because they're often so stiff that only a few hours of operation could do severe damage to your camshaft. Many racing engines feature roller lifters to reduce wear.

Street performance engines must be built with understanding that the engine will last for more than one trip to the local discount store. And their valvetrains are not as rigid, therefore at high engine speeds the valves may begin to float, or remain open, as the lifter "leaps" off of the cam lobe, when it should be well on its way toward the heel of the cam lobe, instead. This may result in the valve occupying the same point in the space-time continuum that the piston is trying to occupy. This is a disastrous and deadly event and has often been responsible for scattering pieces of metal all over the inside of the engine and even all over the ground.

A not very sexy but quite practical way to ensure proper clearance is to mold a 1/8-inch thick layer of modeling clay to the top of the piston. Sprinkle a little talcum powder on the top of the clay to keep it from sticking to the head and valves. This should be done on all pistons to ensure that each has been verified to have the proper clearance. For this method to be accurate, everything must be assembled exactly as it will be when the engine is assembled for the final time. The pistons must be installed on the connecting rods that will be used; the rods

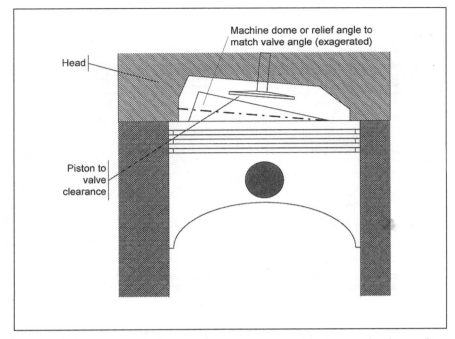

The ideal situation for maximizing the compression ratio, is to make the angle of the valve the same as the angle of the piston dome. Measure the angle of the piston dome then measure the angle of the valve seat. The difference between these two angles is the angle that the cylinder head should be milled.

must be properly installed on the crankshaft and their rod bolts torqued; the crankshaft main bearing caps must be torqued in place; and the same type and thickness head gasket must be used during "mock-ups" as during final assembly.

To get maximum performance from an engine, it is necessary to precisely synchronize the camshaft with the crankshaft. This process is called "phasing," and you need to phase the camshaft when the engine is finally built, so you will also have to phase the camshaft when checking the piston-to-valve clearance. Shortcutting this process can yield perfect results when just testing the clearance but a disastrous lack of clearance when the engine is finally assembled, because the valve timing may be advanced or retarded enough to cause interference.

To phase the camshaft, attach a degree wheel to the front of the crankshaft and rotate the crankshaft until the camshaft pushes the intake lifter for the number one cylinder to its highest point. The point of maximum lift should not be monitored visually, though. For accuracy, measure valve action with a dial indicator. Using the recommenda-

tions of the camshaft grinder, as listed on the "cam card" supplied with the cam, loosen the bolts in the previously slotted cam sprocket holes and align the cam sprocket so that the intake centerline matches the recommended position on the crankshaft.

With all components installed, phased, and torqued in place, rotate the crankshaft several times, then remove the cylinder head. Again, the cross-section of the clay is the piston-to-valve clearance. Now the problem is judging how much clearance is enough, and how you can obtain that clearance.

Sufficient clearance must take into account valve float, connecting rod stretch and thermal expansion of all components. The general rule is that there must be at least 0.080 inch clearance for the intake valves and 0.100 inch for the exhaust valves.

Correcting Insufficient Piston-to-Valve Clearance

If there is insufficient piston-to-valve clearance the real challenge begins. You can try advancing or retarding the cam phasing, but this may sacrifice some performance. You

could have the valve seats reground, but this will affect airflow and therefore possibly rob the engine of some power. The best solution is to deepen the pistons' valve pockets. This is where you really will wish you had a father-in-law with a machine shop. Deepening the valve pockets is beyond the skills of the typical human—well, operating the vertical mill and flycutter required to do so is, at least. The disadvantage (and there is always a disadvantage it seems) of this is that the compression ratio will be lowered a little. A flycutter is a cutting tool with a single bit that rotates around an axis. Racing pistons are often plunge cut, which is a process that removes a minimal amount of metal from the valve relief necessary to provide sufficient clearance, but leaves a crescent of raised metal that helps keep compression ratio loss to a minimum.

Matching Valve Relief-to-Valve Angle

The angle of the valve relief should be the same as the angle of the valve head. This can be measured with a bevel protractor. Measure both the angle of the piston's valve relief plus the valve head angle. This correction procedure will require the machinist to grind the angle of the piston valve relief area to match the angle of the valves. This is usually only necessary in engines where the performance is to be maximized and where the heads have been angle milled. When cylinder heads are milled an extreme amount to maximize compression, the edge of the intake valve seat might be machined away. To prevent this problem, many engine builders may mill the head at a slight angle. This angle will usually result in no more than 0.125 inch difference between intake and exhaust sides. In truly radical cases, some big-block heads are milled at an angle, giving up to 0.250 inch difference between intake and exhaust sides of the head. These radical cases will require the dome of the piston head to be ground at a matching angle.

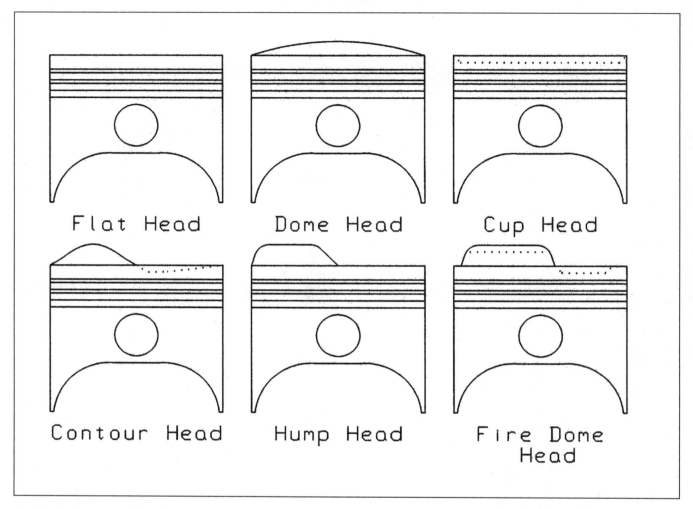

The ideal piston would not have a dome, because a dome inhibits the progression of the flame front through the combustion chamber. If at all possible, avoid the use of domed pistons. Some fuels, especially high octane gasoline, methanol, ethanol, and natural gas give markedly better performance with higher compression ratios, however. If the engine is destined for any of these uses you might consider domed pistons.

Dome Fitting and Radiusing

The purpose of a piston dome is to raise compression, but because the dome rises up into the combustion chamber, it can actually block the travel of the flame front following ignition of the air/fuel mixture, which can result in "pockets" of unburned air and fuel in the combustion chamber, which minimizes fuel and volumetric efficiency, thus reducing power.

Because of this considerable drawback, if it is at all possible, you should avoid the use of domed pistons. Fortunately, you can increase

a street engine's power and performance more with improved intake and exhaust flow than with increased compression and domed pistons. Some fuels, especially high octane gasolines, methanol, ethanol, and natural gas, give markedly better performance with higher compression ratios. If the engine is destined to use one of these fuels, you might consider domed pistons. However, a street machine running on today's pump gases may detonate so badly that any theoretical improvement will be lost in the reality of the pump gas of the 1990s.

Marking Cylinder Positions on the Head

The first step of checking the piston dome-to-combustion chamber clearances is to determine and mark the exact location of each cylinder relative to the head's deck surface. This process begins with coloring the bottom (deck surface) of the head with machinist's dye, then bolting them onto the bare (but fully machined) engine block. From inside the cylinder, you can then use a scribe to trace onto the head's deck surface the circumference of each cylinder. Then, you can remove the cylinder heads.

With the heads off, you'll then be able to work unimpeded as you place each piston dome-first into its respective combustion chamber, taking extreme care to ensure that the piston is positioned precisely within the circle made with the scribe. The next step is to make sure that the piston will have

Radiusing the pistons is a process that ensures proper fit of the pistons in the combustion chamber.

With machinist's dye, color the bottom of the cylinder head and bolt them in place. Use a sharp scribe to mark the circumference of the cylinder on the head (note thin line surrounding each chamber). Remove the heads and place each chamber's respective piston in the chamber.

the proper rotational orientation in the combustion chamber; that is, to make sure the piston isn't "turned" or rotated as it would be in the cylinder. To do this, you need to verify that the center-line of the wrist pin bores is parallel to the long axis of the cylinder head. A quick and dirty way to do this is to slide a wrist pin in the adjacent pistons, so that the pins connect the pistons.

With the piston dome properly aligned in the chamber, the dome should comfortably fill the chamber without interfering with any part of the head or valves. If the piston domes fit comfortably, mold a layer of modeling clay over the top of the piston and press it firmly into the combustion chamber being careful that the piston is precisely positioned within the scribe marks. Then, by sectioning the clay, you can measure the clearances throughout the chamber, which, again, should be at least 0.080 inch for the intake valves and 0.100 inch for the exhaust valves. As simplistic as this method may sound, it works quite well on many engines.

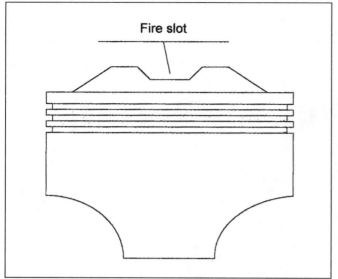

Fire slot

In pistons with extremely high domes, the dome of the piston may mask the spark plug from the rest of the combustion chamber, at least contributing to poor combustion and possibly preventing the engine from running at all. Although a rare requirement, it is sometimes necessary to cut a "fire slot" in the piston dome.

For those who were born with a silver slide rule in their mouth, there is a more scientific—though doubtfully more accurate—method of achieving proper rotational alignment of the piston. In this case, you'll need a machined surface plate that is equipped with a vertical metal rod of the same diameter as the wrist pin, so that you can mount the piston on its side on the plate, by sliding its wrist pin bores over the vertical rod. You'll need to measure the diameter of the piston head, then place marks on each side of the piston (90 degrees from the wrist pin bores) that indicate the middle of the piston (half its diameter). Next, the cylinder head must be

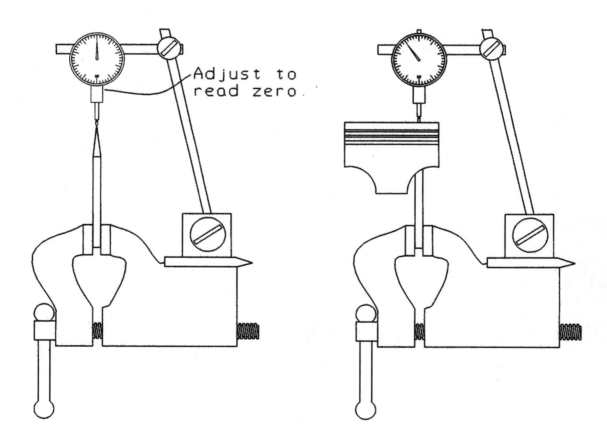

Adjust to read zero.

Checking piston thickness is particularly important before or after any lightening has been done on the piston. If too much metal has been removed, the piston may self-destruct.

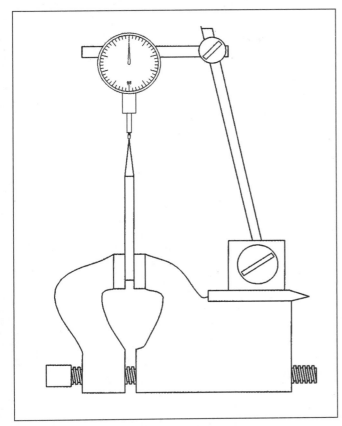

A simple piston thickness gauge can be made from a punch, a dial indicator, and a vise, as illustrated here.

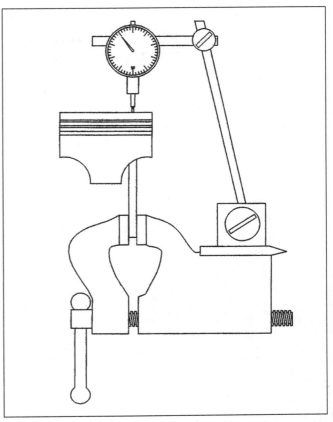

After adjusting the dial indicator to read zero on the tip of the punch, carefully place the piston in between. The dial indicator will then show the thickness of the piston.

marked at a point 90 degrees from the baseline established by the wrist pin. Then with both the head and the piston marked, align the piston in the combustion chamber by aligning the piston's marks with those on the head. From this point on the procedure is the same as described above: put clay on the piston top, press it into the chamber firmly, then section and measure the clay to measure the clearances.

Fitting the Piston Dome

In most cases, checking the piston dome-to-combustion chamber clearances will yield satisfactory clearance. The real problem, however, is what to do if the measurements indicate that the piston will come in contact with the head. The only real solution is to grind either the cylinder head's combustion chamber or the piston's dome, and maybe both. It's natural to feel insecure about grinding your new cylinder

heads or new pistons, but you just have to get over it. But let that insecurity work for you, by allowing it to keep you from grinding carelessly.

There are a few things to remember before you begin grinding away on those new parts that you could easily have paid between $1,000 and $2,000 for: First, don't let your wife find the receipts; second, make sure she is at work or otherwise out of the house when you start grinding, or she'll think you've lost your mind. With these critical items attended to, you'll need to make sure that you have the proper tools to perform the grinding. A high speed, high horsepower grinder is essential. As useful as the small "Dremel" grinders are, they don't have enough horsepower to prevent the grinding bit from binding, which may gouge the head or piston, which would require removing more metal than you planned in order to repair the damage you inflicted. Finally, if high

compression is your goal, remember that every flake of metal removed from the piston or head lowers the compression, and thus reduces maximum power.

With grinder in hand, you'll need to know what you're going to grind: the piston or the head. There's a simple way to determine which you should start with: Pull a large coin out of your pocket, give it a quick flip in the air; heads you grind the head, tails you grind the piston. As whimsical as this may sound, it really makes little difference where the metal is removed. If you prefer to make a logical decision, instead of relying on the fall of a coin, you'll need to consider the type and thickness of the head, and the size of the dome on the piston and its thickness. Use the high-speed grinder to remove the least amount of metal necessary to provide the necessary clearance.

After grinding piston and combustion chambers of the head, it's time to

Lightening the pistons

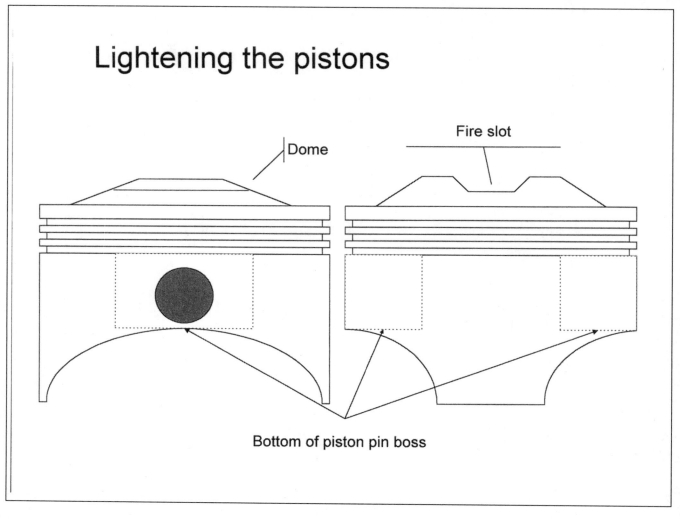

Dome

Fire slot

Bottom of piston pin boss

Lightening the pistons can serve two purposes: First, it reduces reciprocating weight, which makes the engine accelerate faster; second, its how you balance the pistons. The piston pin bosses are one of the best places to remove weight.

waste another head gasket. Install the crankshaft using a set of good main bearings. Install the connecting rods on the pistons and install the piston/rod assemblies in the engine. Use a good but expendable set of rod bearings and torque the connecting rods. Before installing the heads place some more modeling clay on the top of the piston. Be careful not to use an excessive amount of clay, though, which could result in a hydraulic lock situation that can damage the engine. Next, install the cylinder heads using the sacrificial set of head gaskets. Rotate the crankshaft through one complete engine cycle (two revolutions of the crankshaft), then remove the heads, section the clay

and measure it. There must be sufficient clearance when you take into account valve float, connecting rod stretch and thermal expansion of all components. Again, the general rule is that there must be at least 0.080 inch clearance for the intake valves and 0.100 inch for the exhaust valves.

If need be, repeat the grinding and measuring processes until the proper clearance is achieved. And remember that it is very easy to remove metal, but it is very difficult to put metal back. Wasting an extra set of head gaskets as a result of being conservative on the removal of metal from the pistons and cylinder head is a lot cheaper than replacing the heads or pistons.

Relieving the Piston Dome

Many years ago I took a few flying lessons in the town of Renton, Washington. During the course of the lessons, the instructor had me fly toward a mountain. I've got nothing against mountains, but what I didn't like about the exercise was that the instructor had me approach the mountain at what I felt was an insufficient altitude. But, I noticed that the mountain had a notch, or saddle, at the midpoint of its crest, so I aimed for the midpoint.

The flame front in your engine's combustion chamber is a lot like that little Cessna I was flying, and the piston dome is a lot like that mountain, but without the saddle. There is an air/fuel charge on both sides of the piston dome, but with the piston at top dead center, the dome divides the combustion chamber into two separate regions—one directly exposed to the

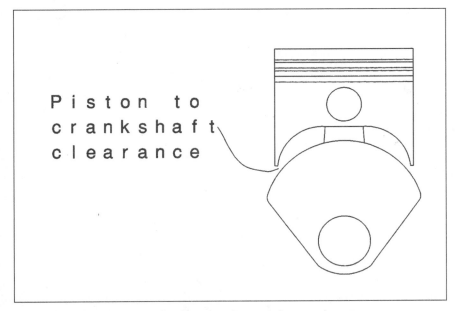

Piston to crankshaft clearance

The slipper skirt piston was developed as the manufacturers began to use counterweights to smooth the operation of the engine. These counterweights would attempt to occupy the same space as the piston with full skirts. When installing a non-stock piston or a non-stock crankshaft, be sure to verify an adequate amount of clearance between the crankshaft counterweights and the piston.

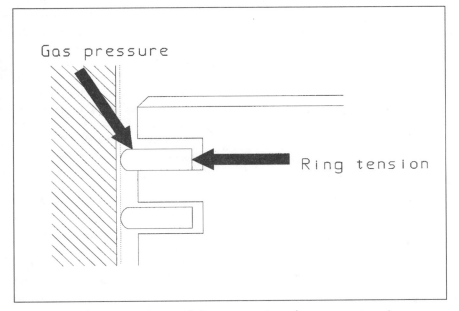

Gas pressure

Ring tension

Gas porting the pistons is one of those operations that, on most engine blueprinting projects, is not necessary. When the piston begins to travel the cylinder on the intake stroke there is a volume of partially or totally burned gases trapped between the top ring and the head of the piston. This can apply enormous pressure to the head of the piston.

spark plug, and one side that has no direct exposure at all. So the problem is how do you get the flame front to get from the spark plug side of the piston dome to the other side of the piston dome to burn the entire air/fuel mixture,

and thus produce maximum power?

Well, although it is rarely required, it may sometimes be necessary to cut a "fire slot" through the piston dome, through which the flame front can travel to ignite the air and

fuel on the other side of the dome. I once had a Mustang that I and some friends rebuilt and took to the local drag strip for some testing. At about 3000 rpm, the engine would begin to misfire. The problem continued throughout the use of the engine. Only years later did I find out that the flame front was probably masked, and thus kept from reaching the unburned gases on the far side of the piston dome, which would explain why the engine ran out of power at relatively low rpm.

The procedure for cutting a fire slot, or tunnel, in the piston dome is like the procedure for the removal of any metal from an expensive component: Begin with a sacrifice to Synchro, The God Of All Things Needlessly Damaged And Therefore Useless. Using a high-speed electric grinding motor or an air-powered grinding motor, grind a notch in the dome to expose the spark to the entire combustion chamber when the piston is at top dead center.

Checking Piston Thickness

There are few things that can happen to a piston that are as potentially catastrophic as detonation. Detonation occurs when high temperatures in the combustion chamber are ignited by the heat of compression. This causes the gases from combustion to begin to expand as the piston is traveling toward the top of the cylinder. This means that the piston must now compress an expanding gas. The result is the violent collision of an expanding gas and metal traveling at several thousand feet per minute.

If the piston head is too thin it will not be able to withstand the extreme pressures of detonation, and can result in catastrophic failure of the piston, metal fragments flying around inside the block, and local auto parts store cash registers drooling at the opportunity to sell you a large number of engine parts. To measure the thickness of the piston head, you could place the piston head down on the surface of the moon, call a buddy at NASA, and have him point a laser at

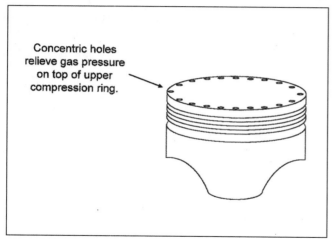

Concentric holes relieve gas pressure on top of upper compression ring.

To gas-port the piston, a series of holes are drilled in a concentric pattern around the perimeter of the head of the piston.

the underside of the piston head. Divide the time it takes for the light to return to the site of the laser by two, then divide that quotient by the speed of light. That will give you the distance from the NASA facility to the bottom of the piston head. Now move the piston and repeat the procedure. This will be the distance to the surface of the moon. Subtract the distance from the NASA facility to the bottom of the piston from the distance from the NASA facility to the surface of the moon. This will give you the piston head thickness. If you do not know anyone at NASA there is an alternative procedure.

Mount a long center punch or similar pointed object in a vise. This will form the lower anvil for the measuring the thickness of the head of the piston. Place a dial indicator on a holder so that the piston or any other object can be measured. Adjust the dial indicator so that it reads zero against the point of the center punch. Place the piston in the measuring tool you have just made, then measure several of what you feel are the thinnest points in the head of the piston. The thinnest point on the head of the piston should not be less than 0.080 if the engine is to be run for less than 15 seconds at a time down a dragstrip. If you

are going to be running any longer, the piston head must be thicker.

A more modern approach to measuring the piston head thickness is to use a sonic measuring tool, which uses sound waves to measure the thickness of metal. Check with some of the machine shops around town. They probably have one and can provide you with accurate measurements.

There are no hard and fast rules about piston head thickness, and you will really only need to check it when planning to modify the head of the piston and when you have finished modifying the head of a piston. I have two pieces of advice. First, do not modify the head of the piston so that it is thinner at any point than it was at the thinnest point before you began. Secondly, call the manufacturer of the piston, explain to them the type of use the engine you are building will get and ask them the minimum recommended thickness. They will take into consideration the type of fuel you are using, the metallurgy of the piston, the speed of the piston at maximum rpm, mean and maximum cylinder pressures, how long the engine will run at one time, the typical and maximum loads on the engine, and then they will calculate these factors on a Cray Supercomputer and then . . . they'll give you their best guess. Remember, this is an area where the faint of heart will save money in the long run.

Most readers of this book are probably not going to be doing any serious piston modifications. Therefore the typical reader might feel that this is an operation they can skip. After all, they might say, I just paid $950 for this set of "Agamemnon Superforged" pistons. They can't possibly have a defect like a thin casting. You might find this to be a rather depressing presumption when you are sitting on the side of the road or track with fragments of your $950 pistons lying in the bottom of the oil pan.

Piston Lightening

In most cases, the only reason to lighten the piston is to balance it. Find a scale accurate to a gram. Measure

Gas pressure

Gas port

Ring tension

The holes in the top of the piston allow the gas trapped on the top of the upper compression ring to vent through the top of the piston. This reduces the pressure against the head of the piston and can prevent piston damage on engines that are designed to run in the 10,000 rpm range.

each piston's weight, then use the lightest piston of the group as your target weight for all the others and then remove metal from the heavier pistons until they weigh the same as the lightest. Remove the metal from the pistons according to the guidelines described below. For most enthusiasts, the best way to ensure a properly balanced set of pistons is to pay a few bucks extra to the manufacturer, in the form of pre-weighed and balanced piston sets. The manufacturer can take the time to weigh the pistons and match them in sets by weight before they ever go out the door and on their way to you.

The ideal piston would be extremely light and extremely strong, and there has been a great deal of experimentation over the years with ceramics as a way of hopefully attaining this goal. Lightening the piston does reduce the inertial forces acting on the piston, but it also weakens the piston.

First of all, lightening the pistons only increases throttle response. Lightweight pistons have no place in engines destined for a vehicle running up and down Alaska's Dalton Highway (known locally as the "haul road")—a nearly 500-mile stretch of gravel heading north out of Fairbanks to Prudhoe Bay on the Arctic Ocean—where reliability is far more precious. With only two places on this stretch of road to buy supplies or gasoline, it's no place for an engine with fragile pistons.

On the other hand, when the ability for the engine to change speeds suddenly and rapidly is more critical than the ability to hang together for 100,000 miles, there is a lot that can be done to lighten most pistons. If you took the time and spent the money to buy quality performance pistons, the only way to significantly and safely reduce their weight is with the skills and trial-and-error experience of a skilled performance machinist. The machinist you would want to use will be someone that has a secret log book of piston lightening successes and failures. In this practice, near-success is when you removed one gram too much from the piston

and it came apart. Total success is when you build a new engine using the same type of piston and don't remove that critical last gram. These types of successes and failures—and the knowledge gained from them—are what make that machinist the one you want to use.

If you are one who is inclined to do this task yourself without the aforementioned experience, there are four places that weight is typically removed:

1. Inside of the skirt
2. The underside of the piston head, near the wrist pin bosses
3. The underside of the ring lands on pistons
4. The piston struts, next to the wrist pin bosses

One thing is absolutely critical to this operation: Don't leave any sharp edges! That means you'll need to use only radiused cutters, which are cutters with rounded tip edges that prevent sharp edged gouges from occurring as the metal is being removed. Sharp edges are the places where stress fractures and cracks can start. And pistons are subjected to such intense pressures and forces that any flaw could be fatal.

A final benefit of the lightening process is that while reducing the reciprocating mass, you're also minimizing the necessary weight of the crankshaft counterweights. And by reducing rotating mass, you're allowing for even more rapid changes in rotational speed. The bottom line is this: lower mass equates immediately to greater changes in speed.

Skirt-to-Crankshaft Clearance

The slipper skirt piston was developed when crankshafts began to need counterweights. The skirt of the standard trunk (full skirt) piston tried to occupy the same space as the crankshaft counterweights. When using a stroker crank or specialty pistons, particularly after custom work or modification to either the pistons, rods, or crankshaft, it is absolutely essential that you check to see that the piston skirts clear the crankshaft counter-

weights through each full range of motion. After the crank is laid into position and the pistons and connecting rods are properly installed, rotate the crankshaft through a minimum of 360 degrees to ensure adequate clearance. Measure any counterweight to skirt clearance that seems questionable, a minimum 0.050 inch of clearance is recommended.

Gas Porting

Gas porting the piston involves precision drilling tiny holes in the top of the piston so that the gases that would otherwise be trapped between the top compression ring and the head of the piston can escape. Located at the back of the ring groove, these holes are typically 0.040 to 0.060 inches in diameter. The holes must be evenly spaced. Only pistons destined for running a quarter mile at a time should be gas ported. In these engines, ring side clearance is often less than 0.002 inch. The gas ports are needed to prevent tremendous pressures from building under the top ring land and tearing the head off the piston at extreme rpm.

Expansion and Cold Piston Clearance

As a piston warms during operation, it expands. Most pistons are designed with a "cam" ground design, which means that the piston isn't truly round, but is instead ever-so-slightly oval shaped—its diameter in one direction is slightly smaller than its diameter in the other direction. The design of the piston, the mass concentrations of the piston, are such that the expansion rates are different on the two axes. When the piston is at operating temperature, the differences in expansion cause the two axes to become equal in diameter, and the piston is then round. But this presents us with a problem when we are trying to measure the piston clearance. The measurement for piston clearance will, out of necessity, be taken cold; therefore, the clearance specs may seem very large to the layman. It would be a mistake to think that power could be

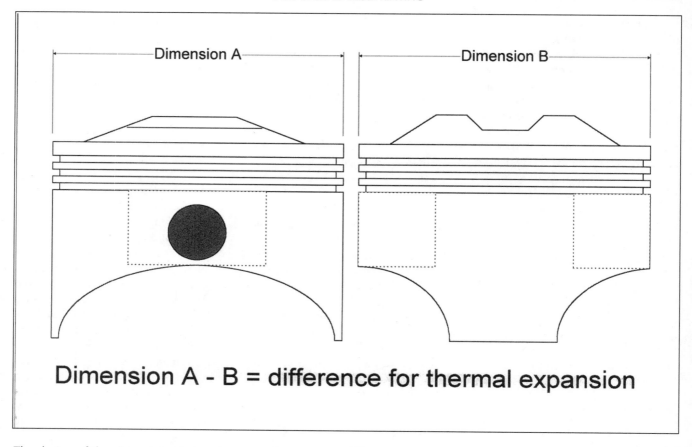

Dimension A - B = difference for thermal expansion

The design of the piston is such that the expansion rates are different on its two axes. When the piston is at operating temperature, the differences in expansion rates cause the two axes to become equal in diameter, so the piston is now round. This presents us with a problem, however, when we are trying to measure the piston clearance. Since the measurement for piston clearance will be taken cold. It also means that the clearance specs may seem very large, but as the piston expands the clearances will tighten up.

improved by tightening up this specification. With a tight piston-to-cylinder clearance, the expansion of the piston as it warms could cause the piston to seize in the cylinder, virtually welding itself in place.

Piston Skirt Preparation

Debur the piston skirts; the procedure here is much the same as the deburring process discussed in previous sections. Remove the casting flash and sharp edges that might form a place for a crack or break to start. Finish the deburring by buffing the entire skirt with 600 grit, solvent soaked paper.

Many builders recommend glass beading the skirt of the piston. This leaves a slightly rough surface that will trap oil and increase lubrication. Before beading the skirt, though, be sure to mask off the circumference of the head of the piston, the ring land, and the ring grooves to prevent them form being blasted. Use fresh glass beads and keep the nozzle in constant motion to prevent unintentional wear to any part of the skirt. After beading, I recommend rubbing the side of a wrist pin over the surface of the skirt. This is to ensure that no sharp edges remain to concentrate heat or scuff the cylinder walls.

Piston Rings

Square inch for square inch, the piston rings may well be the hardest working items in the engine. They slide up and down the cylinders at speeds approaching 46 miles per hour or more. They can be asked to accelerate from 0 feet per minute to over 4,000 feet per minute then back to 0 feet per minute more than 67 times per second. This is like accelerating from 0 to 3,000 miles per hour then back to 0 again in 1 second! If that rate of acceleration could continue for 62 hours, the piston and rings would reach light speed. If you could build a car, or even a rocket, that could sustain this rate of acceleration, it would do you little good, because without inertial dampers, the occupants of the vehicle would be strained through the rear bulkhead of the vehicle like broth through a colander.

This rate of acceleration and deceleration naturally subjects the piston rings to tremendous forces. But that's not all do. Don't forget that several thousand times per minute the rings must also seal the forces of an explosion. In spite of all this, on most Detroit iron or import *voiture d'elegance*, these piston rings hang in there year after year reliably doing there job until finally, after 800,000,000 cycles or more they have the audacity to begin to bypass a significant amount of combustion gases or oil.

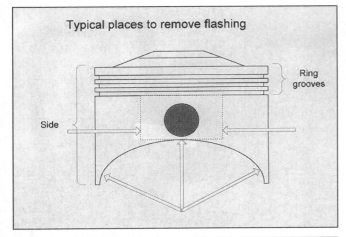

Typical places to remove flashing

Ring grooves

Side

Remove the casting flash and sharp edges that might form a place for a crack or break to start. Finish the deburring by buffing the entire skirt with 600 grit, solvent-soaked paper.

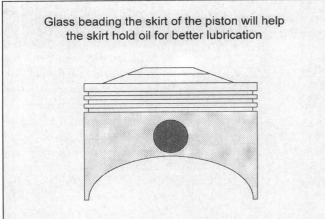

Glass beading the skirt of the piston will help the skirt hold oil for better lubrication

Many builders recommend glass beading the skirt of the piston, which leaves a slightly rough surface that will trap oil and increase lubrication (i.e., reduce friction).

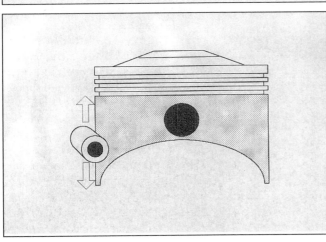

After beading, I recommend rubbing the side of a wrist pin over the surface of the skirt to ensure that no sharp edges remain that might concentrate heat or scuff the cylinder walls.

Like everything else in the world of engine rebuilding and performance modification, there are several different quality grades of piston rings. Let's face it, most rebuild applications are going to do little more than travel to the grocery store and maybe do a little bracket racing. For these applications, less expensive rings will do a very good job and last a long time. If the goal is to get from Point A to Point B in the shortest possible time, however, then something a little tougher will be needed.

The typical spark ignition engine will have three rings: The top two rings are gas sealing rings, while the bottom ring is designed to reduce the amount of oil that migrates up the cylinder walls toward the combustion chamber. The top rings are typically referred to as compression rings; the lower ring is called the oil ring or oil control ring.

Piston Ring Materials
Cast Iron

Cast iron piston rings were the standard of the industry for decades. In the early 1970s, I was driving from Fort Worth, Texas, to Phoenix, Arizona. While passing near Van Horn, Texas, my little Fiat 850, which had been singing along at an impressive 75 miles an hour (almost legal in west Texas at the time), lost most of its reserve power. This little engine had been asked to work like an Indy 500 engine for the past 489 miles. Designed for the Italian market, the engine in this car was designed to go at best a few kilometers at a time. In west Texas, though, the distance from your ranchero to the nearest stock yard might be several hundred miles. I had asked an engine designed for short distance operation in a relatively cool climate to push my little car several hundred miles in the searing heat of the Permian Basin. Not surprisingly, the engine components were not up to the task, and a compression ring on the number one cylinder broke.

Cast iron piston rings are very durable but they are brittle and can be damaged by combustion extremes such as detonation. Very few modern applications use this technology once you look past the performance characteristics of a Cushman.

Moly

The American Heritage Dictionary's definition of *moly*, which is short for *molybdenum*, is as follows: "*Symbol* **Mo** A hard, silvery-white metallic element used to toughen alloy steels and soften tungsten alloy, melting point 2,617°C."

Many alloys used in high performance automotive applications contain molybdenum. It is used to harden and strengthen performance pistons rings. During the manufacturing process, the standard cast iron ring is manufactured with a groove around its outer perimeter. As a final step in the manufacturing process, this groove is spray filled with molten molybdenum. As the molybdenum cools, it becomes molybdenum dioxide—a ceramic material much

Measure any counterweight to skirt clearance that seems questionable. A minimum of 0.050 inch of clearance in recommended.

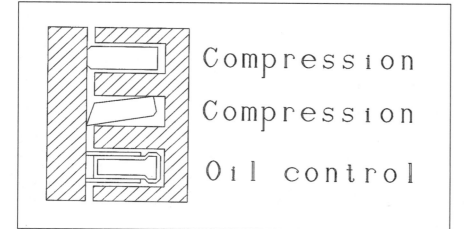

There are two basic types of piston rings. The top two rings are the compression rings, which are designed to seal the expanding gases in the combustion chamber. The third ring is the oil control ring. The job of the oil control ring is to scrape the oil down the cylinder walls and prevent it from entering the combustion chamber.

tougher and harder than the molybdenum itself.

The primary advantage of moly rings is the natural porosity of the molybdenum dioxide coating. This porous layer absorbs oil and allows for extremely good lubrication of the cylinder walls without allowing oil to bypass to the combustion chamber. Early experiments with this technology created a molybdenum dioxide layer that was extremely porous, so porous in fact that dirt and abrasives would be trapped in the coating and would act as an abrasive. Today's moly rings, however, have a porosity of less than 5 percent. Most modern engines feature a moly top compression ring from the factory.

Chrome

Back to *The American Heritage Dictionary*. *Chrome* or *chromium* is defined as follows, "*Symbol* **Cr** A lustrous, hard, steel-gray metallic element, resistant to tarnish and corrosion and found primarily in chromite. It is used as a catalyst, to harden steel alloys and produce stainless steels, in corrosion-resistant decorative platings, and as a pigment in glass, melting point 1,890°C."

Chrome rings are for those who have built an engine with perfect cylinder bores. Because these rings are so resistant to wear, they are intended to be used only in perfect cylinder bores. With lesser rings a little time, and a little patience with the smoking will let the rings seat. With chrome rings, what you have on the first day after an overhaul is what you have from that day forward. In most uses of chrome rings, the rings will easily last as long as or even outlast the rest of the engine.

As perfect as these rings may sound, no component is perfect. Moly will not bond, or weld, to the walls of the cylinder, but chrome will. Also, chrome rings are not recommended for use with gaseous fueled engines. Do not laugh, I know a fellow in Dallas, Texas, who races a compressed natural gas dragster, quite successfully. And given that current EPA regulatory projections imply a requirement for alternative fuels by the turn of the century, someday you might be otherwise tempted to use chrome rings in a natural gas powered street car.

Plasma Ceramic

Plasma ceramic rings are really cool. The facing on the rings is a mixture of titanium oxide and aluminum oxide that is sprayed on the face of the ring. Now this may sound simple, on the surface, but these two substances are a lot like chalk dust. Imagine trying to spray paint with chalk dust and getting it to stick. After spraying the face of the ring, a plasma torch is used to heat the ring surface to between 30,000 to 40,000 degrees Fahrenheit. (This is actually warmer than an August afternoon in Phoenix.) At these temperatures the ceramic titanium oxide and aluminum oxide powder will adhere to the surface of the ring. This process gives the cylinder wall mating surface of the ring a ceramic layer of 0.004 inch to 0.008 inch thick.

Pressure-Balanced Rings

The pressure balanced ring was designed to allow combustion pressure to sneak behind the ring. This pressure

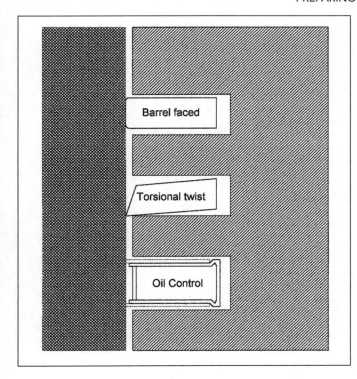

Barrel faced

Torsional twist

Oil Control

There are four common types of compression rings: torsional twist, reverse twist, barrel-faced and low-tension. Often two types are used in combination, one type in the top groove the other in the second groove. This is why it is important to place the rings the right side up in the groove, as recommended by the ring manufacturer.

Nevertheless, TRW claims plasma ceramic rings are five times stronger than a stock cast iron ring. Engines that will be used on the drag strip, especially those that are not naturally aspirated, namely turbocharged or supercharged engines, would benefit from the extra expense of plasma ceramic rings.

Ductile Iron Versus Plain Iron Types

As has already been suggested, there are several ways to classify types of rings. The broadest classifications are by the task the ring is assigned. The basic task of all rings is to seal something. The categories of "some-things" are compression and oil.

Compression Rings
Torsional Twist Rings

For years, I pictured the compression ring as a symmetrical sealing ring. I imagined that it sat more or less statically in the ring groove of the piston, much like the shaft-sealing rings of a transmission shaft. I saw them sitting in place and merely sliding up and down the cylinder, passively preventing blow-by and controlling oil. The reality, of course, is much different from my limited imagination.

A torsional twist ring features a chamfer on its top inner surface. It sits in the ring groove with a twist that forces a line of contact between the upper edge of the ring and the back of the ring groove. When there is a minimum load on the rings, such as during idle and under light coast conditions, this attitude of the rings helps to prevent combustion gases from passing around the back side of the ring during combustion and prevents oil from passing around the back side of the ring during the intake stroke. This clarifies for me why the ring installation instructions always indicated that the chamfered inner edge of the ring should go toward the top. I read this in the installation instructions; I obeyed the installation instructions; but, like so many of my generation eager to "Question Authority," I always wanted to install

behind the ring forces the face of the ring against the cylinder wall. This type of ring typically has a very narrow mating surface with the cylinder wall, which allows for reduced friction, as well as better performance and fuel economy. But the narrow mating surface plus the extra machining for gas passages all add up to extra expense. For maximum performance, pressure-balanced moly or chrome rings are ideal.

Selecting the Best Type of Rings for You

As so many things are, what is ideal for one application is not necessarily ideal for another. The three primary considerations are the general quality of the work being done during the engine rebuild, purpose for rebuilding the engine, and cost. Chrome rings should not even be considered if the engine cylinders are not going to be trued to a perfect circle. The hard, tough surface of chrome rings will prevent them from seating-in properly for thousands of miles, if ever. Nevertheless, chrome rings are the rings of choice in an engine "blueprinted" for power, where price isn't an issue.

Moly rings will seat in nicely in a few hundred miles. However, a common mistake made by the amateur and, sad to say, professional rebuilder is failing to make sure that the cylinders are sufficiently round. As the engine runs during its first life, the cylinder walls are slowly machined into an oval by the rings. Piston offset is the primary agent responsible for this. If these walls are not re-trued during an overhaul, its second life as your rebuilt engine will be a short and unsuccessful one. While the precision of this truing need not be as exact as is necessary with chrome rings, no engine rebuild should include putting rings into old, imperfect cylinders.

In an engine where power and durability are important, like a racing engine, where the dynamic and explosive forces of compression and combustion are very much active, the plasma ceramic ring may be the most appropriate. The expense of these rings makes them impractical and unnecessary in an engine destined to deliver the user to the local grocery store. These rings typically cost $150 to $250 per set—a cost that poorly compares with $30 for a set of cast iron rings and $50 to $75 for a set of moly or chrome rings.

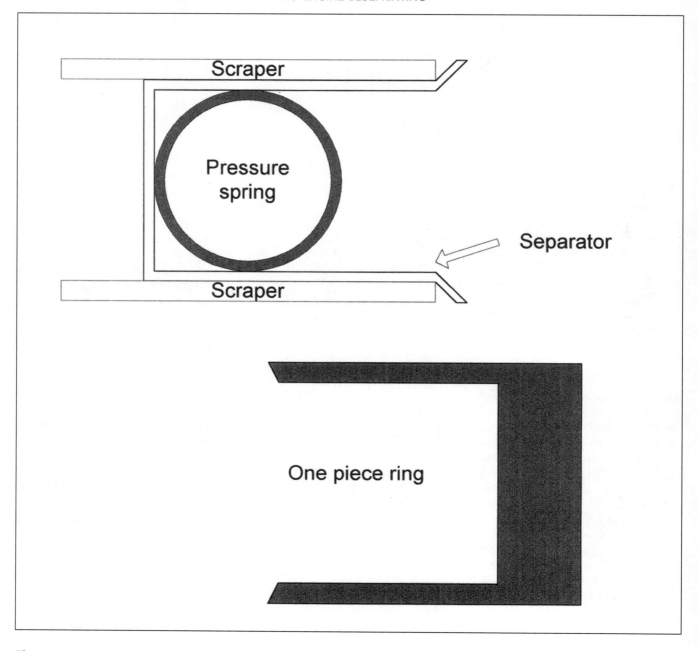

The most common oil control rings are three-piece assemblies. A thin top and bottom spring steel or chrome ring are separated by a springy stainless steel separator or expander. There are some very low-performance applications that use a one-piece oil control ring, but this is virtually unheard of in modern engines.

the rings upside down just because it defied the ill-explained instructions.

During acceleration, as the combustion pressures reach their greatest levels, the torsional twist ring is forced against the bottom of the ring groove. This seals the combustion and prevents excessive blow-by. During deceleration the torsional twist ring is forced against the top of the ring

groove and assists the oil rings. Installing these rings upside down, listening to the temptations of my youth, would have led to low compression and high oil consumption.

Reverse Twist Rings

Reverse twist rings might have served to mollify the rebellious tendencies of my youth. These rings feature a

chamfer on the lower inner edge of the ring. In reality, this would have satisfied no inner craving for rebellion. With these rings the instructions clearly indicate that the chamfer should be installed down; therefore, I would have wanted to install them with the chamfer up, a frustrating dilemma.

In addition to the chamfer being on the lower, inner edge of the piston ring, it is tapered at an extra sharp angle that forces a contact line between the lower edge of the ring and the cylinder wall. The reverse twist maximizes oil control, but is less

You can check ring end-gap with a feeler gauge after squaring the ring in the bore, which can easily be done by setting the ring in the bore, then using an upside-down piston to push it down approximately one inch into the cylinder. Follow the ring manufacturer's specifications for the proper gap.

effective in controlling blow-by gases. A common setup would feature a torsional twist ring as the top ring and a reverse twist ring as the second ring.

Barrel-Faced Rings

The barrel faced ring does not twist but rather remains relatively square in the ring groove. The very slight 0.001 inch curve on the face of the ring allows for any slight misalignment there is in the ring grooves. This curve also allows for a high pressure, though very narrow, contact surface between the ring face and the cylinder wall. Barrel-faced rings often feature a moly or chrome face and may be chamfered to gain some of the benefits of either the torsional twist or reverse twist ring.

Low-Tension Rings

Low-tension rings, as their name implies, minimize the tension at the contact point of the ring with the cylinder wall. This design allows for slower cylinder wear—a feature with obvious advantages. A little less obvious is the fact that the low tension rings reduce energy loss. Their main disadvantage, however, like that of the chrome ring, is that the cylinder must

be in near-perfect machined condition. Maximum allowable cylinder taper is less than 0.006 inch and maximum cylinder out-of-round is just 0.005 inch. This is considerably closer tolerances than can be hoped for from your typical dingleberry hone job.

Ring Combinations

In reality, a package of rings will generally include two different compression ring types. A top ring of the moly barrel variety and a reverse twist second ring would make up a typical set.

Oil Control Rings

The most common oil control rings are three piece assemblies: A thin top and bottom spring steel or chrome ring is separated by a springy stainless steel separator or expander. There are some very low performance applications that use a one piece oil control ring, but this is virtually unheard of in modern performance engines.

The function of the oil control ring is to form a tight seal with the walls of the cylinder. This tight seal makes the oil control ring the greatest offender of all the rings when it comes to power loss as a result of friction between the rings and the cylinder

walls. Engine vacuum rises during deceleration. Actually, during the intake stroke of an engine that is decelerating, the receding piston is creating a low pressure in the cylinder. During acceleration or cruise, air is supplied to the cylinder through the open throttle valve, or butterfly. During deceleration the amount of air that can pass through the throttle bore is extremely limited by the closed throttle valve. This causes the low pressure of the combustion chamber to draw air from any available place. The part of the engine that has both direct connection to the combustion chamber and a high pressure is the crankcase. This is okay, in general, because air drawn from the crankcase would not contain fuel and therefore would not contribute power to the engine, so the engine would still decelerate. However, the air from the crankcase is laden with a mist of engine oil. This mist would enter the combustion chamber and be burned, creating a smoke screen behind the car that would make Agent 007 proud.

Ring Gap Clearance

This is a science unto itself. My best suggestion is that you assign decisions concerning ring gap clearance to an individual that you can blame later if things go wrong. As the engine runs, the rings are heated both by friction and by combustion, and the heated rings expand. If there was no gap between the ends of the rings, they would soon expand to be larger than the cylinder bore, which creates a potentially disastrous condition called negative clearance. To facilitate thermal expansion of the rings, a gap is left between the ends of the rings. When measuring the end gap of a piston ring, always use the engine manufacturer's specifications. If high dollar, "pricey" rings are chosen for use, follow the recommendations of the piston ring manufacturer. If such specifications are missing or unavailable, a typical spec for this gap is 0.0035 inch per inch of cylinder diameter. Using this spec an engine with a 4.00-inch bore should have a gap of 0.014 inch (fourteen thousandths of an inch).

Typically, ring side-clearance should be 0.002 to 0.004 inch.

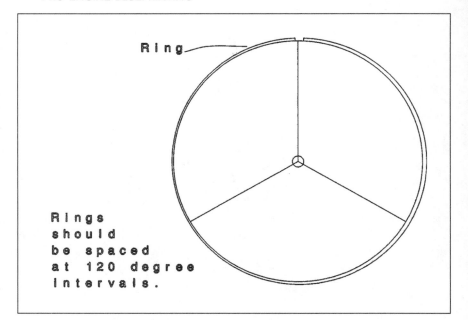

Staggering the gaps of the various rings will provide for a better seal during the early stages of running the engine. As the engine runs, the rings will often rotate. It is essential that the rings on these pistons be staggered at 120-degree intervals to ensure proper operation during the break-in period.

Ring end gap is only highly critical in engines on applications where every last ounce of power is critical. For most engine overhauls, it is far better to have excessive end gap than it is to risk not having enough. In a performance engine, every thousandth of an inch of excessive ring gap translates instantly into a power loss. Therefore specs from the ring manufacturer become critical. Only they know for sure the true expansion rate of the ring.

"File fit" high performance rings are sold with a negative end gap, which allows the installer to set the ring gap as he or she feels is best for the engine he or she is building. A special cutter is required to cut these rings. If you do not already possess such a cutter, purchase it when you purchase the rings. Place each of the piston rings in the cylinder in which it is to be used. With a feeler gauge, measure the gap between the ends of the ring. Performance rings often have no end gap or overlap when installed. K-D Tools makes a special cutting/filing tool that can be used to cut/file the rings to the

Ductile iron top rings	Gap (inches)
Supercharged/ injected nitro engine	0.022–0.024
Supercharged/ injected alcohol engines	0.018–0.020
Supercharged/ injected gasoline engine	0.022–0.024
Oval track (rectangular ring) carbureted engine	0.018–0.020
Oval track (head land rings) carbureted engine	0.024–0.026
Oval track (pressure back rings) carbureted engine	0.020–0.022
Modified drag racing carbureted engine	0.018–0.020
Stock drag racing carbureted engine	0.016–0.018
Street carbureted engine	0.016–0.018
Plain iron second rings	
Supercharged/ injected nitro engine	0.014–0.016
Supercharged/ injected alcohol engines	0.012–0.014
Supercharged/ injected gasoline engine	0.012–0.014
Oval track carbureted engine	0.012–0.014
Modified drag racing carbureted engine	0.012–0.014
Stock, Super Stock drag racing carbureted engine	0.010–0.012
Street carbureted engine	0.010–0.012

perfect gap and yet ensure that the end surfaces of the rings are perfectly parallel to each other. After the rings are cut, any rough edges should be removed by carefully hand filing. Consult the ring manufacturer for the optimum ring gap for your application and usage.

Recommended ring end gap, by engine usage (represented engine has a 4.00-inch bore):

Ring Side Clearance

Ring side clearance should also be checked. A ring that fits too snugly in its groove may become jammed in the groove and fail to seal properly when the engine gets warm. Place a feeler gauge in each of the ring grooves with the ring that is destined for that groove installed. Progressively increase the thickness of the feeler gauge until a snug fit is obtained. Ring side clearance should be 0.002 to 0.004 inch.

Installing Rings on the Pistons

Follow the supplied instructions closely. If you have not done so already, be sure that the ring grooves are clean and clear of debris and carbon using a special tool called a ring groove cleaner. However, for those who have good health insurance and a first aid kit, a broken ring can be used to scrape the carbon from the grooves. Extreme caution should be used when using a ring to clean the grooves, however, because the broken ring is sharp and can leave nasty cuts, so wear gloves.

With the ring grooves clean, install the new rings on the pistons. Stagger the rings before installing the pistons into the cylinder. Staggering will provide for a better seal during the early stages of running the engine. As the engine runs, the rings will often rotate. Some applications employ a pin in the ring groove to the piston is prevented from rotating. It is essential that the rings on these pistons be staggered at 120-degree intervals. The rings are usually identified top, middle, and oil control by the papers covering them in the box. There will also be a mark on the two compression rings indicating which way is up. This mark may be a dot, a bar, or even a

If the cylinders have been bored during this blueprinting project, then they were probably adequately honed as part of that process. Inspect the cylinders closely for evidence of a 45-degree cross-hatch pattern on their surface. If the cross-hatch is inadequate, then hone the cylinders prior to the installation of the pistons. If this project did not include boring the cylinders, then be sure to hone them before installing the pistons.

corporate logo. In a few instances, the rings may be unmarked, in which case there will be instructions in the box.

Two techniques are available for the actual installation of the rings. First, you can start one end of the ring in the correct groove, then rotate the ring around the center of the piston and it will practically fall into place. While this works most of the time, you should plan on breaking an occasional ring using this technique. Piston ring installation pliers can be purchased for only a few dollars at most auto parts stores, and using these pliers virtually eliminates the possibility of broken rings.

Honing Cylinders in Preparation for New Rings

Honing the cylinders is an operation that can be done by anyone. An engine cylinder hone can be purchased for as little as $20. Honing is done to remove the glaze from the cylinder walls. There is a common, but mistaken, belief that honing is used to true the cylinders. Perhaps that belief comes from the common practice of honing the last few thousandths of an inch when the engine cylinders are

bored. The fact is, as the engine is run over the years, the old piston rings polish the walls of the cylinders. Honing breaks up this glaze and provides the rings with a slightly abrasive surface to help seat them.

Correct honing technique will produce a cross-hatch pattern on the cylinder walls. Place the hone in a low-speed electric or air-powered drill motor. It should be noted that in order to produce a 45-degree cross-hatch with an air-powered drill motor rotating at 20,000 rpm, your arm must be capable of reciprocating about 330 times per second. So, unless you're the Six Million Dollar Man, make sure you use a slow drill speed. Hold the drill and hone vertically and move it in and out in slow even movements. Continue the process until there are conspicuous 45-degree cross-hatch marks in each of the cylinders.

Having the engine block professionally honed at a machine shop is advisable. A well-equipped machine shop will have an automated honing machine that will ensure proper cylinder wall alignment and cross-hatching.

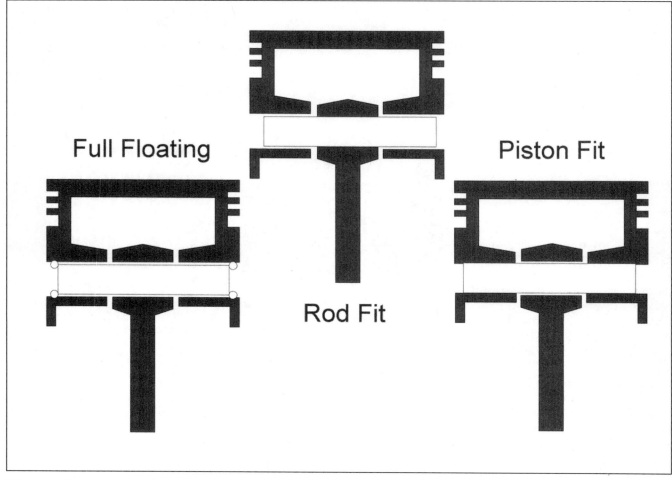

Full Floating

Rod Fit

Piston Fit

There are three ways that the piston pins mount in the pistons. In the full-floating method, the pin isn't pressed into either the rod or the piston, but instead floats freely in both and is held in place by snap rings. In the semi-floating piston pin configuration, the pin is pressed into either the rod or the piston, but not both.

Wrist Pins

The wrist pins are in no way exempt from the stresses and strains of the reciprocating piston and rod assembly. The job of the wrist pin is to transfer the energy from the piston to the connecting rod. The wrist pin is constructed from high-grade steel. For the most part, you need to worry very little about the choice of wrist pins.

When either stock or performance pistons are purchased, they come with wrist pins adequate to handle the loads projected by the manufacturer of that piston. This load is typically not more than 8,000 pounds per square inch. The design of a stock piston permits the assembly to withstand this kind of punishment for only a short time. By comparison, many racing pistons are

designed to allow the piston-to-pin contact surface to handle as much as 20,000 pounds per square inch.

It's interesting to do a few calculations concerning combustion loads. Let us consider the piston to be the moving floor of a cylinder. Now imagine a sealed container with no moving floor. The pressure potential in the cylinder is about 1,743 psi after combustion. This assumes that the pressure in the cylinder was a normal atmospheric pressure of 14.7 psi prior to initial pre-combustion pressurization. If the diameter of the cylinder were 4 inches, and if that load were to be transferred to the 2-square

Charging pressure	Compression ratio	Compression pressure (psi)	Combustion pressure (psi)	Piston surface area	To wrist pin load moment
14.7	8	243.49	905.06	50.24	22,735.20
14.7	9	285.46	1,061.05	50.24	26,653.53
14.7	10	329.09	1,223.23	50.24	30,727.51
14.7	11	374.28	1,391.19	50.24	34,946.80
14.7	12	420.93	1,564.60	50.24	39,302.67
14.7	13	468.97	1,743.14	50.24	43,787.57

inch contact area of the wrist pin, that wrist pin would be subjected to a force of nearly 44,000 psi. Note the chart below.

But, in an engine, we are dealing with a chamber that has a moving floor. The pressures in the cylinder will not build as high as described above, because as the pressure begins to build, the floor below (i.e., the piston) will begin to drop away. As a result, the pressure we are concerned with is the mean effective pressure of the cylinder, or MEP. MEP is calculated by multiplying the horsepower of the engine by 792,000, then dividing by the displacement of the engine times the rpm of the engine. If you are curious about the 792,000 figure, it is not a number pulled out of the air; it is a constant based on the 12:1 conversion factor of inches to feet, times the two crankshaft rotations it takes to complete a full set of cylinder cycles on a four cycle engine, times 33,000—the number of pounds-feet per minute equal to one horsepower.

The formula for calculating MEP looks like this:

$$MEP = \frac{hp \times 792,000}{displacement \times rpm}$$

As you can see from the numbers in the table, the forces exerted on the wrist pin are relatively light and do not increase dramatically as either the horsepower or the RPM increase. Note that when the horsepower increases from a relatively low horsepower to a horsepower eight times greater, the pressure on the piston

wrist pin only increases five fold. At 2,000 horsepower and 10,000 rpm the pressure on the wrist pin is barely out of the acceptable range for a stock unit. This means that the highly resilient pins—those that come with performance pistons—can be shortened. This reduces the contact area and therefore increases the psi on the pin, however it can significantly decrease the reciprocating mass. How important is this? Is it worth the fact that it will probably void the warranty on the piston/pin assembly? Frankly, unless you are trying to squeeze the last hundredth of a second out of your drag car on the quarter-mile, it is hardly worth the effort or the loss of the warranty. However, in the 2,000 horsepower example above, a wrist pin designed to handle 20,000 psi can easily be trimmed of half its contact area with the piston and still maintain a margin of safety.

Wrist pins are relatively trouble free in spite of the repeated forces exerted on them. Many years ago, when I owned a repair shop in Bellevue, Washington, I arranged a car purchase between one of my employees, Pat, and one of my customers. The car's engine had a tapping noise, which is why the customer wanted to get rid of it. Soon, the tapping noise became a rapping noise. Pat turned up his radio. A short time after that, the rapping noise became a knocking noise. Pat turned up his radio still louder. After several months, Pat had the choice of either buying bigger and louder speakers for his radio, or rebuilding his engine. Against my

advice, Pat chose to rebuild the engine. When the engine was disassembled, we found that a retaining clip for the wrist had broken at some point in the distant past. The wrist pin had slipped off to one side and had slowly routed a deep groove in the cylinder wall. The block was useless and had to be replaced. Pat told me he was sorry he had not heeded my advice to buy the new speakers.

Full Floating

Full floating piston pins are held into the piston with lock rings. These lock rings may simply be wire rings, which are the cheapest and least dependable type of lock ring. Higher quality lock rings are used in most pistons. Since the pins are not press-fitted into either the piston nor into the connecting rod, the survival of the engine depends on these little clips. Failure of the clips dooms the engine to at least the aforementioned "Pat" syndrome.

Installing the pistons onto the rods in the full floating wrist pin design is easy, since the wrist pin slides through both the piston and rods with little pressure applied by even the frailest of thumbs.

Semi-Floating
Rod-Fitted

An alternate method of holding the wrist pin in place is to use a press-fit into the small end of the connecting rod. The position of the wrist pin therefore remains stationary relative to the connecting rod and allows the piston to float. The pin is pressed into the small end of the rod with an interference fit

Horsepower	Displacement	RPM	Mean effective pressure	Rod pressure
250	350	6,000	94.29	2,357.14
300	350	6,000	113.14	2,828.57
350	350	6,000	132.00	3,300.00
400	350	6,000	150.86	3,771.43
450	350	6,000	169.71	4,242.86
500	350	6,000	188.57	4,714.29
550	350	6,000	207.43	5,185.71
600	350	6,000	226.29	5,657.14
650	350	6,000	245.14	6,128.57
700	350	6,000	264.00	6,600.00
2,000	455	10,000	348.13	8,703.30

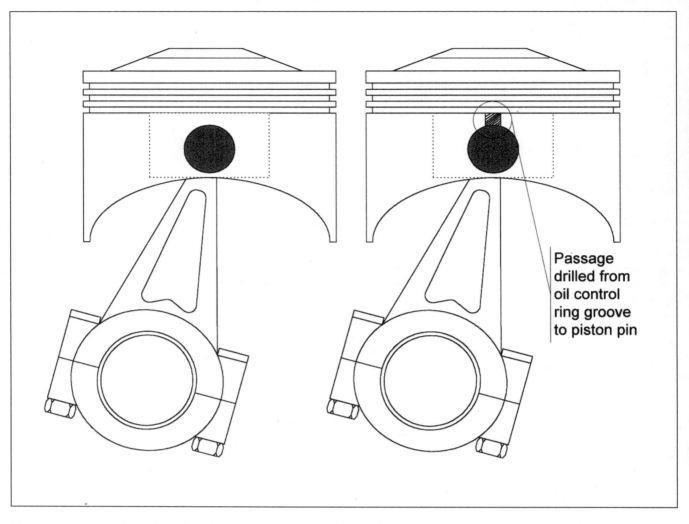

Passage
drilled from
oil control
ring groove
to piston pin

Two primary methods of oiling the piston pin are used. Neither method is perfect, but both work surprisingly well. The first is called splash oiling; this method depends on the crankshaft journals and counterweights to splash oil toward the piston pin. The second method uses the oil scraper rings to force oil through a channel to the piston pin.

of 0.001 inch. An interference fit means that the object to be inserted into the connecting rod, in this case the wrist pin, is larger than the hole in the small end of the connecting rod. This interference fit means that the wrist must be pressed into position with over two tons of force, which makes it an excellent job for a machine shop.

This semi-floating wrist pin is more of a problem to remove and insert than the full floating wrist pin. The safest route is to have the machine shop install semi-floating wrist pins. A press tool can be made to facilitate the pressing of wrist pins in semi-floating applications. Using a piece of hardwood, carve a cra-

dle the diameter of the piston. This will support the piston evenly as the wrist pin is pressed into place. These cradles can also be purchased commercially. Of course, allowing the machinist to install the wrist pins on semi-floating applications may be the best answer, because if they break a piston, they have to buy you a new one.

Piston-Fitted

There are a few applications that feature a wrist pin to be pressed into the piston, but left to float freely in the connecting rod's small end. Otherwise, the premise is the same as Rod-Fitted Semi-Floating wrist pins.

Another Thing to Remember . . .

Pistons are directional. In 1978, I had the fortune, or perhaps misfortune, of rebuilding a Volvo B-28 engine while in Fort Worth, Texas. This engine is particularly interesting, because when fully disassembled, you are left with a workbench full of small pieces. This engine had a bent connecting rod that resulted from a rain storm. While you are probably aware that Seattle has a reputation for a lot of rain, Fort Worth, however, raises images of the semi-arid or even of the desert. But several times a year, the citizens of Fort Worth are blessed with torrential rains, and the owner of this particular Volvo lived in a low area. After one of the more torrential rains of the 1970s, he awoke to find the car almost completely submerged. Later that day, he discovered that the engine would not start. The battery was dead, or at least the engine would not turn over. He towed the car to the top of a hill, and, after turning on the ignition switch and placing the transmission in second gear, he allowed the car to roll down the hill gathering speed. When the car reached about 35 miles an hour, he popped the clutch. Still the engine did not start. He repeated this process several times. Finally he gave up and had the car brought in for a "no-start" problem. Unknown to the car owner, the number one cylinder was full of water and near top dead center on the compression stroke. When he popped the clutch, the connecting rod bent.

After rebuilding the engine I started it. There was a loud knocking noise. When I disassembled the engine again, I found that I had installed the number one connecting rod on the number one piston backward: Every time the piston went to bottom dead center, the piston would touch or tap the top edge of the connecting rod producing the noise. Pistons and connecting rods have directions.

Wrist Pin Oiling

The wrist pin is probably one of the most difficult of the high stress components of the engine to lubricate. Moving up and down the cylinder 500 to 5,000 times per minute or more, it does not stand still to be well lubricated.

On stock pistons, the wrist pin bore is smooth with a hole drilled in the bottom of the bore toward the crankshaft. As the crankshaft rotates, oil is splashed toward the piston. The oil is then expected to migrate along the wrist pin to the form the lubricating film between the pin and the piston. This actually works pretty well on a low-performance, stock engine. However, if you plan on racing your newly rebuilt engine, this type of oiling might not be good enough.

A second method forces oil picked up by the oil scraper ring and forces it into a grove cut in the piston pin bore. This groove helps move the oil along the length of the wrist pin. On some perfect world this oiling method for the wrist pin might be totally superior, but

back here on planet Earth, combustion is not always perfect, so partially burned hydrocarbon particles can be picked up by the oil scraper ring and carried along with the wrist pin lubricating oil into the groove. After a few thousand miles, the groove becomes restricted and will eventually cut off wrist pin lubrication entirely.

No matter what type of wrist pin lubrication system your old or new pistons were designed with, almost all of them can be improved. Drill a hole perpendicular to the flat part of the wrist pin boss on the underside of the piston. The hole should be 0.125 inch and drilled so that it will intersect the wrist pin bore at its centerline.

Wrist Pin and Bore Location

When the connecting rod is pushing the piston up the cylinder, it does so at an angle. This causes the piston to tilt, pushing the skirt of the piston against the cylinder wall. When the spark plug fires the air/fuel charge, the piston is pushed down the cylinder, forcing the connecting rod and crankshaft to move. The angle of the connecting rod now causes the piston to rock in the opposite direction. The closer the wrist pin is to the top of the piston, the less rocking there will be. The closer the wrist pin is to the top of the piston, the longer the connecting rod has to be. The longer the connecting rod is, the less sharp the angle at which it applies lateral force to the piston, which further reduces piston tilting. Tilting increases the friction between the piston and the cylinder walls, which reduces potential engine power and increases the stress and strain on the piston and cylinder.

If the wrist pin were located on the same plane as the highest part of the piston that actually contacts the cylinder wall, rocking of the piston on the compression stroke would be minimized. However, pressure on the top edge of the piston where it contacts the cylinder wall will be maximized. Again a compromise is required.

Wrist Pin Bore

There is an old *Star Trek* episode called "Amok Time" where Spock gets all lusty for his betrothed. Kirk decides to protect Spock in a battle for the affections of the lovely Vulcan in question by fighting him to the death. Since the air on Vulcan is hot and thin Kirk soon has difficulty supplying his lungs with enough oxygen to properly convert the food he had eaten into the energy necessary to kill Spock, Dr. McCoy complains about the unfair advantage Spock has in being more accustomed to the Vulcan atmospheric pressure and climate. The Vulcan leader, T'Pau, responds, "The air is the air, what is to be done?" Thus, I say: The location of the wrist pin bore, is the location of the wrist pin bore, what is to be done? Very little is to be done. If you have plenty of money—money enough to afford failure—the wrist pins can be set closer to the head of the piston. This may improve the thrust angle. Bore the wrist pin bore off-center toward the head of the piston for an oversized wrist pin. This will locate the wrist pin closer to the head of the piston by 50 percent of the increase in wrist pin diameter. All of this work may give you a better thrust angle, but it will come at a price that will be paid in the loss of compression ratio. More work will now need to be done to boost the compression ratio back up to ideal.

It's a lot of work and expense for only a little improvement. Your best bet is to simply purchase a set of replacement, performance pistons designed by someone who has already taken the best possible thrust angle into consideration when designing the pistons. The designer will also make sure that the design does not suffer a loss of compression ratio.

Oversized Wrist Pins

Since the piston's wrist pin bore is much softer than the wrist pin itself, you will find that the wrist pin almost never wears significantly. The piston bore does wear, however, and can be machined and fitted with a larger, or oversized wrist pin. Let us

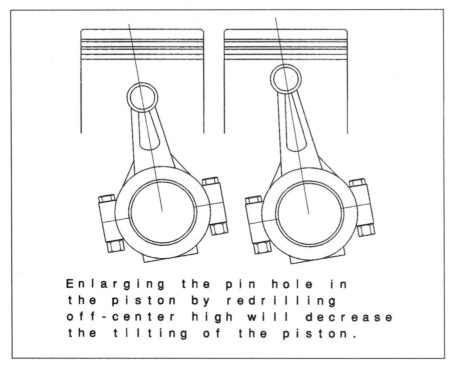

Enlarging the pin hole in the piston by redrilling off-center high will decrease the tilting of the piston.

When the connecting rod is pushing the piston up the cylinder, it does so at an angle. This causes the piston to tilt, pushing the skirt of the piston against the cylinder wall. When the spark plug ignites the air/fuel charge, the piston is pushed down the cylinder, forcing the connecting rod and crankshaft to move. The angle of the connecting rod now causes the piston to rock in the opposite direction. Tilting increases the friction between the piston and the cylinder walls, which reduces potential engine power and increases the stress and strain on the piston and cylinder. Pistons with a higher wrist pin bore will rock less than similar pistons with a lower bore, due to reduced rod angularity.

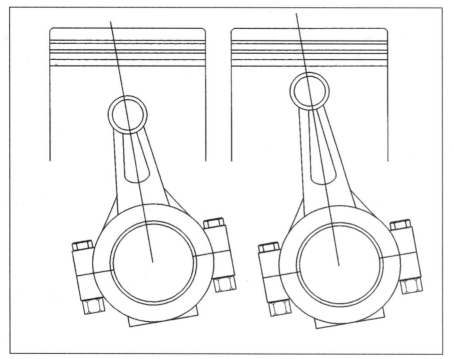

look at the logic of this operation. A new set of pistons will cost in the neighborhood of $320. The machining of the pistons will cost in the neighborhood of $80 to $120. Now, granted there is a big difference in these two neighborhoods. However, if the pistons have been in the engine long enough to damage or wear the wrist pin bores, then they have had a good, long life and deserve to be retired. Besides, would you rather assault the Al-Can Highway or Death Valley with fresh pistons, or with pistons that have had the wrist pin bore machined and an oversized pin fitted? It seems that when they will charge you $5 per mile for towing on the Al-Can, reboring may be false economy. On the other hand, if the engine you are working on is from a 1929 De Soto 3.2-liter side valve six-cylinder, then almost any amount of machining could be justified.

Balancing the Pistons

Rebuilding an engine is a really simple and fun procedure. On more than one occasion, I have managed to rebuild an engine in a day. The real challenge of rebuilding an engine is to take the time to create as perfect a machine as possible. The dynamic forces of the reciprocating components of the engine becomes amplified as the engine speed increases. An imbalance puts the crankshaft and other components under fluctuating stresses that create a vibration. The vibration is energy being lost to rocking the engine, instead of being used to push the vehicle down the road. Bottom line: Balancing the engine's reciprocating components will decrease the vibration and thus increase the power to the ground.

The closer the wrist pin is to the top of the piston, the less rocking will occur. The closer the wrist pin is to the top of the piston the longer the connecting rod has to be. And the longer the connecting rod is, the less sharp the angle at which it applies lateral force to the piston, and therefore less tilting of the piston will occur.

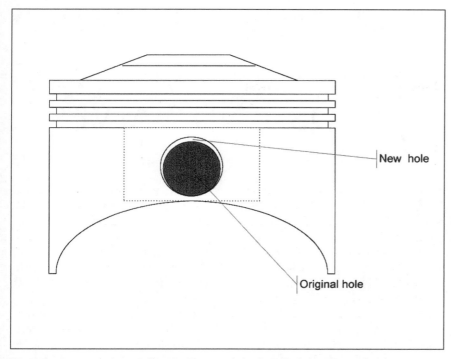

Bore the wrist pin bore off-center toward the head of the piston for an oversized wrist pin. This will locate the wrist pin closer to the head of the piston by 50 percent of the increase of the wrist pin's diameter. This will give you a better thrust angle but will reduce the compression ratio slightly.

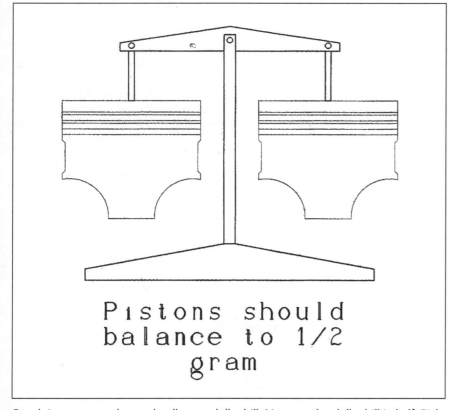

Reach into your pocket and pull out a dollar bill. Now cut the dollar bill in half. Pick up one half. Note the weight. It is about one half gram. This is how closely the pistons should be balanced, in fact, this is how closely each of the reciprocating masses—the piston, wrist pin, connecting rod, and bearing—should be balanced.

Reach into your pocket and pull out a dollar bill. Now cut the dollar bill in half. Pick up one half. Note the weight. It is about one half gram. This is how closely the pistons should be balanced. In fact, this is how closely each of the reciprocating assemblies—the piston, wrist pin, connecting rod, and bearing, together—should be balanced.

Begin the balancing procedure by installing the wrist pin and its retaining clips, if applicable, into the pistons. Place each of the piston assemblies, in turn, on the scale. You will now remove metal from the heaviest ones to make them all weigh the same as the lightest ones.

Mount the first piston in a lathe. Use the lathe cutting tool to remove metal from the wrist pin bosses inside the piston. Repeat the process for each of the remaining pistons. Remember that you will still have the connecting rods to balance, therefore a little extra exactness will mean less balancing work when the pistons are mated to the connecting rods.

The valves seal the cylinder during the combustion process and provide a passage for the fresh intake air to enter the cylinder and for the exhaust gases to exit the cylinder.

CHAPTER TEN

PREPARING CYLINDER HEADS AND VALVES

Okay, you've read every magazine article ever written about cylinder heads for your engine, and you've spoken with everyone in your state who's ever rebuilt an engine to find out what their favorite cylinder heads are and why. Armed with that knowledge, you went out and purchased the absolute best heads money can buy for your new engine. But you know what? They're still not good enough for it.

No cylinder head is ever perfect out of the box, and especially not off a rack at the local salvage yard. Even new fancy-shmancy Computer Numerically Controlled (CNC) machined heads can benefit from fine tuning to better suit your particular combination of components and intended application. After all, stock heads and aftermarket heads, alike, are built to fit a wide variety of engines that can use an almost endless combi-

nation of parts. What on Earth would make you think that they would be optimized for your engine in their as-purchased condition?

Blueprinting cylinder heads is, without a doubt, probably the most time-consuming task of your engine build. You'll spend so much time checking dimensions, checking for warpage, checking for casting flaws, and correcting any imperfections that you'll likely wish you had never embarked on an engine build-up project.

But there's really no easy way out of matching your heads to your engine, other than to just dig in and do it. You'll know, better than anyone else, when you've done all that can be done to maximize their port flow rates, perfectly prepare their block and manifold mating surfaces, equalize the combustion chambers, optimize the valvetrain geometry, and more.

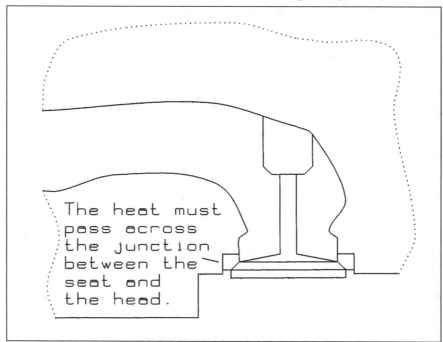

The nominal angle for the valve faces on most engines is 45 degrees.

Now, if this sounds like a lot of hard work, that's because it is. But it's also essential work. And when it comes to your heads, can you really trust them to someone else?

Valves and Seats
Resurfacing the Valve Faces

This process requires a valve grinding machine. At several thousand dollars each, it is probably unreasonable to purchase a valve grinding machine for just one or two engine rebuilds. Plus, this procedure is one that requires skill and practice. Your machinist should always do both this procedure and the grinding of the valve seats.

Resurfacing of the valve face usually begins with chamfering the valve tip. This increases the accuracy of centering when the valve is chucked up in the arbor of the valve grinder. The next step is to insert the valve in the arbor of the grinder and adjust the arbor head to the correct angle. The face angle for most applications is 45 degrees.

The valve is held in the arbor and rotated at a relatively low speed. A grinding stone is also rotated at a relatively low speed. As a cooling oil is poured on the valve face, the machinist moves the arbor assembly across the stone. An adjustment wheel determines how much contact there is between the valve and the grinding stone. Metal is slowly removed from the face of the valve until it looks smooth and even all the way around. Any valve that shows a narrow band perpendicular to the valve margin during the first couple of passes is burned and should be replaced. If, when the face is smooth and even, an inspection of the margin reveals a sharp edge instead of a margin, replace the valve. Some machinists will cut a new

margin on the valve, but for a few dollars more it is better to have a valve that can be trusted for 150,000 miles rather than a valve that has been 150,000 miles already.

Based on that preceding statement, you may be tempted to replace all the valves, which isn't a bad idea, except that valves can be bent and damaged during transportation and storage. For these reasons, even new valves should be refaced.

After each of the valves is refaced, the stem tips should be ground smooth. If the tip is badly worn, grinding it smooth would remove the hardened surface of the tip, which is only a few thousandths of an inch thick. If in doubt about having passed through the hardening when grinding the tip, replace the valve.

If the valve neck accidentally comes in contact with the grinding stone, replace the valve. There is little doubt that this has weakened the valve in a critical area. Reusing it may cause

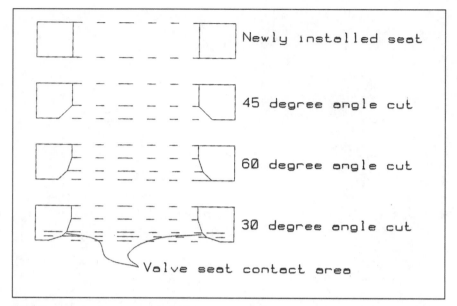

Grinding the valve seats requires a stone grinder. Generally, three stones are needed. The first stone, usually ground to a 45 or 46 degree angle, determines the seat angle. A second stone, usually ground to a 60 degree angle, narrows the seat from the bottom up. The third stone, usually ground to a 30 degree angle narrows the seat from the top down. Correct seat width is important to proper transfer of heat from the valve to the valve seat and eventually to the cylinder head.

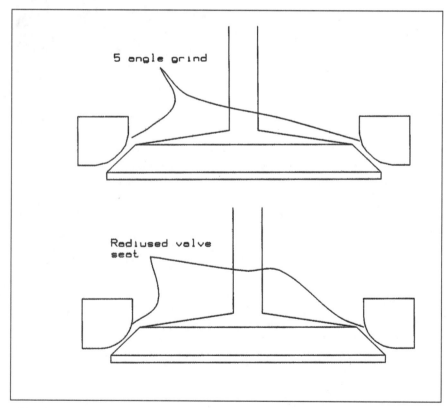

Although it requires very specialized equipment, some shops can perform a filleted valve grind. Instead of a simple three-angle grind, which can impede airflow, the valve seats are rounded. Some machinists will perform a five-angle grind, which very nearly emulates the filleted grind.

the valve to break off the stem and become embedded in the piston in the future. While this can generate some unusual sculptures, it is hardly worth the trouble.

NOTE: Some applications use valves filled with metallic sodium. If enough metal is removed to expose the sodium to atmospheric moisture, *it will burst into flames!* Grinding these valves is extremely dangerous! It is recommended that either these valves be replaced instead of ground, or that the job be left to a professional, experienced machinist. If you are going to grind the valves yourself, and if you are possibly working with sodium filled valves, first contact your local fire department for tips on how to extinguish the fire.

Resurfacing the Valve Seats

Because the valve seat must be concentric to the guide, all valve guide repairs must be made before the valve seats are ground.

Valve Lapping

Back in the days of ducktails, white socks, and cuffs in your blue jeans, you might have found Billy Joe down at the local drive-in grinding his valves with a suction cup on a stick to impress the girls and lesser males. This method is known as lapping the valves, and it involves dabbing a spot of valve grinding or valve lapping compound, which is really just an abrasive grit suspended in a lubricant, on the valve seat, then, as the valve is placed on the seat and rapidly rotated back and forth, the valve imperfections and the seat imperfections are theoretically matched. The reality of the situation, however, is that matching two imperfect surfaces still results in imperfection; two wrongs don't make a right. Another shortcoming of lapping is that is doesn't do anything to correct incorrect valve seat width, either. So, while lapping valves is valid when minor repairs are made, it is wholly inadequate during an engine overhaul.

In short, lapping valves was never an effective method of ensuring an effective seal between the valve and the

Valve lapping in most engine building went out with the British invasion. However, a blueprinted engine is often asked to perform immediately, without the break-in period allowed for most engine overhauls. Lapping the valve during head assembly, and after a three-angle grind, ensures a good seal from the moment the engine is started.

seat. In the days of the Model T, this was often done when the carbon was scraped from the cylinder head. Even in those days, though, it was an unsatisfactory method of grinding the valves.

Valve Seat Grinding

A second method of grinding the valve seats requires a stone grinder and, generally, an assortment of three stones. The first stone, usually ground to a 45 degree angle, determines the seat angle. A second stone, usually ground to a 60 degree angle, narrows the seat from the bottom up. The third stone, usually ground to a 30 degree angle, narrows the seat from the top down. Correct seat width is important to proper heat transfer from the valve to the valve seat to the cylinder head. When no specifications are available, the intake valve seat width should be no more than 0.0625 (1/16th) inch while the exhaust seat must be no less than 0.078 (5/64th) inch.

The process, itself, starts with a machined pilot that is inserted into the valve guide from the combustion chamber side. This pilot ensures the centerline of the grinding stone is perpendicular to the ground surface of the

valve seat. Next, the grinding stone holder—with stone installed—is slipped over the pilot. A large electric motor, resembling a drill and called a driver, is then lowered onto the stone holder. The driver is powered briefly, and removed from the stone holder while the stone is still spinning. Extreme care must be taken not to allow the weight of the driver to rest on the stone holder at any time, because the weight of the driver can seriously affect the quality of the grind, as well as cause excess wear on the grinding stones. The holder must also be removed before it stops spinning, otherwise it will produce an uneven grind as the stone slows and begins to bounce on the seat surface.

After the initial 45 degree grind is made, the valve to be used in that seat should then be tried in the seat. Place a spot of Prussian Blue on the valve face, slip the valve into the guide, and, using a lapping stick, rotate the valve against the seat at least twice, then remove the valve and inspect its face. The Prussian Blue should form a stripe roughly centered in the face of the valve. If the stripe is high on the valve, the machinist will use a 30-degree

stone on the seat to lower the contact point between the valve and the seat. If the stripe is too low, he will use a 60-degree stone on the seat to raise the contact point. If the contact stripe is too wide, he will use both the 30-degree and a 60-degree stones to narrow the seat contact stripe. If the contact stripe is too narrow, he will use the 45 degree stone to widen it.

Many manufacturers and machinists will recommend grinding the seats to 44 degrees, while the valve faces are usually ground to 45 degrees. This provides an interference angle of one degree. This slight, deliberate mismatching of angles is intended to help the valves seat. After as little as 100 miles, the interference angle disappears.

"Performance" Valve Grinds

The so-called "performance" valve grind is one of my favorite marketing terms. What happens if you don't buy the performance grind? Does the engine run slower and safer? *All* valve grinds should be performance grinds; anything less is shoddy work. If the machinist insists there is a difference, don't argue. Instead, just pay the few dollars extra for the performance grind. Some shops, when doing a "standard grind," will hit the seat with only a 45-degree stone, which fails to ensure proper seat contact width or depth. Nevertheless, there is a distinction between the valve grind commonly sold as a "performance" valve grind and the "precision" valve grind, which will be discussed later in this book.

Valve Guides
Inspect and Measure the Valve Guides

Measuring the valve guides now will help you coordinate the work your machinist will be doing for you more effectively. Use a split ball gauge to measure the diameter at the top, just below the edge, at the bottom, and in the middle. If the valve guides are worn, the machinist will have several options for you.

First, if the guides are removable, he can replace them. In fact, for those with a spirit more daring than the

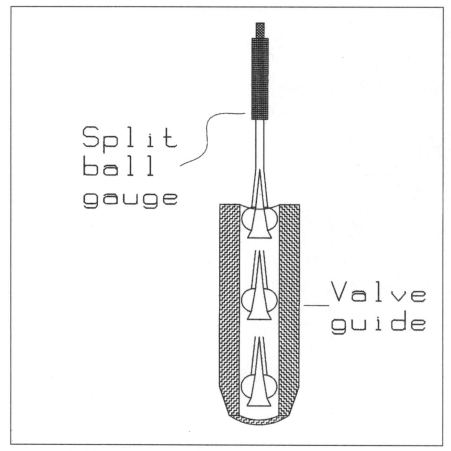

Use a split ball gauge to measure the valve guide diameter at the top, just below the edge, at the bottom, and in the middle. If the valve guides are worn, the machinist will have several options for you.

valve guide drift be larger in diameter than the outside diameter of the guide, but this isn't usually a problem for drifts designed for this purpose. Still, if the diameter of the drift is too small it will damage the new guide.

Types of Replacement Guides

Most replaceable factory guides are made of cast iron, which are brittle and require a large clearance between the guide and the valve stem—0.001 inch to 0.003 inch for the intake guides and 0.002 to 0.004 inch for the exhaust—for proper lubrication. Excessive wear is considered anything greater than 0.005 inch.

The trick replacement for cast iron guides is the phosphor bronze

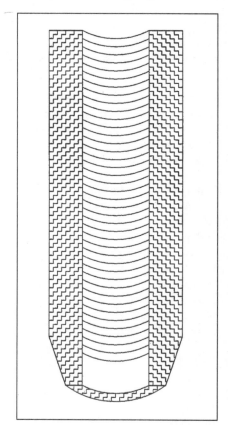

Knurling is one of those few repair procedures that may actually improve the operation of the item being repaired. Knurling creates parallel grooves perpendicular to the centerline of the guide. These grooves help to control oil slipping down the guide to be burned in the combustion chamber, plus the grooves hold oil in the guide to improve valve stem lubrication.

average mortal, you can procure a set of valve guide drifts and a press, and replace them yourself. If the guides are a cast part of the head, they can be either knurled or sleeved.

Valve Guide Knurling

Although it is strongly recommended that this be done by an experienced individual, do-it-yourself kits can be purchased at a reasonable price.

Knurling the valve guides involves using a special tool to pull metal from the worn guide toward the center, which reduces the inside diameter of the valve guide to less than the diameter of the valve stem. A precision ream is then used to size the guide for the valve. While this may sound like a flaky repair, in reality, this is an excellent way to repair the guides. Knurling leaves behind parallel grooves perpendicular to the centerline of the guide.

These grooves help to control oil that might otherwise be able to slip down the guide until they enter the combustion chamber and are burned, resulting in a bluish smoke out your tailpipes.

If the guides are not replaceable, knurling makes good sense in a repair. However, many cylinder heads are designed with removable and replaceable guides, in which case replacement is the better option.

Valve Guide Replacement

Replacing the valve guides is a much easier operation than it might at first seem. The only special tools required are an appropriate valve guide drift and a press or hammer. Slip the drift into the old guide and gently tap it out with a hammer. When the old guides are removed, install the new guide by tapping them into place. It is critically important that the step of the

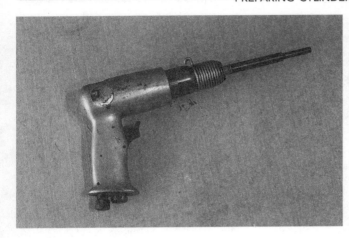

Some heads are designed with replaceable valve guides. This air-chisel is fitted with a special drift used to remove and install guides.

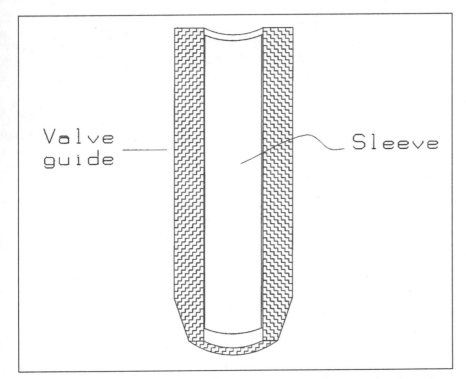

Valve guide — Sleeve

Most replaceable factory guides are made of cast iron. These are brittle and require a large clearance between the guide and the valve stem for proper lubrication. This clearance is 0.001 to 0.003 inch for the intake guides and 0.002 to 0.004 inch for the exhaust. The trick replacement for cast iron guides is the phosphor bronze guide. These guides are porous in nature, which results in a self-lubricating quality. The porous lubricating qualities of the guide allow the guide-to-stem clearance to be very small. In a performance application, the reduced clearance can provide better stability for the valve.

guide. These guides are porous in nature, which gives them a self-lubricating quality that allows the guide-to-stem clearance to be very tight. Although some machinists claim as little clearance as 0.0005 inch is acceptable with this type of guide, it is advisable to follow factory specs. In a performance application, the reduced

clearance can provide better stability for the valve. Once the guide is pressed into the head, it must be sized with a ream. The ream is designed with a reverse flute that will carry the bronze shavings up and out of the guide as it is reamed. A special bronze cutting lubricating oil should be used during this procedure, although many

machinists advise that 90 weight oil works, too. Equally important as properly lubricating the ream is allowing it time to thoroughly cool between guides. In a professional machine shop, the machinist will use two reams, which allows one to cool while the other is being used.

Even bronze guides are limited by their individual metallurgy and design, however. Water-cooled Volkswagen products of the mid-1970s had a severe problem with worn guides. In one case, I personally experienced guides worn so badly that I could rock the valve back and forth in the guide over an eighth of an inch with the valve spring still installed! The problem was resolved by installing an updated guide.

Another unusual problem is when a guide comes loose in the head. Usually limited to more exotic engines such as Mercedes Benz, this condition usually destroys the head. As the guide moves up and down in the head, it softens the metal around it. If the head is irreplaceable, a highly skilled machinist may be able to remove the damaged metal and either manufacture an over-sized guide, or replacement-weld the damaged area.

Valve Seals

There are as many kinds of valve seals on the markets as there are poisonous insects in west Texas.

A very popular valve seal on domestic engines is the umbrella seal, which just slips onto the valve stem forming an umbrella over the top of the valve guide. The umbrella shape serves to shield the droplets of oil from the top of the valve guide, which reduces the amount of oil that slips between the guide and the valve. Don't think that new valve seals will cure oil burning resulting from worn valve guides, though. Valve guide repairs are the only way to fix worn valve guides.

Some valve seals snap onto the valve guide and are held in place through friction. Many import manufacturers prefer the snap-on type. Unlike the umbrella seal, which tends

101

There are many types of valve seals available for engine builders to choose from. The most common is the umbrella seal. This seal simply slips over the top of the intake valve guide and reduces the amount of oil mist that can accumulate on the valve stem and around the guide. As a result, less oil can pass down the valve guide to be burned in the combustion chamber.

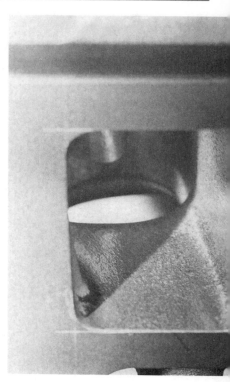

Porting the intake and exhaust ports of the cylinder head may be the single most significant step that can be taken to improve the air flow in and out of the cylinders. People that port heads every day, all day long tell me that the greatest improvement occurs within the first few minutes of work on each port. Beyond that, a great deal of effort can be spent making only fractional improvements in performance.

to move up and down on the valve stem, friction holds the snap-on seal firmly on the guide. Because they're stationary, snap-on seals have the additional benefit of wiping the valve clean of oil every time it travels down into the guide.

A few words of caution are warranted here, though: When selecting the type of valve stem seal to be used, make sure it is compatible with the valve springs selected. While this is almost never a problem with stock valve springs, many performance springs sport a larger diameter coil stock, or an inner spring, either of which reduces the space available within the spring for the seal. Often these springs can conflict with the valve stem seals. Select your valve springs first, then test the compatibility of the valve stem seal chosen. The man at the local performance parts house should be happy to help you find a seal that fits; if not, his competitor will be.

Porting for Street Performance

In porting a head for street or track performance use, there are four areas that need attention: The valve pocket; the short-side radius; the valve bowl; and the intake ports.

Valve Pocket

Use a carbide grinder to smooth the area immediately behind the intake valve, where the seat transitions into the intake port and around the bottom of the valve guide. When the

head is manufactured this area is left with a rough surface, which disturbs the air flow into the cylinder. Smooth this area while trying to remove as little metal as possible.

The Short-Side Radius

The short-side radius is the bump in the floor of the intake port of the head. It is the area where the air has to turn the corner on its journey to the cylinder. Your goal is to straighten out the path the air must follow through the port as much as possible. By lowering the hump in the port floor, you make the corner that has to be turned a more shallow angle, which improves air flow. At high velocities, the air responds to this hump in much the same way as air would respond to a wall in the port. If the short side radius rises 0.5 inch into the straight-line shape of the port, and if the height of the port is 2.0 inches, then the port height is effectively reduced by one fourth. In reality the effect is not really that great, because it is unlikely the air flow rate through that section of the port would ever be at the port's maximum capability. Calculate your air flow requirement based on displacement and maximum desired rpm and ensure that when the head is flow tested its flow rate exceeds the requirements of each cylinder.

$$\frac{(C.I. \ Displacement/1728) \times RPM}{2} = CFM$$

$$CFM \times 1.5 = Required\text{-}head\text{-}airflow$$

The Valve Bowl

The valve bowl is the area behind the valve, where the valve guide protrudes into the port. The valve guide is positioned in a boss, or mount, that protrudes into the air stream on most cylinder heads. Additionally, the valve stem itself inhibits air flow. While the ideal head would be a forcefield that could be switched off during the intake and exhaust strokes, the second-best head would be one without a guide or valve stem. Unfortunately, neither of these is possible; therefore, we must minimize the valve guide boss and leave the valve stem. Taper and streamline the valve guide boss to minimize its disruptive effects on airflow.

Intake Ports

The intake ports of stock heads can almost always benefit from being matched to the port openings in your intake gasket. To do this, paint the gasket surface of the head with a light mist of your favorite color of paint. There are professional dyes designed specifically for this purpose, but the paint can work equally well. Then, set the gasket you intend to use during final assembly on the head and install intake manifold bolts to hold the gasket in the proper position. Then, tape the gasket securely in place and carefully trace the gasket's port openings with a scribe, then remove the gasket. The metal between the scribed marks and the port opening is the material you are going to remove to match the head's port to the gasket.

If you need to enlarge a port, and there are many heads which will *not* require port enlargement, emphasize enlargement of the top of the port (i.e., its roof), by making the top of the port higher and wider. Transition this enlargement smoothly into the valve bowl.

You can use this same process to match the ports of the intake manifold to the intake gasket, and the cylinder head's exhaust ports and the exhaust manifold ports to the exhaust manifold gaskets, too. However, if the bottom of the exhaust port does not match the exhaust manifold gasket, do not try to make them match. The misalignment normally found here is intentional—it forms a reversion dam that keeps the exhaust gases from reentering the combustion chamber as the exhaust pressure pulses vary.

Cardboard Templates

When modifying port sizes for high-performance or racing engines, after the desired shape for the first intake and exhaust port has been determined, cut, and flow benched, you will want to match the characteristics of the other ports to this port. From stiff cardboard or plastic, make a set of templates for the short side radius, the manifold port width at the top, the manifold port width at the bottom, and the height of the manifold port. Additional templates should be made of the valve pocket and the guide boss. The real art—and what will really prove your skill—will be how closely you can match the other ports to this port.

Checking With Silicone Goop

By now, you finished grinding and trying to match the ports with the cardboard templates. If you are anal retentive you have probably spent several weeks perfecting the ports, if you are a ritalin candidate, you have probably changed your hobby from performance engines to quilt making. If you are an anal retentive ritalin candidate (as I am) you are doubtless talking to yourself. This is one skill where dedication, patience, and the desire for perfection are absolutely necessary.

Now it's time to check your work. Chicago Latex and Permaflex Mould Company both make a latex compound that is used to check the relative size and shape of the ports. Spray all the surfaces of the intake and exhaust ports with WD-40 or a similar lubricant then slightly slant the head so that one set of ports is slightly above the other side. Tilting the head reduces the possibility of bubbles being trapped in the latex when it is poured into the port. Next, place the valves in their appropriate guides, but suspend the valves so that they are high enough above the seat to permit pouring the latex into the valve pocket and port. After placing duct tape over the intake and exhaust ports, mix the latex according to instructions provided with the latex, and fill the intake port with the compound through the open valve, pouring slowly to reduce the possibility of an air bubble being trapped. Once the intake port is filled, fill the exhaust port. Once both ports are filled, fill the combustion chamber portion of the head and push both valves through the latex firmly into their seated positions and finish filling the combustion chamber. Then repeat this process for the other cylinders.

Once the latex has set, carefully remove the molds along with the valves. When they are all out, you will

There are three areas that require attention when porting a head: the short side radius, valve bowl, and the intake ports (shown).

have a three-dimensional representation of the ports. Now all you have to do is retouch the ports to match your first "model" port.

Polishing

When an engine builder speaks of "polishing" cylinder head ports, he's not talking about the same kind of "polishing" that is commonly done to aluminum wheels or valve covers that results in a mirror-like surface. In fact, it has been shown in many industries that when a surface is too polished it can impede flow rather than help it, because a slightly rough surface creates turbulence that helps keep the fuel suspended in the flowing air.

Instead, when polishing cylinder head ports you should look for casting ridges and places where the walls of the port become abruptly rougher than the rest of the port and smooth out these areas because ridges and sudden increases in the roughness of the surface can decrease air-flow through the port.

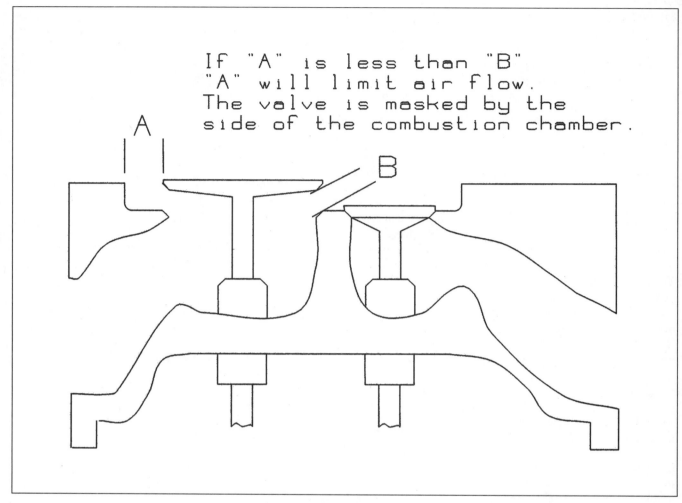

If "A" is less than "B"
"A" will limit air flow.
The valve is masked by the
side of the combustion chamber.

A

B

Valve masking occurs when the distance between the edge the open valve is less than the distance between the valve face and the valve seat in the cylinder head. Now all the work that has been done to ensure good air and exhaust flow through the valves has been wasted because the maximum air flow will now be determined by the distance from the valve to the wall of the combustion chamber.

Using the grinder motor that was used to port the head along with a grinding bit that is finer than the one used to port the head, remove the casting ridges and ensure that the steps and grooves that might have occurred while porting the head are smooth to allow good flow.

Valve Masking

Due to the basic design of the overhead valve engine, there will always be some valve masking, which is the effect of a pressure that builds up between the valve margin and the walls of the in-head portion of the combustion chamber because the valve is too close to the in-head portion of the chamber.

The amount of air flowing through the valves in and out of the cylinder head should only be limited by the valve lift. If the valve lift is greater than the clearance between the margin of the valve and the side of the combustion chamber, then this clearance and not valve lift will limit airflow through that side of the valve.

Most diesel engines offer a virtually perfect situation when it comes to valve masking: their cylinder heads are perfectly flat on the bottom, because there is no combustion chamber in the cylinder head. The result is that there is no part of the cylinder head combustion chamber that interferes with the flow of air and exhaust gases around the valves. However, masking can even occur in these engines, because the valve hangs into the cylinder when it is open and the cylinder wall itself can mask airflow around the valve. This type of masking problem can only be resolved by redesigning the heads and relocating the valves. At least on most gasoline engines the problem can be reduced or maybe eliminated.

Unfortunately, resolving the problem of valve masking is a very expensive and/or time consuming project. This is the first major operation of working a cylinder head that really separates the mature articulate primates from their offspring, or as the politically non-correct might say, the men from the boys. First, you need to acquire the proper power tool. I have seen the results of guys trying to port, polish, or otherwise re-work their cylinder heads using the quarter inch drill motor that their wife bought

It takes a brave person indeed to take a grinder to an expensive cylinder head. If you have hesitated to port your heads for this very reason, but have discovered a valve masking problem, it is now time to get out the grinder. Resolving a valve masking problem is simply a matter of grinding metal away from the walls of the combustion chamber of the cylinder head until the distance from the head to the valve is equal to or greater than the distance from the fully open valve to the valve seat.

them for Father's Day to remove the last excuse for not hanging the portrait of Uncle Ed in the living room. It is not pretty (their port work, not Uncle Ed's picture). This operation requires a high-speed electric- or air-powered tool with a power rating in full horsepower not fractions. The grinding tool itself should be a high-speed carbide-grinding bit.

In the ideal world, you would now obtain an X-ray of the areas of the head immediately around the combustion chambers. I have often wondered how my doctor would react if I asked him for a radiologist referral to X-ray a pair of Chevy heads. Second-best would be accurate drawings of the inside of the head locations of water jackets, oil galleries, and other hazards. You might as well try to find an efficiently run government program before bothering to look for head plans, though. Without knowing the locations of the jackets, galleries, etc., you are at a disadvantage and risk grinding through the metal into one of these areas. Trust me, you will be at a disadvantage; you will be at risk.

To begin, paint the bottom of the head with a light mist of your favorite color of paint, or purchase one of the professional dyes designed specifically for this purpose. Next, carefully measure and scribe the outer limits of the metal you are going to remove to resolve the masking problem.

As you begin to remove metal, remember it is important that the sizes of each of the combustion chambers be of equal volume. This is more important than eliminating the masking. Talk to as many people who have performed this operation as possible to find out about the risks of penetrating a water jacket or oil gallery before diving into this procedure.

Finally, grind the area that masks the valve. Try to get a clearance between the valve at all points of the opening process that is equal to the valve lift. Calculating the valve lift will require knowing the cam lift and rocker ratio. Therefore the cylinder head work again should not be done until the cam and valve lift decisions have been made.

I hope you won't have 4 pounds of aluminum shavings on the floor before you read this paragraph, because every ounce of metal you remove from the combustion chamber reduces your compression ratio in that cylinder. Are you frustrated yet? Again, each time you resolve one problem you affect another aspect of the performance modification. As you remove the metal, CC the cylinder head combustion chambers several times. Each time you CC the head, calculate the new compression ratio. Keep in mind also that the compression ratios must be equal in all cylinders to ensure smooth performance.

Milling

Generally, the cylinder head is only milled to make the mating with the cylinder block flat. Milling the head increases the compression ratio, therefore the head can be milled deliberately to increase the compression ratio. Use the following formulas:

$$\text{compression ratio} = \text{displacement ratio} + 1$$

$$\text{displacement} = \frac{\text{cylinder volume}}{\text{chamber volume}}$$

$$\text{amount to mill} = \frac{\text{new displacement ratio} - \text{old displacement ratio}}{\text{new displacement ratio} \times \text{old dispacement ratio} \times \text{stroke}}$$

Let us say that the current compression ratio of our engine with a 3.00-inch stroke is 9.5:1 and we wish to raise the compression ratio to 11.0:1.

$$\text{amount to mill} = \frac{10-8.5}{10 \times 8.5} \times \text{stroke}$$

$$\text{amount to mill} = \frac{1.5}{85} \times 3$$

$$\text{amount to mill} = 0.052941$$

To raise the compression ratio to the desired level, you would need to mill a little over 50 thousandths of an inch off the head.

Of the machining operations done during an engine rebuild, resurfacing the cylinder head may be the most common. Constant changes of temperature, coupled with inadequate maintenance such as routine retorquing of heads, or incorrect retorquing of heads, can result in warping.

Resurfacing the head involves milling off several thousandths of an inch of metal, which, in effect, removes the high spots, making the head flat again.

Several things must be taken into account when the head is resurfaced. If the engine is an overhead cam design, removing several thousandths of an inch will cause the camshaft to be closer to the crankshaft, which can

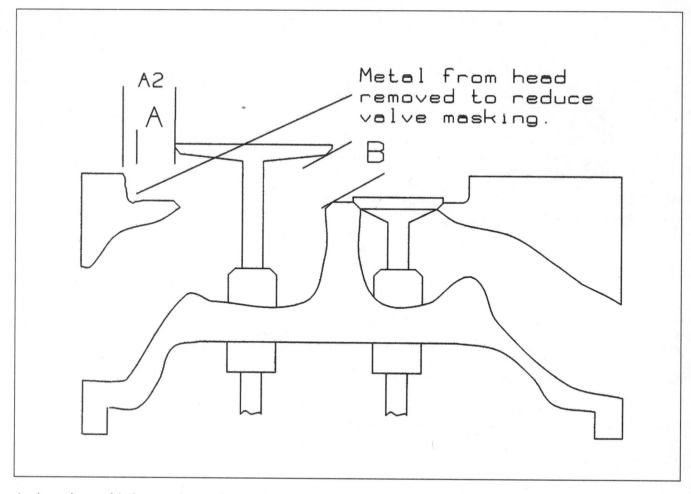

As always, be careful when grinding on the cylinder head, because on most cylinder heads, the potential areas of valve masking are very close to the water jacket.

$$\text{Amount to mill} = \frac{(\text{new compression ratio -1}) - (\text{old compression ratio-1})}{(\text{new compression ratio -1}) \times (\text{old compression ratio-1})} \times \text{stroke}$$

affect the tension or amount slack in the timing chain or belt. Additionally, a warped head mating surface may indicate that the top of the head is warped, too. And if the top of the head is warped, the cam bearing alignment may be mis-aligned, which can cause them to bind, damaging or even breaking the camshaft.

Of course, there are a few solutions to these problems. First, in case it crossed your mind, taking a link out of the chain to shorten it is not the

answer. Within one or two revolutions of the crankshaft, the camshaft would be far enough out of phase to bend every valve in the head. As you read this you are probably thinking, "Oh, come on, no one would actually do that." Well, I once witnessed a professional technician in a hurry to finish a job do that very thing. He knew better, he just wasn't thinking. Think.

For many applications automatic chain and belt adjusters will take up a great deal of this slack. When too much

metal has to been removed, though, the slack can be corrected by shimming the cam bearing towers, assuming that the application you are working on has removable cam towers. Shims can be obtained through your machinist or in some cases through the appropriate dealer. For the applications where the cam towers are not removable, your machinist might be able to line-bore the cam journals of the towers and install oversize cam bearings. There are head designs that do not lend themselves to

Milling the cylinder head is a common procedure in most regular engine overhauls. In these projects, the cylinder head is machined in order to ensure that it is flat. In blueprinting projects, the cylinder head is often milled to increase the compression ratio.

this solution either, though, leaving you with one final solution: to replace the head.

Straightening the head may be another way to eliminate many of the problems addressed above. The technology for this procedure is not available everywhere, however, and the success of the procedure seems to vary a great deal depending on the skill and knowledge of the technician. The process involves heating the head to a high temperature with it bolted to a machined flat plate. While this may seem simple enough to do in your oven at home, overheating the head can soften the metal or make it brittle, but not applying enough heat will be ineffective. Given the cost and questionable success of head straightening, you may be ahead of the game if you simply replace the head.

Misaligned cam bearings can be corrected by the same procedure described in the preceding discussion about tightening the chain or belt. Your machinist should be able to line-bore the cam journals of the towers off-center and install oversize cam bearings.

If the engine is a V-design, both cylinder heads should be machined the same amount. Since resurfacing the cylinder head alters the size of the combustion chamber and therefore affects the compression ratio, machining the heads differently will create unequal power and performance characteristics from each side of the engine. Additionally, removing metal from the heads can affect the interference angle between the intake manifold and its mating surface on the cylinder head. No more than 0.024 inch should be removed from these heads.

If the head is badly warped, your machinist will need to machine the mating surface of the cylinder head with the intake manifold. Not doing so creates several potential problems in terms of port alignment, valvetrain geometry, and compression ratio.

If the heads are milled but the intake manifold is not, the ports of the intake manifold may not line up properly, which can cause air leaks (often, and incorrectly, referred to as vacuum leaks), oil leaks, and coolant leaks, none of which is fun to deal with.

You might also run into problems since the rocker arm shaft or studs will be closer to the camshaft, which changes your valvetrain geometry, possibly causing the rockers to bottom out the valve springs. It should also be noted, here, that this problem is not unique to V-4, V-6, and V-8 engines—it can happen on any overhead valve design pushrod engine. There are several solutions to this problem, ranging from shorter-than-stock pushrods to shorter installed-height valve springs (though these do not actually correct the deficient geometry, but rather compensate for it).

And, of course, removing metal from the mating surface of the head and/or block increases the compression ratio, which increases the potential for detonation or pinging. Imagine yourself, after having occupied that precious corner of the garage that is normally reserved for your wife's car, after having spent $1,000 or more pursuing automotive excellence in the fine art of engine building, only to find out that your boss can now hear your new engine from five blocks away as you accelerate up the hill on your way to work, late as usual. With oil companies shifting their emphasis away from anti-knock additives and toward emission control additives, make every effort to retain the same compression ratio unless you are willing or desire to take some extraordinary steps to prevent spark knock. Raising the compression ratio may require the use of the most expensive gasoline available or the habitual use of a spark prevention additive.

The simplest solution to this problem is to use a specially designed shim or a thicker head gasket. Gasket maker Fel-Pro offers 0.020-inch shims for several engines. Fel-Pro and other gasket companies also make head gaskets in various thicknesses. Check into these options with your local parts house and consult with your machinist. This solution solves all the potential problems.

Another option: If shims or thicker gaskets are not an option for the application you are working on, the intake manifold can be machined to ensure a proper fit. This machining still leaves the problem of the shorter pushrods being required. Refer to the chart for how much to machine.

Measuring Port Volume

Many readers probably see the internal-combustion gasoline engine as a precision piece of equipment. Other readers probably laughed at the last statement. The truth is, production engines are often highly impre-

Head angle	Amount machined from head, times:	Amount to remove from manifold
5 degrees	1.1	=
10 degrees	1.2	=
15 degrees	1.4	=
20 degrees	1.7	=
25 degrees	2.0	=
30 degrees	3.0	=
35 degrees	4.0	=
40 degrees	8.0	=

cise chunks of iron. The manufacturers vary in their level of precision. Even heads that are supposedly identical can have port volumes that vary tremendously.

On some ideal world, the performance engine builder would be able to go into a cylinder head warehouse and measure the port volumes until he found the heads with the largest and most closely matched volumes. Measuring the port is easily accomplished with Z-argon n-band scanning-tunneling sonar resonometer. Okay, the burette will work good too. With the valves installed and held in place with the valve springs, fill the port from the burette and record the amount (in cc's) of fluid necessary, then repeat this for each of the remaining intake and exhaust ports. This procedure is particularly important if the head is being selected for a racing engine in a class that does not allow head modifications. Several heads should be measured and the ones with the largest ports chosen.

Again on the ideal world, there would be reference specifications for port volumes. But, back on this world, the most important thing is that the head with the largest, most evenly sized ports be chosen. For most uses, the ports can be modified and equalized with a grinder later.

Checking Port Shape

Actually, the shape of the port can have more to do with its ability to flow air than the volume of the port. Visual inspection and estimation of the shape of the ports is impractical for even the most experienced eye. The solution is latex rubber. This stuff

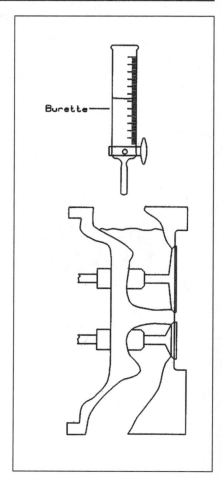

Measuring the port volume is another task for the burette. The volume of each intake port should be equal to the others, and each of the exhaust ports should be equal. This will help to ensure even operation of the cylinders.

is hard to come by through traditional auto supply sources. The phone book should have a few (very few) listings of local companies that can probably supply you with the needed materials, or at least lead you in the right direction. If

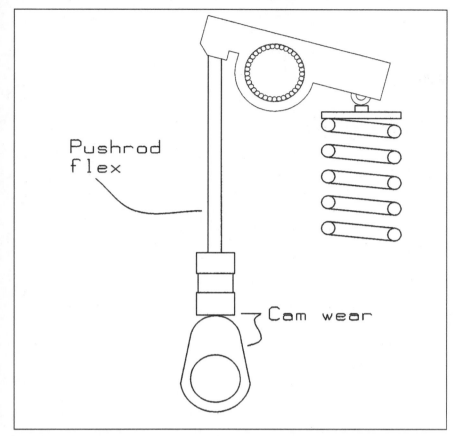

Pushrod flex

Cam wear

Valve springs must be stiff enough to make sure the valve will snap closed before the piston has a chance to smack it, but soft enough to prevent damage to the valvetrain. Extremely stiff springs can cause wear, warping, and distortion of the camshaft and lifters.

all else fails, kits can be ordered from Chicago Latex Products. However or wherever you get it, mix the latex according to the instructions. Next, spray a penetrating oil into the ports to prevent the rubber from sticking. A spray lecithin mixture, such as the commercial product "Pam," also works well. Then pour the mixture into each of the ports and allow it to set for several hours. Once cured, remove the valves and pull the rubber out through the valve opening. To ensure even air flow, the molds of all the same-type ports (intakes to intakes, exhausts to exhausts) should be as similar in shape as possible. Later in this book we will discuss how to use these initial molds and subsequent molds to port the head.

Spring Pressure

Ignoring the tendency of pistons to disintegrate when their maximum rated velocity is exceeded, the single most limiting factor to engine rpm is valve float, which occurs when the cam's toe attempts to begin to lift the lifter or follower before the spring has had time to close the valve from the last opening. The greater the spring tension, the faster the valve will be closed. But, excessive spring tension can cause cam lobes and lifters to self-destruct as a result of excessive friction. The spring tension, therefore, must be a compromise between the speed that will keep the valve closed when needed, and the amount of punishment the rest of the valvetrain can take.

There is a tool specially designed to measure spring tension. One of the more common manufacturers of this tool is Rimac. The valve spring is placed in the tool and a lever is moved to apply tension to the spring. The tension should be carefully measured at the installed valve height and again at the spring height when the valve is fully open. The valve open height of the spring can be calculated by subtracting the net valve lift from the length of the valve from its seat to the bottom of the valve retainer. Compare these measurements to the specification provided by the engine or camshaft manufacturer. If either measurement is below spec, there are two alternatives: to shim the springs, or to get new springs.

The cheapest way to correct a below-spec spring is with hardened valve spring shims. Commonly available in thicknesses of 0.015, 0.030 and 0.060 inch, these shims can be added in combinations to get the tension specs up to where they belong.

A better way to correct the problem is to replace the springs. Your cam manufacturer should be able to recommend a matching set of springs. Replacement shims can be used to balance the tension of the springs. Note that aluminum and alloy heads require the use of at least one shim under each spring of each valve to prevent the spring from digging into the head.

This is also a good time to check the valve springs for binding. Compress the valve spring to the valve's fully open height. Check this measurement carefully. Now compress the spring another 0.060 inch. If the spring is now in a bind (i.e., two or more coils are touching each other), either the spring must be replaced with one that has the correct tension and does not bind, or the net valve lift will have to be altered. For engines that are going to see extended service between overhauls, which really only excludes the most ardent and well financed drag and sprint car racers, the figure of 0.060 inch should be adjusted up to 0.100 inch.

Not all of us are blessed with a Rimac or equivalent machine. Fortunately for us, a rather accurate and inexpensive valve spring tension

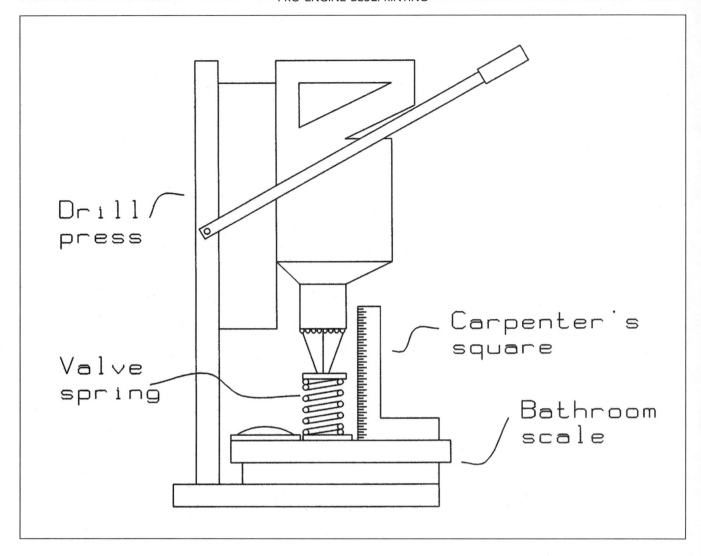

Spring pressure can be balanced by measuring the amount of pressure required to compress the spring to a predetermined height. Special equipment can be purchased to do this, for the amateur an excellent tester can be made from a steel rule, a drill press, and a bathroom scale.

tool can be constructed from a drill press and a set of bathroom scales. Place the scales on the platform of the drill press. Place a piece of plywood on the scales, place the spring on the piece of wood and use the drill press chuck to depress the spring. Control the pressure with the drill press lever.

A few words of caution are in order: When checking valve springs tensions, it is extremely possible for the spring to shoot out of the tensioner with tremendous force, which could result in serious injuries. If possible, take precautions, such as putting a

small barrier between you and the spring, to deflect it should it pop out toward you.

Spring Seat

In a performance engine, it is usually desirable to increase the tension of the valve springs. Often the laws of physics will require the stiffer spring to have a larger diameter, which means that the spring may no longer sit properly on its seat. Since the seats are often cast with an inward taper from the bottom to the top. Cutting metal away from the flat surface of the seat may therefore increase the diameter of

the seat. A vertical mill or special spring seat cutting tool can be used to perform this operation. Shims may then be employed to make the installed valve spring height correct. As always, keep in mind that this operation carries with it the risk of cutting into the water jacket. Unless you are trying to and need to get every last fractional horsepower out of the engine, simply buy the stiffest springs that will fit your stock spring seats. Also keep in mind that stiffer springs increase valvetrain wear and therefore reduce durability.

Retainer-to-Guide Clearance

One cheap but easy and effective trick to increase valve lift is to use higher ratio rocker arms. As the valve lift increases, whether through the use

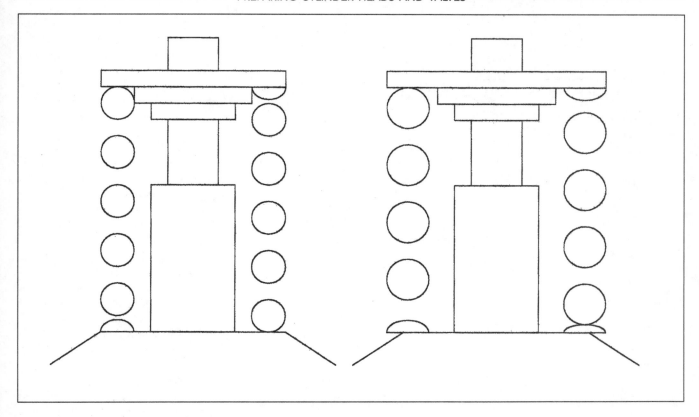

When high performance valve springs are purchased, you may find that they are larger in diameter than the stock springs, which means that the new springs may not seat properly.

of a high-lift camshaft or through the use of high-ratio rockers, the valve spring retainer gets closer and closer to the top of the valve guide. Before the engine is fully assembled, insert the valves into the valve guides and hold them in place with a blob of modeling clay. Snug the cylinder in place with a head gasket installed. Rotate the crankshaft until the pushrod is at its highest point, then install and adjust the rocker. Install the retainer and valve keepers on the valve. Be careful not to drop the valve into the cylinder! The distance between the bottom of the valve keeper and the top of the valve guide should be a minimum of 0.060 inch. Repeat this procedure for each of the valves.

Rocker Arms

There are many types of performance rocker arms available. One of the most common types of rocker arms is the stud-mounted, stamped-steel rocker. These are so common

because they are inexpensive to manufacture and do a very adequate job in grocery-getter usage. For performance usage, however, these are wholly inadequate. The rockers are mounted on studs and held in place by a semi-hemispherical washer called a pivot ball, while a nut secures them. There is nothing to offer lateral stability. Additionally, a high-lift cam, combined with high-tension valve springs, can exert extreme forces on the rocker arms. I have seen the rocker arm pulled off the stud, and I've seen pushrods perforate rocker arms.

When the engine is destined for performance use, stamped-steel rockers should be replaced with cast aluminum rockers. Most of these rockers are a higher ratio than stock or may offer a choice of ratios. They feature a short shaft and roller bearings, and do not need a pivot ball. The short shaft bolts onto the stock stud and provides increased stability, while the roller bearing offers increased durability.

Most of these rockers have a roller that makes contact with the end of the valve, too. This roller eliminates the increased wear at the contact point between the top of the valve and the rocker. The cast aluminum design prevents pushrod perforation, as well.

A second type of stock rocker arm mounts the rocker on a shaft. These rockers can either be stamped steel or cast. Inherently more stable than the pivot-ball rocker arms, the shaft-mounted rocker arms *can* be retained when performance modifications are done. The cast rocker arm runs very little risk of pushrod perforation when high-lift cams and high-tension valve springs are used. The only reason to replace these rocker arms is to decrease wear between the rocker and the shaft. When a high-lift cam or high-tension valve springs are used, replace the stock rocker arms with roller rockers.

While rarely a problem, you should nevertheless take the time to examine rocker arm-to-valve spring retainer clearance throughout the full movement of the arm, as it is possible—especially when changing to a

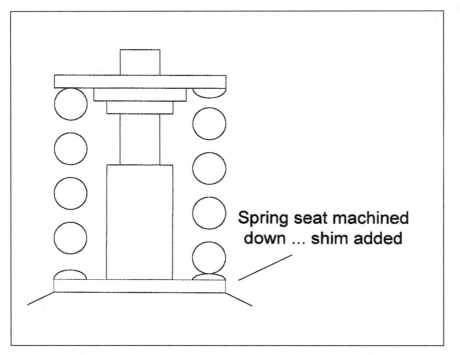

Spring seat machined
down ... shim added

Since the casting of the seats is usually tapered in from the bottom to the top, cutting metal away from the flat surface of the seat may therefore increase the diameter of the seat. A vertical mill or special spring seat cutting tool can be used to perform this operation. Shims may then be employed to correct the installed valve spring height.

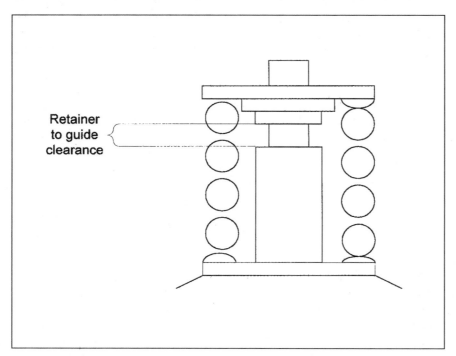

Retainer
to guide
clearance

When high-lift cams and long-ratio rockers are employed, it may be possible for the valve to be pushed down so far that the valve spring retainer will contact the top of the valve guide. This could knock the retainer off the valve, resulting in very serious damage to your very expensive engine.

different type or ratio rocker, or a high-performance or racing cam—for the rocker to contact the spring retainer, which can allow the keepers to become loose, fall out, and then allow the valve to drop down into the cylinder causing very expensive damage.

Guide Plates

Rocker arm guide plates are available for stud and pivot ball rockers to keep them properly aligned. These are not nearly as effective at maintaining a properly aligned valvetrain than shaft-mounted rockers.

The guide plate mounts on the stud and has a groove for the pushrod to travel in. Because the pushrod rubs against the guide plates as the engine runs, stock, soft-metal pushrods will self-destruct in a short time, so hardened pushrods should be used.

Pushrods

Rocker arm geometry is affected when you deck the block, use a camshaft with non-stock base circle, or mill the cylinder heads, because in all three cases you are changing the distance from the base circle of the cam lobe to the rocker arm. You can correct for any changes by installing different length pushrods; Longer-than-stock or shorter-than-stock pushrods can be used as needed to cure the effects of these machining operations. Most pushrod manufacturers offer adjustable pushrods that can be used to measure the needed length, eliminating the old trial and error method that required buying several different size pushrods before finding the right size.

One of the drawbacks to using high-ratio rocker arms is the possibility that the new arm will cause the pushrod to rub against the side of the hole through which it passes through the head. As you begin to adjust the valves, be sure to check for rubbing or binding.

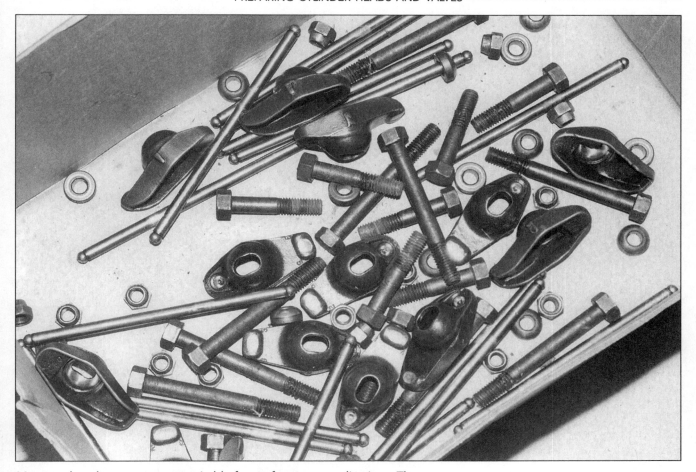

Most stock rocker arms are not suitable for performance applications. They tend to be of a design that offers poor lateral support and are often made of stamped steel that can be perforated by the pushrods when high tension valve springs and high-lift camshafts are used.

These stamped steel rockers are mounted on a steel shaft, which does offer good lateral support, but they are still prone to the perforation problem.

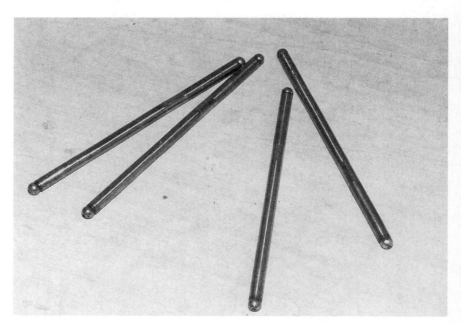

Decking the block, milling the cylinder heads, or using camshafts with non-stock base circles can all affect rocker arm geometry. The problems created by these operations can be corrected by installing different length push rods.

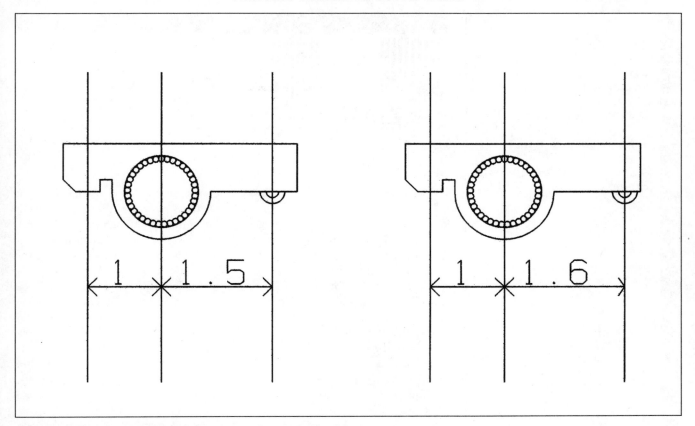

Long-ratio rocker arms are used to increase the total valve lift.

To ensure the stability and alignment of the pushrods, most performance engine builders use guide plates. This is particularly important on applications where the design of the cylinder head does not permit the installation of a more stable rocker design.

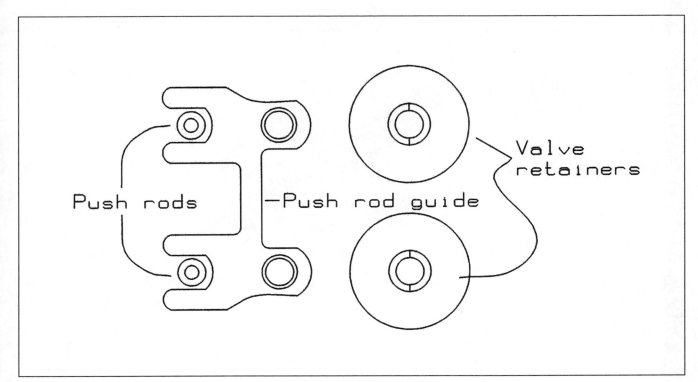

Those effective at selecting the correct camshaft may be among the most erudite, or maybe most lucky, gearheads in the automotive enthusiast community. I have spent hours with formulas arriving at the same decision that had been suggested to me by a friend. There are many good sources in getting help with camshaft decisions. Some of the best sources of advice are the camshaft manufacturers themselves.

CHAPTER ELEVEN

CAMSHAFT BASICS AND PREPARATION

The cylinder head and its air flow capabilities are only as efficient as the control of the valves, which are opened and closed by the camshaft. Up to this point, the air flow calculations we have made have assumed that the intake and exhaust valves are always open. Anyone who has ever been so much as called a motorhead knows that they are open only a percentage of the time. In a rather simple example, let us assume that the camshaft has a duration of 360 degrees on both the intake and exhaust lobes with zero time opening and closing ramps. (This is an impossible design, but makes the explanation easier.) The 360-degree duration means that both the intake valve and the exhaust valve are open half the time—one full crankshaft rotation each. With a camshaft like this, the flow rate of the valves need only match the theoretical cfm of the engine. The square cam lobe would

open the valve to its maximum height at the beginning of the intake stroke. If the flow rate through the head's intake port was exactly equal to the cfm at that engine speed, 100-percent volumetric efficiency would be achieved.

Unfortunately, camshafts cannot be built without opening and closing ramps, so the valves both open and close rather slowly—much, much slower than our instant-open/instant-close example above. This means that the air flow potential through both the intake and exhaust valves will be virtually nothing when the valve begins to open, and the flow will increase gradually as the valve opens farther. Fortunately, this gradual opening of the valves coincides with the piston velocity: The intake valve opens a few degrees before top dead center, and as the crankshaft crests over TDC, the piston speed drops to zero momentarily, so at this point, the cylinder has no potential for drawing in air. As the crankshaft

Cam lift is the difference in the distance from the centerline of the camshaft to the heel of the cam and the distance from the centerline of the camshaft and the toe of the cam.

swings past TDC, the piston begins to accelerate, which creates a low-pressure area that draws air into the cylinder. The piston speed and air flow reach their maximum as the crank journal for that piston swings past 90 degrees from TDC. After 90 degrees, the speed of the piston and potential air flow begins to decrease. But this decrease coincides with the closing of the valve, as the lifter rides down the cam lobe's closing ramp. If the piston displaces 0.022 cubic feet on each intake stroke, the bulk of the air needed to fill that cylinder must enter the cylinder while the piston velocity is at its greatest—between 45 degrees after TDC and 45 degrees before BDC (bottom dead center). Eighty percent of the air must be drawn in during 50 percent of the intake stroke. At 5,000 rpm, this example engine would be demanding 436 cubic feet of air per minute, but most

of that air must be drawn in during half the intake stroke, which means that the air flow rate will be well in excess of 436 cfm for half the intake stroke. The heads, therefore, must be able to flow 654 cfm—a figure equal to 81.75 cfm per cylinder. In fact, this flow rate can marginally support engine speeds approaching 7,000 rpm.

$$\frac{\text{c. i. displacement}/1728 \times \text{RPM}}{2} = \text{CFM}$$

CFM x 1.5 = Required Head Airflow

Keep in mind that the airflow in the above formula is the required airflow for *all* cylinders. The result should be divided by the number of cylinders for a per-cylinder airflow measurement.

Up to this point in the examples, we have worked with a figure of 5,000

rpm as maximum rpm. This was a convenient number to work with in the illustrations and is a good maximum rpm for a street engine. What, other than use, determines the maximum rpm of an engine? Although there are many moving parts in an engine, none are subjected to more stress than the piston. A stock engine, with stock pistons, rods, and crankshaft will have a maximum piston velocity of 3,500 feet per minute. The maximum rpm with this piston speed in a 302 cubic inch engine is 7,000 rpm. So you can see that the figures used up to this point are very conservative. Full-race forged cranks, heavy-duty rods, main bearing caps, and pistons can support piston velocities of 6,000 feet per minute. With this type of bottom end preparation, engine speeds approaching 12,000 rpm are theoretically possible.

$$\text{RPM} = \frac{\text{FPM x 6}}{\text{Stroke}}$$

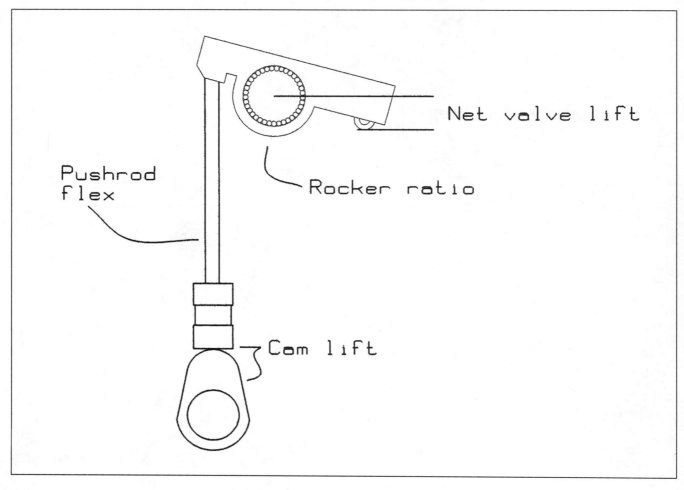

Net valve lift

Rocker ratio

Pushrod flex

Cam lift

Remember that rocker ratio can have a tremendous effect on total valve lift.

For our imaginary 302, an engine speed of 7,000 rpm would require a per cylinder air flow rate of 114 cfm.

Selecting a Camshaft

When the cylinder head is being flow tested, the technician will measure the air flow at various lift points for the valve. The camshaft should be able to lift the valve to the point where the desired airflow can be achieved. A camshaft with a lift of 0.500 inch will open the valve one half inch. If 114 cfm is our target, then the head must flow a minimum 114 cfm when the valve is opened 0.500 inch. On many overhead cam engines that do not incorporate a rocker arm, the formula for cam lift versus valve lift is just that simple. For engines that use rocker arms, the ratio of the rocker arm must be considered.

Cam Lift, Valve Lift, and Rocker Arm Ratio

Cam lift is the difference between the largest diameter of the cam lobe minus the smallest diameter of the cam lobe. Camshaft manufacturers advertise lift measured in inches of gross valve opening, assuming a stock rocker arm ratio.

If the rocker arm ratio is 1.5:1, it means that a 0.500-inch movement of the push rod will result in a 0.750-inch movement of the valve. In our above example, the target airflow was 114 cfm. After having the finished heads flow tested, it is determined that this air flow rate is achieved at 0.500 valve lift. The camshaft could have a 0.500 lift, or we could use a milder cam with 0.450 inch of lift in conjunction with a 1.5:1 ratio rocker arm—a combination that would provide a valve lift of 0.675

inches. The result is more than adequate air flow, without the extremely high stress factors that would be placed on a high lift camshaft. A rocker ratio of 1.5:1 is typical of a stock rocker arm. Some performance rocker arms have ratios of 1.7:1. Using the same example, the 1.7:1 rocker would increase the valve lift to 0.0765 inch (0.450 inch x 1.7 = 0.765 inch). This example is very radical and would probably either result in the valve spring retainer bottoming on the valve guide or the spring coils binding. And if neither of those happened, the valve would surely smack the piston.

Net lift (valve opening) is equal to the cam lift, less any camshaft flex, times the rocker ratio, less valve clearance, and less any valvetrain flex. Therefore a cam of 0.300 inch, less cam flex of 0.010 would yield a net cam lift of 0.290 inch. A 1.5:1 ratio rocker would yield a gross valve lift, then, of 0.435 inch. If the valvetrain

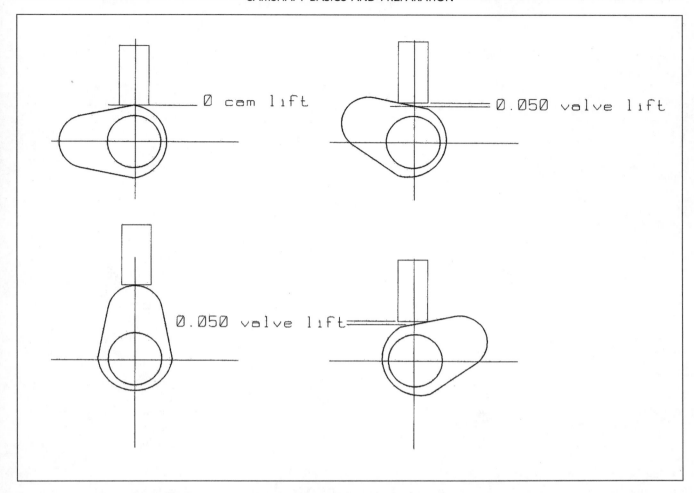

Camshaft duration is measured between the valve being opened a specified amount and that same amount prior to closing. Society of Automotive Engineers (SAE) standard for measuring duration is at 0.006 inch of valve lift, while the performance industry measures at 0.050 inch of valve lift. Never try to compare SAE figures to the aftermarket's "at .050" figures.

flex (flexing of the pushrod for instance) amounts to 0.004 inch, and the valve clearance is 0.018 inch, the net valve opening will be 0.413 inch.

Now we have arrived at a quandary: Do we select the camshaft and rocker arms based on predicted cylinder head air flow, or do we maximize the efficiency of the heads, have them flow tested, then select the camshaft and rockers. The obvious conclusion is that the flow rate through the cylinder head is the variable over which the engine builder has the least control. So, maximize the cylinder head flow, have the head flow-bench tested, then select the camshaft lift and rocker ratio.

Duration

Camshaft duration is the difference, in degrees, between a specified valve open height and that same height just prior to the valve's closing. Society of Automotive Engineers (SAE) standard for measuring duration is at 0.006 inch of valve lift, while the performance industry measures at 0.050 inch of valve lift. This means that one must be careful to compare apples to apples when dealing with different camshaft manufacturers; it's best to use the "at 0.050-inch" spec, since that is the accepted industry standard. Increasing the duration raises the rpm at which the engine achieves maximum power. A stock, early production 302 Ford has an intake duration of 266 degrees and an exhaust duration of 244 degrees. This provides good low-end power, with the power peak being reached at less than 4,000 rpm. By increasing the duration to 320 degrees for the intake and 320 degrees for the exhaust, the peak power band is moved up to somewhere between 4,800 and 8,200 rpm. When selecting a camshaft, depend on the specs provided by the camshaft manufacturer for the best duration for the peak power rpm band desired.

Valve Overlap

Valve overlap is the measurement, in degrees, between the point at which the intake valve begins to open and the point at which the exhaust valve fully closes. Lots of valve overlap increases the efficiency of cylinder filling at high rpm, but sacrifices low-rpm idle vacuum and therefore low-speed performance, and results in a rougher idle.

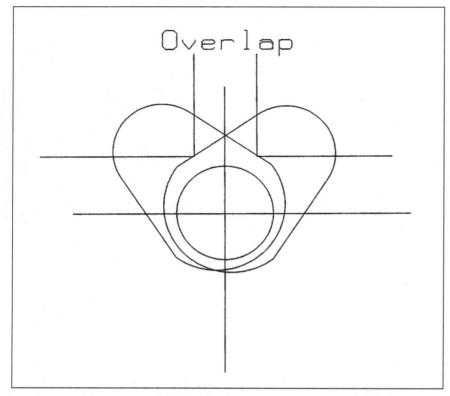

Valve overlap is the number of degrees of crankshaft rotation that the intake valve and the exhaust valve are simultaneously open.

During the 1970s, increased valve overlap was used to draw exhaust gases back into the combustion chamber to cool the combustion process and reduce the emissions of oxides of nitrogen.

In a performance engine, the greater valve overlap allows the average velocity of the gases flowing through the combustion chamber to remain high. The higher velocity increases the inertial flow of these gases, ensuring that the cylinders fill better on each intake stroke and scavenge better on each exhaust stroke.

The down-side of increased valve overlap is the *lumpy* or loping idle that is characteristic of most racing engines. This lumpy idle results in erratic manifold vacuum that can seriously affect the operation of carburetors and fuel injection systems, or even just power brake systems. Although NOx emissions might be reduced at high engine speeds, carbon monoxide and hydrocarbon emissions at lower speeds are usually greatly increased. Use of a high overlap camshaft on a street application will almost ensure the vehicle will fail the local emission standards, not just in California, but in all 50 states.

A Less-than-Professional Example

Deep in the recesses of a garage in Fort Worth, Texas, a "racing" engine, which had been assembled from junk parts in 1973, was found. This racing engine started life as a 1967 Ford 289, was fitted with a crankshaft from a 1968 302 and a set of 12:1, 0.030-inch-over TRW pistons. The camshaft that was installed had 0.297-inch lift on both the intake and exhaust lobes. Since stock rockers had a 1.6:1 ratio, the valves could potentially open 0.4752 inch. Since solid lifters were installed, a potential 0.015 inches of valve lift was lost to the lash adjustment and 0.003 inches was lost to flex in the pushrod, which meant that the net lift was really only 0.4572 inch.

valve lift = (cam lift x rocker ratio) - (valve lash + valvetrain flex)

The bore of this engine was 4.030 inches, and its stroke was 3.00 inches. The displacement of the engine was 306.13 cubic inches.

displacement = π/ x bore^2 x stroke x no. of cylinders

$$cfm = \frac{rpm \text{ x } displacement}{3456}$$

At 5,000 rpm, this engine will move about 443 cubic feet of air per minute, which equals 55.38 cubic feet of air per minute per cylinder.

$$cfm \text{ per cylinder} = \frac{([rpm \text{ x } displacement]/3456)}{Number \text{ of cylinders}}$$

The intake and exhaust ports of the cylinder heads must be able to flow a minimum of 83 cfm per cylinder (55.38 x 1.5).

After shopping the phone directory for a shop with a flow bench, a small machine shop specializing in racing heads was located in Arlington, Texas, near my home. As the first cylinder head was fitted on the bench, it was noticed that they must have come out of the factory in about 1962, mounted on a 221 cubic inch V-8 engine. At 5,000 rpm, the original 221-inch engine would only have required an air flow rate of 60 cubic feet per minute per cylinder (40 cfm times 1.5).

$$\frac{(5000 \text{ x } 221)/3456}{8} \text{ x } 1.5 = 60$$

If the air flow capacity of this head is no better than what was required for the 221, the 306 cubic inch engine will not receive sufficient air.

When the cylinder head is mounted on the flow bench, the air flow rate was set to 200 cfm. Air flow readings were taken at progressive valve openings of 0.050 inch. The results of the test are listed in the following table.

Cam timing is critical to peak performance from an engine. To degree the camshaft, it is first necessary to identify the exact point of TDC for the number one cylinder on the compression stroke. A piston stop is required to do this job. Piston stops can be purchased commercially, or can be manufactured from a piece of angle iron and a few bolts.

	Exhaust	Intake	Exhaust	Intake	20 Inches
0.05	13.00%	13.00%	26.078	25.922	18.51538
0.1	20.00%	17.50%	40.12	34.895	28.4852
0.15	28.00%	37.00%	56.168	73.778	39.87928
0.2	35.00%	46.50%	70.21	92.721	49.8491
0.25	40.50%	57.50%	81.243	114.655	57.68253
0.3	43.50%	66.00%	87.261	131.604	61.95531
0.35	45.50%	69.50%	91.273	138.583	64.80383
0.4	46.50%	71.80%	93.279	143.1692	66.22809
0.45	48.00%	74.00%	96.288	147.556	68.36448
0.5	48.50%	76.40%	97.291	152.3416	69.07661
0.55	48.50%	—	—	—	—

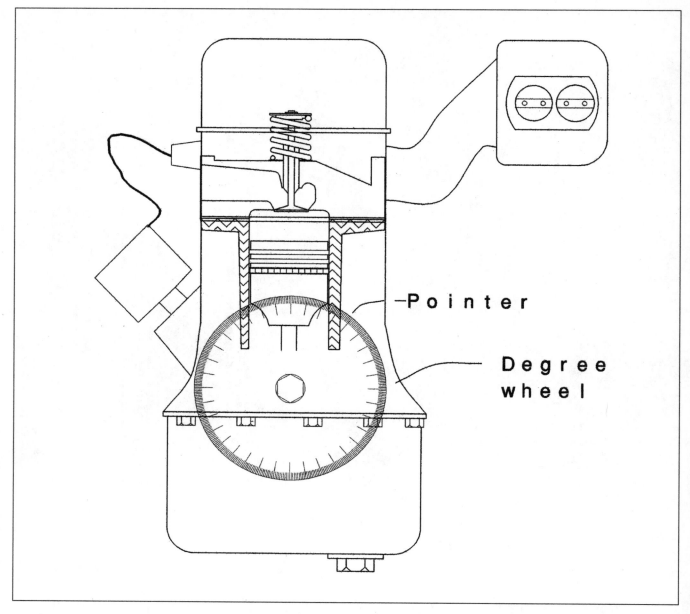

Pointer

Degree
wheel

Install a degree wheel on the front of the crankshaft. Position the degree wheel so it is near the top-dead-center mark when the number one piston appears to be near TDC. The adjustment is not critical at this point. A pointer to mark TDC can be manufactured from a coat hanger or other wire laying around the shop. Set the piston stop so the piston will only travel within 1/4 to 1/2 inch of the top of its travel.

At 0.05 inch of valve opening, the exhaust valve flowed at a rate of 13 percent of the 200 cfm. The crude results of this test is an air flow rate of 26 cfm. The manufacturer of this particular flow bench recommended a correction factor of 1.003 be used to adjust for inaccuracies in the bench. The adjusted air flow rate through the exhaust valve was therefore 26.078

cubic feet per minute. The correction factor of 1.003 is recommended by the manufacturer of the flow bench to adjust for known measurement errors. Although correcting for an error of 3/10 of 1 percent may seem nit-picky, nit-picky is the difference between the front row of Indianapolis and spending the week before Memorial Day driving back to Houston.

When the valve was opened to 0.10 inch, the flow rate increased to 20 percent. Using the above formula, the airflow rate became 40.12 cfm. When the valve was opened to slightly less than the calculated exhaust valve opening height, the flow rate reached 96 cfm. This is slightly better than the desired flow rate of 83 cfm. The problem with this reading relates to what goes on in the engine when the air flow increases toward wide-open-throttle. As the throttle opening increases, the load on the engine increases and the engine vacuum drops. The readings in the fourth and fifth columns of the above chart were taken at 24 inches of

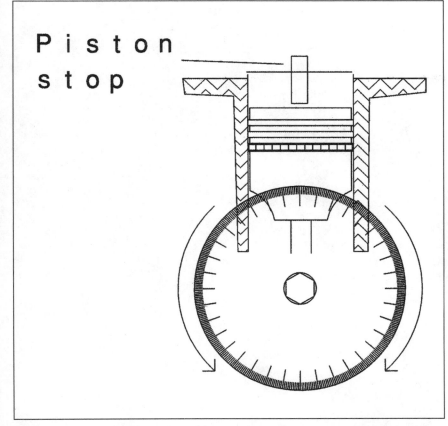

Piston stop

Rotate the crankshaft clockwise until the piston comes against the stop. Note the reading on the degree wheel. Rotate the crankshaft counter-clockwise until the piston comes against the stop. Note the reading on the degree wheel. Top dead center is halfway in between. Bring the crankshaft back to TDC and readjust the degree wheel to read zero (TDC).

beginning to accelerate rapidly, so the low pressure (high vacuum) is at its greatest. As the valve approaches its maximum opening, the piston velocity begins to decrease, so the low pressure begins to rise as the velocity decreases. If the throttle is wide open, there is minimal restriction to the flow of air into the intake, so the intake fills with air rapidly and vacuum drops.

In a gasoline-powered spark-ignition engine, the ratio of fuel to air in the combustion chamber must be precise. Not only is the air used as an expansion medium to drive the piston downward, it is also used as a medium for evenly distributing the fuel particles in the combustion chamber. Igniting the fuel with the spark plug only begins a process that must then be supported by the evenly distributed fuel itself. As the flame front travels through the combustion chamber, it leaps from one fuel droplet to another much like a forest fire leaps from one tree to another. If there is a gap in the trees, a fire break, the forest fire will stop at the break. If there is a break in the fuel particles, the flame front will stop at the break. An inadequate amount of fuel will result in large gaps in the fuel particles, these large gaps will then result in some of the fuel not being burned. Unburned fuel results in high emissions and a loss of potential power.

Changing Cam Phasing

Cam timing is critical to peak performance from a performance engine. To degree, or phase, the camshaft it is first necessary to identify the exact point of TDC for the number one cylinder on the compression stroke. A piston stop is required to do this job. Piston stops

vacuum. The last column shows exhaust port readings at 20 inches of vacuum, and there is a considerable difference between it and the preceding column. As the throttle responds to the driver's demand for more power and more speed, the engine vacuum can drop to virtually nothing. This presents a serious inhibition to air flow.

High-lift, long-duration camshafts and a wide open throttle can team up to reduce the vacuum created by each

cylinder. On a stock engine in good condition, each cylinder creates an average of about 20 inches of vacuum. The Allen Smart Engine Analyzer creates a vacuum wave form pattern. This pattern reflects changes in manifold vacuum as each intake valve opens and closes. When the intake valve opens, the piston is about to begin its decent down the cylinder. This creates a low pressure area above the moving piston. As the valve first opens, the piston is

Net (actual) valve lift =

cam lift - camshaft flex X rocker ratio - valve/rocker gap - pushrod flex

Install a dial indicator on the intake lifter and rotate the crankshaft against normal rotation until the dial indicator is at its most extended reading. Now rotate the crankshaft in the direction of normal rotation. When the valve lift reaches the point recommended by the camshaft manufacturer, the degrees shown on the degree wheel should also match the readings recommended by the camshaft manufacturer on the cam card.

can be purchased commercially or can be manufactured from a piece of angle iron and a few bolts. Install a degree wheel on the front of the crankshaft. Position the degree wheel so that it is near the top dead center mark when the number one piston appears to be near top dead center. The adjustment is not critical at this point. A pointer to mark TDC can be manufactured from a coat hanger or other scrap wire laying around the shop. Set the piston stop so the piston will only travel within 1/4–1/2 inch from the top of its travel. Rotate the crankshaft clockwise until the piston comes against

the stop. Note the reading on the degree wheel. Rotate the crankshaft counter-clockwise until the piston again comes against the stop. Note the reading on the degree wheel. Top dead center is the halfway point in-between the two readings. For example, if it first comes to 14-degrees *before* TDC on the wheel, then the second reading says 6 degrees *after* TDC, the mid-point is 4 degrees before TDC (14 + 6 = 20; 20 ÷ 2 = 10; 14 - 10 = 4 degrees, and 6 + 10 = 16 degrees). Bring the crankshaft to the point of TDC (4 degrees BTDC, in our example), then readjust the degree wheel to

read 0 degrees (TDC) by either rotating the degree wheel (if it's way out of adjustment) or bending your pointer to point to 0 degrees.

Now, install a dial indicator on the intake lifter and rotate the crankshaft against normal rotation until the dial indicator is at its most extended reading. Now, rotate the crankshaft in the direction of normal crankshaft rotation. When the valve lift reaches the point recommended by the camshaft manufacturer, the degrees indicated on the degree wheel should also match the readings recommended by the camshaft manufacturer (shown on the cam card).

124

The compression ratio is the relationship between the volume of the cylinder when the piston is at bottom dead center and when it is at top dead center.

CHAPTER TWELVE

COMPRESSION RATIO AND BALANCING

Let's face it: Who wouldn't want to be able to say, "Yeah, my big-block's balanced and blueprinted and has 12-and-a-half to one forged pistons!"? It just sounds cool. Unfortunately, stratospheric compression ratios are far from practical in today's world, given the pathetic substances we affectionately still call fuel.

Sure, in the good old days of 104-octane Sunoco 260 you could run 12.5:1 pistons and not worry too much about burning a hole through one or more of them by the time you drove to the end of your driveway. But, today, with 94-octane "Super" unleaded, a more realistic maximum streetable compression ratio is in the neighborhood of 10–10.5:1, depending on cylinder head design and camshaft profile, among other factors.

Of course, attaining that theoretically acceptable compression ratio isn't quite as simple as ordering up a set of 10.0:1 pistons in the proper bore size. Since you've been doing all sorts of work to the block, the cylinder heads, the cam, the crank, and the rods, you've been altering a bunch of factors that could result in a compression ratio that will either be measurably higher or lower than the 10.0:1 written on the side of the pistons' box.

The only way to know your compression ratio for sure, and thus have a snowball's chance in Hades of correcting it, is to properly measure your engine's assembled static compression ratio. It might sound like a tough task, but it's actually quite simple—once you know what you're doing.

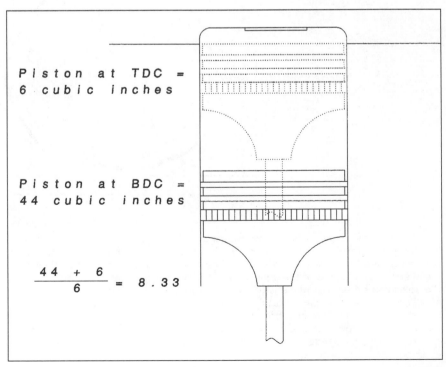

Piston at TDC = 6 cubic inches

Piston at BDC = 44 cubic inches

$$\frac{44 + 6}{6} = 8.33$$

swept volume = pi/4 X (bore X bore) X stroke

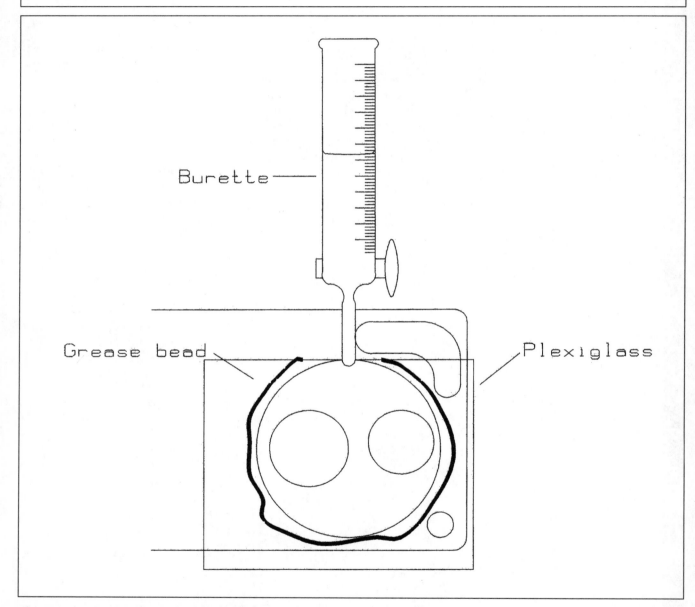

Burette

Grease bead

Plexiglass

The easiest way to measure the volume of the combustion chambers is with a light oil poured from a burette. Uneven-sized combustion chambers result in uneven power from the cylinders. Use a graduated burette. With the valves installed, place a piece of Plexiglas over the combustion chamber. The Plexiglas can be held in place with a little petroleum jelly. There should be a small hole in the Plexiglas through which mineral oil can be metered out of the burette. The volume drained from the burette is the volume of that combustion chamber. Repeat this process for each of the combustion chambers. Use a carbide grinding bit to enlarge each of the combustion chambers to match the largest.

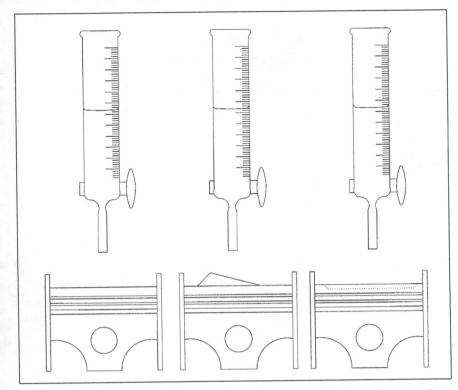

To accurately determine the compression ratio, you need to know how much volume the piston dome displaces in the cylinder head. Position the piston a measured amount down in the cylinder. Use the volume formula to determine what the volume of the cylinder would be with a flat-topped piston. Seal the area between the circumference of the piston head and the cylinder wall with a light coat of grease. Fill the area on top of the piston with light oil from a burette. Note how much oil is required to fill the cylinder. The difference between the formula calculation and the amount of oil required to fill the cylinder is the piston displacement of the combustion chamber.

Calculating the Cylinder's Swept Volume

Tradition has it that Euclid, a motorhead from the third or fourth century BC, was the first to calculate the swept volume of a cylinder. His theory was that if you square half the bore, multiply that times pi (π) then multiply the product of that calculation by the stroke, we would know the swept volume of the cylinder. This was revolutionary at the time. Most of the competition were still moving the piston to bottom dead center, filling the bore with cream cheese up to the deck of the block, then scooping the cream cheese into the stomachs of a goat. The typical big-block of the day featured an average of three goat stomachs per cylinder.

Euclid's formula was as follows:

cylinder volume (swept) = $(0.5 \times \text{bore})^2 \times \pi \times \text{stroke}$

Example:

$(0.5 \times 4.00)^2 \times 3.14 \times 3.00$ = swept volume

$(2.00)^2 \times 3.14 \times 3.00$ = swept volume

$4.00 \times 3.14 \times 3.00$ = swept volume

37.68 cubic inches = swept volume

In the example above, every cylinder has a swept volume of 37.68 cubic inches. Each cylinder therefore displaces 37.68 cubic inches of air, as the piston moves from bottom dead center to top dead center. Multiply this result by 16.387 to convert cubic inches to cubic centimeters. The swept volume of this cylinder is 617.46 cubic centimeters. If this example were an eight cylinder engine, it would be a 301.44 (302 if you round as Ford does) cubic inch engine. (That is a 0.052 cubic cubit engine.)

Calculating Combustion Chamber Volume

Now this is an exercise well suited for cream cheese. Instead of cream cheese, though, we use mineral spirits today. Find a piece of Plexiglas. Form a circle around the combustion chamber

Unlike high compression, balancing an engine's reciprocating and rotating assemblies just makes good sense, for any engine, from your grandma's Sunday driver to your Saturday night sleeper. Equalizing and minimizing the weight of the piston and rod assemblies, as well as the crankshaft, will dramatically cut-down on harmful vibrations that can pound out bearings, hammer away at fasteners, and otherwise shake things apart. And, best of all, balancing is neither a difficult nor expensive process.

Computing Compression Ratio

For those of us who struggle with math, there is intense fear associated with the word "calculate." For me, it brings back memories of Mrs. Maujer, my seventh grade math teacher at Jeanne d'Arc high school near Toul, France. Mrs. Maujer had the reputation of being merciless in her teaching of math skills. She was the one who taught me that one could have *negative* apples. Rest assured that calculating compression ratio is not nearly as complicated as what happens to Johnny's positive apples if Freddy combines them with his negative apples.

To begin calculating our compression ratio, we must know the total volume of the cylinder, which will include both the swept and unswept portions of the cylinder. The swept portion of the cylinder is that part where the piston travels, and the unswept portion is the remaining volume of the cylinder and cylinder head that is never invaded by the piston.

$$\text{Compression ratio} = \frac{\text{cylinder swept volume} + \text{combustion chamber volume} - \text{piston displacement of combustion chamber} + \text{valve relief displacement}}{\text{combustion chamber volume} - \text{piston displacement of combustion chamber} + \text{valve relief displacement}}$$

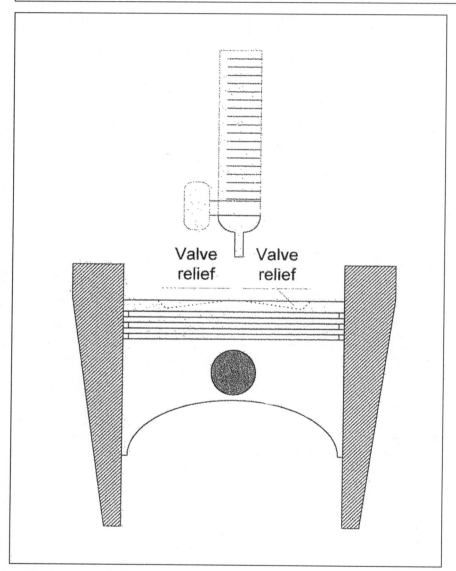

Compression ratio formula.

in the head with grease to form a seal when the Plexiglas is laid on the cylinder head. Place the Plexiglas on the head so that there is a small gap at the top of the mating point between the head and the Plexiglas. Using a burette, fill the combustion chamber with mineral spirits, noting how much fluid from the burette is used. Let us say that the volume of our example is 96 cubic centimeters.

Calculating Piston Displacement in Combustion Chamber

Now, if all pistons were flat on top, this step would not be necessary, but because many high-performance pistons feature piston domes or some have piston dishes or at least valve reliefs, we have to adjust our volumes appropriately. Move the piston down the cylinder until it sits about 1/2 inch below the deck of the block. Make sure the highest point of the piston is below the deck of the block. Now use the burette to fill the cylinder. Record the volume of mineral spirits necessary to fill the cylinder. Work fast, because the mineral spirits will leak past the rings. If you prefer not to work fast, or prefer to be as accurate as possible with your measurements, the leaking past the rings can be reduced by carefully sealing the gap between the piston and the cylinder wall with grease. As the grease is applied, be careful not to let any of the grease take up space in the combustion chamber! Now, accurately measure the distance from the block deck to the top of the piston. Use Euclid's little formula to calculate how much volume the cylinder above the top of the piston would have taken up if the top of the piston

To accurately determine the compression ratio, you also need to know how much volume there is in the valve reliefs of the piston. The technique is just like calculating piston dome displacement. Position the piston a measured amount down in the cylinder. Use the volume formula to determine what the volume of the cylinder would be with a flat-topped piston. Seal the area between the circumference of the piston head and the cylinder wall with a light coat of grease. Fill the area on top of the piston with light oil from a burette. Note how much oil is required to fill the reliefs. The difference between the formula calculation and the amount of oil required to fill the reliefs is valve relief volume.

had been flat. Now subtract the amount that flowed from the burette to fill the cylinder from the flat top piston volume. The difference is how much to subtract from combustion chamber volume, measured with the Plexiglas and burette. The difference is the actual size of the combustion chamber when the piston is at top dead center. For our discussion, we will say that the top of the piston fills 10 cubic centimeters of the combustion chamber.

The thickness and the volume of the head gasket must also be considered in your compression ratio calculation.

I suppose that it would be appropriate to note at this point that Mrs. Maujer was right: There is a place for math in the real world. If the piston top is depressed or recessed, then the piston design will add to the size of the combustion chamber. It might be said the combustion chamber size is reduced by a negative amount.

The Final Calculation for Compression Ratio

Armed with our swept volume and combustion chamber size, we can now calculate the compression ratio. The formula looks like this:

$$Compression\ Ratio = \frac{Total\ Cylinder\ Volume}{Compressed\ Cylinder\ Volume}$$

$$= \frac{(Swept\ Volume + (Chamber\ Volume - dome\ volume))}{(Chamber\ Volume - dome\ volume)}$$

$$= \frac{(617.46 + (96 - 10))}{(96 - 10)}$$

$$= \frac{617.46 + 86}{86}$$

$$= \frac{703.46}{86}$$

$$= 8.18\ (:1)$$

In our example, the swept volume was 617.46 cubic centimeters, the combustion chamber size was 96 cc's, and the piston dome volume was 10 cc. The total size of the cylinder—swept volume plus *net* combustion chamber volume—is 617.46 plus 86, which equals 703.46 cubic centimeters. We then divide the 703.46 by 86 to get our compression ratio of 8.18 to 1.

Valve Relief Volume

The valve reliefs in the pistons lower the compression ratio. The volume of these areas needs to be *added* to the volume of the combustion chamber in the compression ratio calculation. The volume of the reliefs is very easy to measure, the technique is similar to the technique used to measure the combustion chamber volume itself. Fill the valve reliefs with the burette, monitoring the amount of oil, or for that matter cream cheese, that it takes to fill the reliefs. Add the total volume of all valve reliefs to the volume of the combustion chamber before doing your final compression ratio calculation.

Power and Compression Ratio

I began this discussion of compression ratio by talking about my adolescent misconception of its importance. There is little doubt that a confined burn will make a bigger bang than an unconfined burn. The real question is, does a bigger bang mean more power? As far as big bangs go, a former racing foe of mine, Alf Gephardt, had a BMW 2002 that took the cake. The unofficial ground rule of the Green Valley Racing Association was to never let Alf pass on your left. Over the sound of your own engine, over the noise suppression of your Bell Star helmet, over the cotton stuffed in your ears, Alf's little Beemer was still deafening. Its bark was much worse than its bite—and its bite was considerable.

Compression ratio has a lot to do with how confined the charge is when it is ignited. The larger the confined space, the less pressure will be created when ignition occurs. The smaller the confined space, the greater the pressure that will be created when ignition occurs. Now, imagine a room full of undisciplined children. The passion with which you desire to leave the room is inversely proportional to the size of the room. In a big room, you'll want to get out; in a small room, you'll want to get out *fast!* The same is true of the burning gases inside the combustion chamber. The more passionate the burning gases are, the greater the pressure they create and the more force (power) is generated.

To give you a more graphic representation of what this means, picture a 300 square foot room, which we'll use to represent the volume of the combustion chamber when the piston is at bottom dead center. Now put 30 kids in the room with you. Now begin to move the walls closer together, as you feed the kids jelly doughnuts and Kool-Aid. By the time the moving walls have shrunk the room to 30 square feet, which represents the piston at top dead center, each of the kids has consumed three doughnuts and 16 ounces of Kool-Aid. There is pressure in that room, wouldn't you say?

The Down-Side of High Compression

For most things in life, there is both a good side and a bad side, and compression is no exception. High-compression engines survive well on high octane fuels—such as methanol, ethanol, natural gas and the mythical high-octane gasolines of the 1960s—that burn or burned slowly and evenly in the combustion chamber. The slow, even burn reduces hot spots and produces a more even temperature in the combustion chamber. A more even temperature in the combustion chamber yields a more even expansion of gases. For high-compression engines, this is particularly important, since the average temperature of combustion is already elevated. With an elevated average temperature, the spot temperatures are close to or past the point that melt metal. Today's gasoline is not very compatible with high compression engines. In fact, high compression and low octane can be a deadly combination for the engine.

Several years ago, while working as an import car technician at an independent shop, a six-cylinder Mercedes was brought into the shop by the owner. The primary complaint was a lack of power. The compression test indicated that four of the six cylinders had no compression at all. When the cylinder head was removed, the pistons in these four cylinders had holes in them at least the size of quarters. These holes had been burned into the pistons by high temperatures associated with detonation. The most likely cause of the detonation was a relatively high compression engine running for an extended time on low octane fuel.

Detonation occurs when the air/fuel mixture in the combustion chamber ignites prematurely. This early ignition may be caused by over-advanced timing, high compression, low flash point for the fuel, or sharp, glowing edges in the combustion chamber. When the air/fuel mixture ignites with the piston on the upward stroke, the gases resulting from combustion begin to expand rapidly. The piston, therefore, must compress combustion gases rather than simply the relatively low pressure of air that has been drawn in from the atmosphere. One of the results is the classic "marbles in a tin can" sound familiar to all

who have had the pleasure of experiencing detonation. Another result is that the rapidly expanding, heated gases are further pressurized, and therefore heated, as a result of their confinement. The final results are extremely high temperatures and pressures that can each damage pistons and other expensive components.

Detonation is a clue that something more sinister is happening. The same high pressures and temperatures that produce detonation also cause oxygen to combine with nitrogen, producing NOx. This was, as mentioned earlier, the main reason compression ratios were lowered in the 1970s. In the late 1980s and early 1990s, computer-controlled timing systems were developed to reduce the possibility of detonation. This also reduced the instances in which the conditions were right for the formation of oxides of nitrogen. This development allowed the compression ratios to creep back up during the mid-1990s.

Balancing
Rotating and Reciprocating Weight

The real challenge of rebuilding an engine is taking the time to create as perfect a machine as possible. The dynamic forces of the reciprocating components of the engine become amplified as the engine speed increases. An imbalance puts the crankshaft and other components

under fluctuating stresses that create a vibration. Those vibrations are energy being lost to rocking the engine instead of pushing the vehicle down the road. Bottom line: Balancing the engine's reciprocating components will decrease the vibrations, and this will increase the power to the ground. Reach into your pocket and pull out a dollar bill. Now cut the dollar bill in half. Pick up one half. Note the weight. It is about one half gram. This is how closely the pistons should be balanced. In fact, one half gram is how closely matched each of the reciprocating masses, piston, wrist pin, connecting rod, and bearings should be balanced.

Begin the balancing procedure by installing the wrist pin and its retaining clips (if applicable) into the pistons. Place each of the piston assemblies, in turn, on the scale. You will now remove metal from the heaviest pistons to make them all weigh the same as the lightest one.

To shave off the weight, mount the first piston in a lathe. Use the lathe cutting tool to remove metal from the wrist pin bosses inside the piston. Then repeat the process for each of the remaining pistons. Remember that you will still have the connecting rods to balance, therefore a little extra exactness will mean less balancing work when the pistons are mated to the connecting rods.

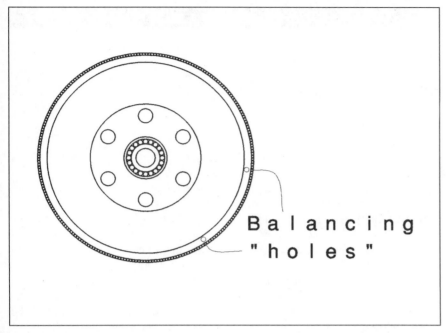

Balancing "holes"

Do not forget to balance the rotating components that mount on the engine. The flywheel should be balanced.

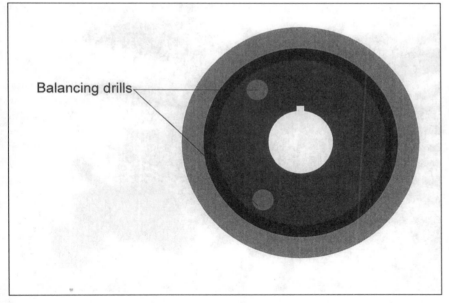

Balancing drills

The name "harmonic balancer" is often used for this component. The name would lead you to believe that it is in balance or performs the act of increasing balance. Actually, it's a harmonic (vibration) damper. Whatever you want to call it, get it balanced, too.

With the main bearing caps torqued in place, it is now time to install the rods into the pistons. It is critically important to make sure the piston and rod are mated properly. Each has a front and a back to it. Normally there will be a notch in the top of the piston indicating how the piston is oriented to the front of the engine (notch to the front). The rods should have been marked during disassembly. If new rods are being used refer to the instruction sheet in the box. If the rods were purchased from a machine shop, ask them.

CHAPTER THIRTEEN

ENGINE ASSEMBLY TIPS

You probably thought you were done with the tedium of measurements. All the parts are back from the machine shop and you are ready to reassemble, right? Sorry, it's time to get those micrometers, dial indicators, and feeler gauges back out. Confirming the measurements as the new parts are installed is a crucial part of the reassembly process.

The Block and Crank

Turn the block upside down. Clean the main bearing saddles thoroughly with a light solvent. The oil clearances of the main bearings will be less than 0.002 inch. Even a small piece of sand could distort the bearing and bind the crankshaft. Place the main bearing shells in the saddles. Be careful to do two things: First, install the main bearing with the thrust surface on the correct saddle; second, if only half the bearing shells have an oil supply hole in them, be sure that the hole lines up with the oil gallery port in the block's saddle. Take it from experience, the engine will make a very annoying knocking sound if the oil cannot get through the bearing to the crank journal. With the bearing shells properly laid in the saddle, smear assembly lube across the bearing surface, then carefully lay the crankshaft in the block.

Lay a short piece of Plastigage on each of the crank journals. Clean the main bearing caps to remove grit and place the bearing shells in them. Install the main bearing caps and torque them to the proper specification. Remove the bearing caps and use the Plastigage packaging to measure its width on the journal. Typical bearing clearances for passenger car and light duty truck engines are 0.0015 to 0.002 inch. If the bearing clearance is incorrect, you either measured your crank diameter incorrectly, have the wrong bearings, or are suffering from a mistake made in

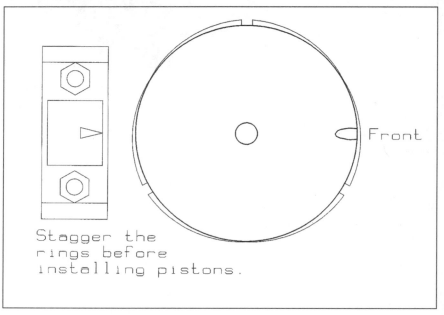

Stagger the rings before installing pistons.

Front

Place each of the piston rings to be used in the cylinder in which it is to be used. With a feeler gauge, measure the gap between the ends of the ring and compare to specifications for your application.

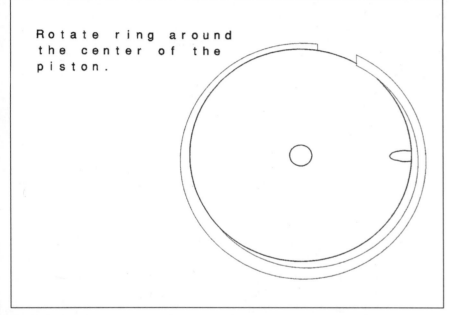

Rotate ring around the center of the piston.

Rotate the ring around the center of the piston and it will practically fall into place. Plan on breaking an occasional ring using this technique. Piston ring installation pliers can be purchased for only a few dollars at most auto parts stores, and will virtually eliminate the possibility of breaking rings.

the machining process. Remove the bearing shell from the bearing cap. On the backside of the shell, near one end, there should be a small marking indicating the undersize of the bearing (e.g., ".010" for ten thousandths undersize). Be sure this marking coincides with the marking the machinist stamped on the crankshaft near one of the main journals. If those numbers match, measure the crank journals—it was probably machined to a size other than that indicated.

If the Plastigage shows the oil clearance to be correct, apply assembly lube and install the main bearing caps and torque them to the proper specification. Some people like to remove the Plastigage before installing the bearing caps, but it is not really necessary, since the Plastigage is oil-soluble.

After all the main bearings are torqued, check the crankshaft end play. Install a dial indicator on the block to detect movement in the crankshaft. Using a pry bar, gently force the crank as far back in the block as possible. Adjust the dial indicator to zero and pry the crank as far forward as possible. The dial indicator will show crankshaft end play. Although allowable end play differs from application to another, a general rule of thumb is 0.003 to 0.008 inch. If the end play is incorrect, the crankshaft thrust surfaces will need to be repaired.

If you do not have access to a dial indicator, an alternative, though slightly less accurate method is to use a feeler gauge. Pry the crankshaft all the way to the rear and place the largest feeler gauge blade possible between the crank thrust surface and the main bearing thrust surface.

Installing the Connecting Rods to the Pistons

With the main bearing caps torqued in place, it is now time to install the rods into the pistons. It is critically important to make sure the piston and rod are mated properly. Each has a front and a back to it. Normally, there will be a notch in the top of the piston indicating which side of the piston should face the front of the engine (notch to the front). The rods should have been marked during disassembly. If new rods are being used, refer to the instruction sheet in the box. If the rods were purchased from a machine shop, ask them.

The wrist pin is installed into the piston and rod in one of two ways: As a full-floating pin or as a semi-floating pin.

Full Floating

Installing the pistons onto the rods with full floating wrist pins is easy, since the wrist pin slides through both the piston and rods with minimal pressure applied by even the frailest of thumbs.

Semi-Floating

Installing semi-floating wrist pins is more of a problem. The wrist pin either slides through the piston and presses into the rod, or it presses into the piston and slides through the rod. Either one of these offers a perfect opportunity for the rebuilder to damage the piston. The safest route is to have the machine shop install semi-floating wrist pins.

A press tool can be made to facilitate pressing the wrist pins, in

With the ring compressor in place, protect the crank journal and the rod bolts from one another with a couple of pieces of rubber hose on the rod bolts. Long pieces of rubber hose can even help guide the connecting rod into its proper position on the crankshaft. Gently lower the piston into position. With a small, soft mallet, tap the edges of the piston ring compressor to ensure that it is firmly seated against the deck of the block. Tap the piston into position with firm application of the blunt end of the mallet. If the piston should be stopped by a ring slipping from between the ring compressor and the block, start again.

Remove the oil pump cover and pack a little light grease into it. This will help to prime the pump for initial start up. Torque the cover plate back on to the proper spec.

semi-floating applications. Using a piece of hardwood, carve a cradle that is equal in diameter to that of the piston. This will support the piston evenly as the wrist pin is pressed into place. These cradles can also be purchased commercially. Of course, allowing the machinist to install the wrist pins on semi-floating applications may still be the best answer. After all, if they break one of your pistons, they'll have to buy you another. You can't make yourself that same guarantee.

Ring End Gap

Place each of the piston rings into the cylinder in which they will be used. With a feeler gauge, measure the gap between the ends of the ring and compare those figures to the specifications for your application. If the ring end gap is incorrect, you have the wrong rings or the cylinders have been bored or honed incorrectly.

Installing the Rings

If you have not done so already, be sure that the ring grooves are clean and clear of debris and carbon by using a special tool called a ring

groove cleaner. For those who have good health insurance and a first aid kit, a broken ring can be used to scrape the carbon from the grooves, but extreme caution should be used when using a ring to clean the grooves, because the broken ring is sharp and can leave nasty cuts. Wear gloves.

With the ring grooves clean, install the new rings on the pistons, using one of the two methods described in the following paragraph. Stagger the rings before installing the pistons into the cylinder. Staggering will provide for a better seal during the early stages of running the engine. The rings are usually identified top, middle, and oil control by the papers covering them in the box. There will also be a mark on the two compression rings indicating which side faces up. This mark may be a dot, a bar, or even a corporate logo. In a few instances the rings may be unmarked, in which case there will be instructions in the box.

Two techniques are available for the actual installation of the rings. Start one end of the ring in the correct groove, then rotate the ring

around the center of the piston and it will practically fall into place. But you should plan on breaking an occasional ring using this technique. Piston ring installation pliers can be purchased for only a few dollars at most auto parts stores, and they virtually eliminate the possibility of breaking rings.

Installing the Piston and Rod Assembly

With the rod installed in the piston and the rings in place, put a piston ring compressor around the rings. There's no such thing as a piston ring compressor that really works well, so good luck with whatever style you choose. With the ring compressor in place, protect the crank journal and the rod bolts from one another with a couple of pieces of rubber hose slipped over the rod bolts. Long pieces of rubber hose—about 10 inches or so—can even help guide the connecting rod into its proper position on the crankshaft; all you have to do is slip the hoses onto the rod bolts, then place one piece of hose on each side of the rod journal before installing the piston. Gently

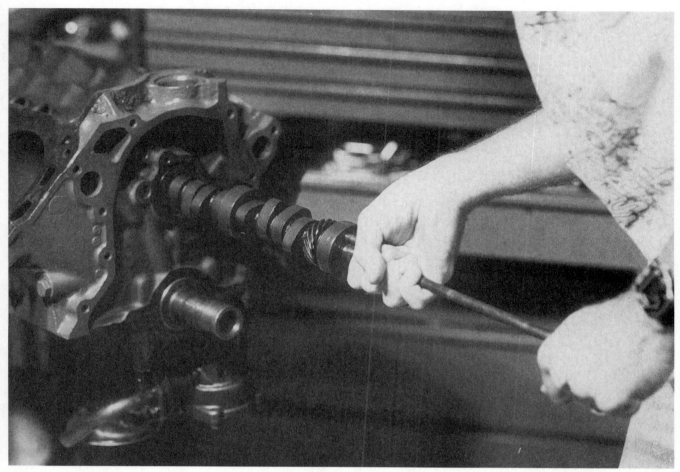

Installing an OHV camshaft is a lot like pushing a rope uphill. The part that you can hold on to is too short to be able to support it while you thread it through the journals. The answer to this is a camshaft installation tool, which can often be made from a simple piece of long threaded rod of the proper size to screw into the cam bolt holes.

lower the piston into position. With a small, soft-faced mallet, tap the edges of the piston ring compressor to ensure that it is firmly seated against the deck of the block. Tap the piston into position with firm application of the blunt end of the mallet. If the piston should be stopped by a ring slipping from between the ring compressor and the block, start again. After installing the first piston, Plastigage the journal using the same method described measuring the main bearing oil clearance. If the oil clearance on the first rod journal is correct, proceed to the next piston. Repeat this process until all the pistons are installed. It may be a little obsessive-compulsive, but it's a good idea to Plastigage each rod journal before proceeding to the next piston.

After the pistons are installed and the connecting rods are torqued, check the connecting rod side clearance for each rod. Hold the connecting rod as far to one side as possible and measure the side clearance using a feeler gauge. Verify the acceptable range of clearances with the specifications. Typical side clearances are 0.010 to 0.020 inch. If the side clearance is outside the specified range for this application, replace the connecting rod. If the side clearance is still incorrect, there is a problem with the crankshaft.

Install the Oil Pump

If the oil pump mounts in the oil pan, it should be installed at this point. Many applications mount the oil pump outside the engine, for instance

as part of the timing cover, and these style pumps should be installed later. Remove the oil pump cover and pack a little light grease into it. This will help to prime the pump for initial start up. Torque the cover plate back on to the proper spec. Many OHV applications use the gears of the distributor, by means of a shaft, to drive the oil pump. If your engine is configured in this manner, now is the time to install this shaft. Be sure to inspect the shaft for twisting and straightness, which could be a foreshadowing of future problems. Install the oil pump.

Installing the Camshaft

Installing the camshaft on an overhead cam engine is done when the head is assembled. On an overhead valve engine, the camshaft is installed into the block and should be done at this time. Installing an OHV camshaft is a lot like pushing a rope uphill. The part that you can hold on to is too short to be able to support it while you thread it through

Typically, there will be marks, usually dots, on both the cam gear and the crank gear. These dots normally line up opposite one another and as close together as possible. There is some variation in this industry standard and the factory service manual for that engine should be consulted when in doubt.

An important step of head assembly involves proper valve seal installation. Most engine rebuild gasket kits or valve seal kits come with a little Mylar sheath that fits snugly over the end of the valve stem to protect the seal as it is slid over the stem. Failure to use this sheath can result in the seal being cut and oil being burned.

the journals. The answer to this is a camshaft installation tool, which is essentially just a long handle that bolts to the front of the cam. These can be purchased or made from a piece of all-thread that matches the center bolt hole of the camshaft. Lube the cam lobes and bearings with assembly lube. Be sure that the assembly lube is high-pressure lube. Forces at the cam lobes exceed 100,000 psi. Using the all-thread to shift the center of gravity and as a handle, install the camshaft. Care should be taken to ensure the cam lobes do not damage the cam bearings, so work slowly and cautiously.

Installing the Timing Gears

On an overhead cam engine, this procedure is not usually done until the cylinder head is installed.

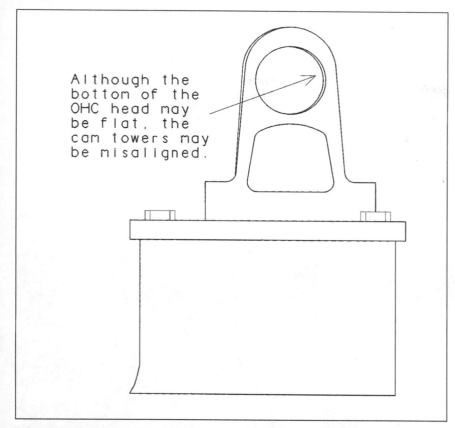

Although the bottom of the OHC head may be flat, the cam towers may be misaligned.

If the engine is an overhead cam design, install the camshaft now. Some applications use a bucket/shim cam follower. These should be installed after checking the cam for free rotation and removing the cam. The installed followers would bind the camshaft preventing it from rotating freely. If the cam does not rotate freely, it will be necessary to have the cam journals line bored.

On an OHV engine, however, the timing gears should be installed now. Typically, there will be marks, usually dots, on both the cam gear and the crank gear. These dots normally line up opposite one another and as close together as possible. There is some variation in this industry standard and the factory service manual for your particular engine should be consulted when in doubt.

If the engine uses a chain to drive the camshaft, the gear can be placed in the chain, the cam gear started first, then the crank gear; cam gear and chain all slide into place together. Usually only gentle persuasion from a soft hammer is necessary to position the gears. In many cases, the larger gear, the cam gear, has nylon teeth. The nylon teeth can be damaged by a hammer, so be careful.

Where meshed timing gears are used, the cam gear is usually fiber. Part of the factory tool kit with these applications is a fiber gear puller and installer. Removing the gear when disassembling the engine was no problem because you did not care about the condition of the old gear. The center of the cam gear, where it mates with the camshaft, is usually metal. Drive the gear into place using a round, hollow driver on the metal area. As the cam gear slides into place, it will be necessary to be sure the cam continues to rotate freely. Should the gear bind, it can damage the teeth as it slides into place.

Note that some engines, like the Volvo B20 OHV four cylinder have a "freeze-plug" at the back of the gallery for the camshaft. If the cam gear is driven on too hard, this plug will pop out of position. Nor-

mally it will not begin to leak immediately—it will wait until several weeks after the engine installation to pop out, undoubtedly at the least opportune time. Use care and inspect this plug thoroughly.

Reassembling the Cylinder Head

Most likely, when you got the cylinder head back from the machinist it was fully assembled—the valve seals, valves, and springs had been installed. If not, begin by sliding the valves into place, then install the valve seals. Some valve seals snap onto the valve guide and are held in place through friction. These valve seals are popular on domestic engines. Another type is the umbrella seal, which just slips onto the valve stem forming an umbrella over the top of the valve guide. The umbrella seals are very popular on domestic engines, too. New seals are critical, but don't expect new valve seals to cure oil burning as a result of worn valve guides; valve guide repairs are the only way to repair valve guide problems.

Most engine rebuild gasket kits or valve seal kits come with a little mylar sheath that fits snugly over the end of the valve stem to protect the seal as it is slid over the stem. Failure to use this sheath can result in the seal being cut, which will cause oil to be burned.

With the valves and the valve seals in place, install the valve springs, retainers, and keepers. The valve spring compressor you used to take the head apart needs to be used again to reassemble it.

If the engine is an overhead cam design, install the camshaft now. Some applications use a bucket/shim cam follower. These should be installed after checking the cam for free rotation and removing the cam. The installed followers would bind the camshaft, preventing you from assessing whether the cam can rotate freely. If the cam does not rotate freely, it will be necessary to have the cam journals line bored.

With the camshaft's free rotation confirmed, remove the camshaft (if

Installing the heads is the part of reassembling the engine that requires the best technique and care. Be sure both the head and the block mating surfaces are clean. Place the head gasket on the block deck. Look carefully to ensure that the proper side is up. Head gaskets are not always marked for proper installation. The ports in the water jacket and other ports between the cylinder head and block should line up through the head gasket.

Place the cylinder head gently on the head gasket. Be careful not to allow an edge of the head to dent or otherwise damage the head gasket. Many head gasket failures are as a result of damage to the head gasket when the head is installed.

necessary) to install the cam followers. For most applications that use a rocker type follower, the rockers will slip into place when the valve is partially depressed. Many professionals line up the rocker and drive it into position with a hammer. While this may not do any obvious damage to the rocker, cam lobe, or the rocker support, it can damage the cam lobe's surface hardening and lead to premature component failure.

Installing the Cylinder Head

This is the part of reassembling the engine that requires the best technique and care. Be sure both the head and the block mating surfaces are clean. Place the head gasket on the block deck. Look carefully to ensure that the proper side is up. Head gaskets are not always marked for proper installation. The ports in the water jacket and any oil gallery ports between the cylinder head and block should line up through the head gasket. I once purchased an aftermarket head gasket for a Japanese car. This next point could not be stated better than it was stated on the packaging for that gasket, "Do not smear sealers and all sorts of other things on this gasket." If the head is properly machined and flat, sealers are not needed. If the head is not properly machined or flat, it should be repaired or replaced.

If the cylinder head was resurfaced on the bottom, the combustion chamber volume has been reduced, which raised the compression ratio. If the engine has a four-inch bore, removing 0.030 inch from a head will decrease the combustion chamber by 0.4 cubic centimeters. This would raise the compression ratio by only in the range of 1/2 percent. However, if you are building a relatively high compression engine that you plan to feed pump gas, you may want to consider using a thicker than stock head gasket, or if available, a shim.

Place the cylinder head gently on the head gasket. Be careful not to allow one of the edges of the head to dent or otherwise damage the head gasket. Many head gasket failures are as a result of damage to the head gasket when the head is installed.

Now comes the most critical part in the head installation process: torquing. In general, cylinder heads are torqued from the center to the ends, in steps. This prevents warping the head. Some heads are torqued to an angle, rather than the more common foot-pounds specification. The most notable of these is the Volvo V-6 engine. If possible, consult the factory service manual for the proper torque spec. If no service manual is available, it is usually acceptable to begin with the center-most bolt, torque it to 25 percent of the spec, go to the bolt next closest to the center and begin tightening the bolts in an hourglass pattern, criss-crossing the head until all are torqued to 25 percent of the spec. Repeat this process at 50 percent of the torque spec, then 75 percent, and finally at 100 percent. On applications with aluminum heads, it's a good idea to retorque the head after the engine has been run for a few hours and allowed to cool.

OHC Cam Timing

During the middle part of the 1970s I worked at a Lotus dealership in Texas. One of the older mechanics, one old enough to know better, installed the cylinder heads on a DOHC (dual overhead cam) Lotus engine. Curiosity got the better of his judgment and he cranked the engine over before installing the timing chain. His motive, of course, was to confirm that the engine turned over smoothly. At several points, the engine bound up and was difficult to turn over. With more leverage, he was able to eventually get the engine to rotate smoothly. This of course was after he bent the valves that had been interfering with the pistons. The moral of the story is that after the cylinder heads are installed, never attempt to rotate the crank until the timing belt or chain is installed. This is especially important on OHC and DOHC engines, but also applies to OHV engines.

If the engine is an overhead cam design, now is the time to adjust the cam timing, install the timing chain or belt. If a timing belt is used, be aware that many timing belts are designed with a front side and a backside. These belts should only be installed as intended. Consult the factory service manual for details.

OHV Lifters and Pushrods

Install the lifters. Do not use new lifters on an old camshaft; do not install a new camshaft without new lifters. Put a little assembly lube on the sides and especially on the bottom. The lifters should fall into place with only the slightest pressure.

Set the pushrods through the heads and into the lifters. Install the rocker arms.

Adjust the Valves

Almost all of today's engines have hydraulic lifters or hydraulic valve compensators. These will probably require readjustment after a few minutes of running. No matter whether the lifters are hydraulic or solid (i.e., mechanical) they should be adjusted at this point.

Mechanical Lifters

Mechanical lifters are generally adjusted to a hot specification, this specification can be found on the EPA sticker located under the hood. If no cold specification is given, adjust the valves to 0.002 inch tighter than the hot specification.

Rotate the crankshaft and observe the lifters on the companion cylinder to the one you are going to adjust. When one of the lifters on the companion cylinder stops moving down and the other lifter starts moving up the valves on your cylinder are ready to adjust. The companion cylinder is the one opposite in the firing order. Check the factory service manual for the firing order to the engine you are working on.

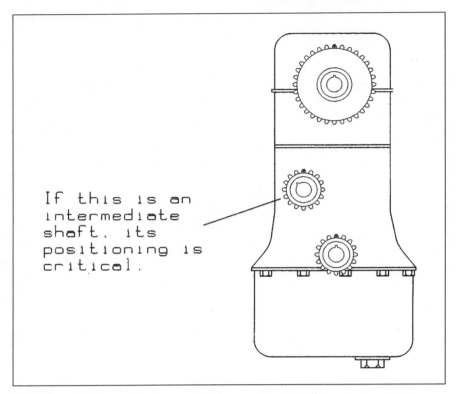

If this is an intermediate shaft, its positioning is critical.

If a timing belt is used, be aware that many timing belts are designed with a front side and a backside. These belts should only be installed as intended. Consult the factory service manual for details.

Some typical firing orders are:
Common Inline Engine Firing Orders:

4 cylinder	1-3-4-2 or
	1-2-4-3
5 cylinder	1-2-4-5-3
6 cylinder	1-5-3-6-2-4 or
	1-2-4-6-5-3 or
	1-4-2-6-5-3 or
	1-4-5-6-3-2
8 cylinder	1-6-2-5-8-3-7-4 or
	1-3-6-8-4-2-7-5 or
	1-4-7-3-8-5-2-6 or
	1-3-2-5-8-6-7-4

Common V Engine Firing Orders:

4 cylinder	1-3-2-4
6 cylinder	1-2-5-6-4-3 or
	1-4-5-6-2-3
8 cylinder	1-6-3-5-4-7-2-8
	1-5-4-8-6-3-7-2
	1-8-3-6-4-5-2-7
	1-8-4-3-6-5-7-2

Common Pancake
Engine Firing Orders:

4 cylinder	1-4-3-2

A rule of thumb for finding the companion cylinder is to divide the cylinders at the midpoint, then the first cylinder on the first half is the companion to the first one of the second half, and the second one on the first half of the cylinders is the companion to the second of the second half, and so on. In the V-8 engines with the firing order 1-5-4-8-6-3-7-2, 1 and 6 are companion cylinders, so are 5 and 3, 4 and 7, 8 and 2. Note, however, that this does not always hold true; Chevrolet V-8 engines (firing order 1-8-4-3-6-5-7-2), for instance do not follow this rule.

With the lifters of the companion cylinder rocking, insert the correct thickness feeler gauge between the rocker arm and the valve stem tip. Tighten the rocker arm against the feeler gauge until the gauge slides snugly in and out with a slight resistance. Repeat this process for each of the cylinders.

An alternate method for determining when you can adjust a cylinder's valve clearances involves rotating the engine until that cylinder is on either its compression or power strokes. To determine this, simply watch the cylinder's exhaust valve open then start to close. As the exhaust valve closes, the intake valve will start opening. As you continue rotating the crankshaft, the intake valve will close and the piston will begin the compression stroke. Rotate the crankshaft an extra 90 degrees to be sure the piston is well into the compression stroke, or even just beginning the power stroke. The valves will be completely closed and you can adjust their lash (clearance) with a feeler gauge, as described above.

A third method—and perhaps the toughest to foul up—is to adjust the exhaust valve just after the intake valve closes. Then, rotate the engine again until the intake valve just begins to open and adjust the intake valve.

Hydraulic Lifters

The preliminary process of adjusting the valves in an overhead valve engine with hydraulic lifters is the same as for adjusting mechanical lifters. However, final adjustment of the lifter must be made with the engine running. New lifters, or even old hydraulic lifters that have bled down during the rebuilding or cleaning process will compress easily as the rocker is adjusted, which would allow the valve to open too far after the engine starts and the lifters pump up. This could result in potential damage when the valves are in overlap, on the transition between the exhaust and intake strokes. For a moment, the intake and exhaust valves are both open as the piston is approaching the top of its stroke. Should the lifters be adjusted too tightly when they're pumped up, the valves may meet the piston. Generally speaking, it is devastating to an engine to have two metal objects attempting to occupy the same space at the same time. To ensure the lifters will not cause damage to the valve once the engine is started, be careful not to depress the lifter as the valve is being adjusted.

Do not use new lifters on an old camshaft. Do not install a new camshaft without new lifters. Put a little assembly lube on the sides and especially on the bottom of the lifters, then the lifters should fall into place with only the slightest pressure.

Overhead Cam

In many cases, the machinist will have made preliminary adjustment of the valves when he did the valve grind. Be sure to ask about this when you pick up the cylinder head. Different overhead cam configurations will require different techniques for adjustment. The three most common configurations for overhead cam valve adjustment are: rocker arm; shim on top of the follower bucket; and shim under the follower bucket.

The adjustment procedure for the rocker arm design is exactly the same as for the overhead valve engines. Rotate the crankshaft until the valves of the companion cylinder are in overlap. Notice the heels of the cam lobes on the cylinder you are adjusting are both in contact with the rocker. Adjust the valves with the adjusting screws at the ends of the rockers.

For applications with the shim located on top of the follower bucket, a special tool is required to depress the follower and valve spring to change the shim. This tool slips between the camshaft and the follower, depressing the follower as the tool is levered downward. Measure the clearance for each valve. If the valve clearance is incorrect, remove the old shim using the special tool and replace it with a shim that is the correct thickness. These shims are easy to come by from the dealer and are even available from the aftermarket. The thickness of the shims usually increases in increments of tenths of a millimeter. In many cases, the old shim may be difficult to remove from the follower. Although a special

pair of pliers resembling snap ring pliers can be purchased, a pick generally works just as well.

Another type of adjustment shim design places the shims under the bucket. Replacing this type of shim requires removal of the camshaft. The easiest way to adjust these valves is to check the adjustment of all the valves, determine how much of a change needs to be made on each, then remove the camshaft only once and replace the shims. As you reinstall the camshaft, after replacing the shims, make sure the valve timing is correct.

With the valves adjusted, install the oil pan, the intake manifold, the valve covers, the exhaust manifolds, and the flywheel or automatic transmission flexplate.

Priming and Installing the Oil Pump

If you haven't already done so, remove the cover plate on the oil pump and pack light grease between the gears of the pump. This will prime the pump and get oil to the bearing surfaces as quickly as possible on initial start-up.

Oil Pan and Valve Covers

The only thing that is not obvious about installing the oil pan and valve covers are gasket dimples. Gasket dimples occur as the oil pan or valve cover is bolted into place. The stamped steel units tend to dimple as they are torqued. Check for this and repair by peening from the backside before installing.

Installing the Intake Manifold

Set the intake manifold gaskets in place. If this is a "V" engine, the gaskets may not want to stay in place as the manifold is set into position, but a light film of grease on the gasket surfaces will solve this problem. Torque the manifold in a decreasing hourglass shaped pattern starting at the outer ends. Torque in 25-, 50-, 75- and 100-percent stages, just as with the cylinder heads.

Installing the Distributor

This may be the trickiest part of the reassembly process. Set the crankshaft to top dead center number one compression. Drop the distributor into place so that when the distributor is in the seated position, the rotor points to the number one position on the distributor cap. While this does not ensure that the ignition timing is correct for driving the car, it gets the timing close enough to get the engine started. The gear at the bottom of the distributor has a helical cut. When the distributor slides into position, the distributor shaft will rotate the equivalent of about two teeth. Therefore, the teeth of the distributor gear should be aligned about two teeth out of phase as you begin to drop it into position.

Installing the Exhaust Manifolds

It is a good idea to make sure the exhaust manifolds are flat and true before installing them. Many applications depend on a machine fit between the exhaust manifold and the head, rather than using a gasket. Torque the manifold in place from the ends to the center in stages.

Installing the Flywheel/Flexplate

Use new bolts and torque them to spec with an accurate torque wrench.

Reassembly Measurements to Check
Plastigage rod journals
Plastigage main journals
Piston ring end gap
Crankshaft end-play
Camshaft end-play
Rod side clearance
Timing gear backlash

Procedures
Honing the cylinders
Installing the camshaft
Installing the crankshaft
Aligning the timing gears and chain
Installing the pistons on the connecting rods
Installing the rings
Installing the pistons in the cylinders
Reassembling the cylinder heads
Installing the valve seals, types
Installing the cylinder heads
Installing the valvetrain
Adjusting the valves
Priming and installing the oil pump
Oil pan and valve covers
Installing the intake manifold
Installing the distributor
Installing the exhaust manifolds
Installing the flywheel/flexplate

INDEX